# WHO
# WE ARE

# ROBERT

PRINCETON UNIVERSITY PRESS

PRINCETON AND OXFORD

# H. WIEBE

# WHO WE ARE

*A History of*
*Popular Nationalism*

PUBLISHED BY PRINCETON UNIVERSITY PRESS, 41 WILLIAM STREET,
PRINCETON, NEW JERSEY 08540
IN THE UNITED KINGDOM: PRINCETON UNIVERSITY PRESS,
3 MARKET PLACE, WOODSTOCK, OXFORDSHIRE OX20 1SY

LIBRARY OF CONGRESS CATALOGING-IN-PUBLICATION DATA

WIEBE, ROBERT H.
WHO WE ARE : A HISTORY OF POPULAR NATIONALISM /
ROBERT H. WIEBE.
P.    CM.
INCLUDES BIBLIOGRAPHICAL REFERENCES AND INDEX.
ISBN 0-691-09023-8 (ALK. PAPER)
1. NATIONALISM.   2. NATIONALISM—HISTORY.   I. TITLE.

JC311 .W464 2002
320.54'09—DC21                              2001036272

THIS BOOK HAS BEEN COMPOSED IN ITC GARAMOND

PRINTED ON ACID-FREE PAPER. ∞

WWW.PUP.PRINCETON.EDU

PRINTED IN THE UNITED STATES OF AMERICA

10  9  8  7  6  5  4  3  2  1

# Contents

## Foreword

I first met Bob Wiebe in 1972 when he came to teach at Harvard University for a year. At that time, five years after the publication of *The Search for Order*, he was the star among American historians. Throughout his career he was continually sought for panels and presentations. His gentle manner, attentive listening, and willingness to attempt large synthetic hypotheses when we all cowered within our specialties never failed to draw our admiration.

In 1972 some magic drew us together as fast friends. From this vantage point I learned of Bob's growing frustration that no one was listening. Although Bob remained steadfast in his core concerns, with each book, fewer and fewer of us paid attention to his ever-sustained concern for the changing fortunes of American democracy.

*The Search for Order* became the profession's best seller in 1967, and remained so for the next 30-odd years because it continued the core tradition of American history: it examined the life and health of the American experiment with democracy. This was

Wiebe's lifetime scholarly question, the center of his patient discussions with students, the impulse behind his many synthetic historical lectures, articles, and books. We professionals didn't listen, but we liked Bob a lot.

*The Search for Order* was everything that the series editor, David Donald, promised: "the take-off book." In 1967 the social sciences were flying high as the best methods for explaining contemporary life. Historians were then struggling to adapt their approaches: quantitative economic, social, political and demographic history; urban history; detailed social studies of immigrants; and estimates of social mobility rates. Such initiatives divided the profession between the new historians and the old. In the midst of these aggrandizements and wounded egos, Bob's *Search for Order* appeared as a triumphant synthesis of the old and the new.

Prof. Wiebe was always the conscientious professor, an avid and thoughtful reader of the relevant literature. He was not an archives man. For the decades from the Reconstruction through World War I he crafted a wonderful synthesis of historical events and 1960s social science. His history explained the world we were all then living in, and I would argue it is, even more, an explanation of 2001.

What we professional American historians did not do was to attend to Bob's concern for the democratic experiment. Yet this was the question that drove all his work. Few attended to his crucial study of small-scale communities in the United States, *The Segmented Society* (1975), where he set forth his thesis that democracy was practiced inside these communities, but that outside their boundaries they feared strangers and manifested all manner of intolerance for the new and the liberal.

Bob never gave up. In effect he wrote a whole social-political history of the United States from the eighteenth century to the present. His last volume, *Self-Rule* (1995), was an attack on the bankruptcy of the media, public relations, and corporate, bureaucratic, and judge-ridden contemporary America. The book called for a renewal of trust in the competence of local democratic decision making. I still hear his voice, as many of his friends and students do, when I read the daily news.

*Sam Bass Warner, Jr.*
*April 2001*

# Foreword

Writers on nationalism can be divided into two diverse but distinguishable groups. The first is composed of the nationalists themselves, who view nationalism as a natural, irresistible force—the expression of a deeply rooted collective identity formed by language, ethnicity, religion, history. National history, therefore, is the history of the nation's growing consciousness of its own existence and the fulfillment, often against terrible odds, of its common destiny, which usually means the formation of a territorial state. The second group is made up of nationalism's critics and victims, who emphasize its historicity, artificiality, sometimes even its pathology. It is no surprise that many of the most prominent members of this group are émigrés or exiles—George Mosse, Eric Hobsbawm, Ernest Gellner, Benedict Anderson—who have felt the lash of national hatred or discrimination.

Among the virtues of Robert Wiebe's approach to nationalism is that he has learned from both groups, but belongs to neither. Here is Wiebe's definition of his subject: "Nationalism is the desire among people who believe they share a common ancestry and a common destiny to live under their own government on land sacred to their history." He has chosen his words with characteristic precision: a people's common ancestry and common destiny may be imagined or invented, they are often matters of belief rather than fact; but a people's aspiration to live under their own government is real and must be seen as part of a larger movement for self-determination. While Wiebe is at pains to show how often national aspirations have been misused, corrupted, and perverted, he never doubts their fundamental authenticity and legitimacy. The world, he believes, is full of divisions and diversity; cosmopolitanism is an idle, empty dream. People, therefore, have the right to decide who they are and who they wish to be, a right that cannot be rejected in the name of an essentially bogus, often hypocritical universalism, which he regards as just "another form of provincialism." In a series of extraordinarily well-informed, wide-ranging, and provocative chapters, Wiebe traces the origins of nationalism in Europe and its spread throughout the world.

He begins by establishing nationalism's relationship to democracy and socialism, which he sees as the other two emancipatory movements produced by the growing mobilization of European society. Each movement builds on immediate human experiences—the family, public life, work—and then extends them into visions of those extended communities that a mobile society seems to require—nation, political community, and class. In the end, all three are subverted by their relationship to states, the most significant sources of organized political power in the modern world. The state is the snake in Wiebe's garden; it entices nationalists into a "Faustian bargain" in which, in exchange for promises of power, nationalists sell their democratic souls. "Wherever nationalism disappeared inside state patriotism," he writes, "the mongrel results bristled with aggressive, coercive qualities." Nationalism for Wiebe is essentially populist and potentially democratic; states are essentially authoritarian and characteristically repressive.

Wiebe's final chapters push off from nationalism's European sources and follow its often tragic history in the second half of the twentieth century. He ends with an extraordinary analysis of the contemporary world and an eloquent plea for accepting humanity's deep and indelible diversities. Does Wiebe have the answer to the new century's discontents? Probably not. But his final chapter is a beautiful illustration of Raymond Aron's admonition that while we may have lost our taste for prophecy, we should never forget our duty to hope. Like all true believers in democracy, Wiebe never loses the hope that men and women eventually will find a way to determine for themselves who they want to be.

*James J. Sheehan*
*April 2001*

*Preface*

For at least a century and a half, nationalism has been one of the most effective answers to questions of identity and connectedness in a fluid world: who (identity) we (connectedness) are. This study traces nationalism's rise and decline as a popular movement, first in Europe and its offshoots, then elsewhere around the world. Nationalism rose and fell along with two other great movements, democracy and socialism. A history of nationalism does not make sense without them or, for that matter, without proper attention to the most important alternative ways of dividing people in modern times: by languages, races, religions, and states.

It scarcely needs saying that in a study of this length I have not written a comprehensive history of anything. I pick and choose unashamedly. In particular I concentrate on popular movements. By popular I do not mean either democratic or spontaneous; I mean movements with widespread appeal, both in space and among diverse people in many walks of life. Elites who have communicated among themselves about nationalism over the past two centuries do not interest me very much. Nationalism's ability to mobilize a general population does. How do we account for its waxing and waning fortunes? What has happened to it as it has spread around the world? The uncontestable truth that nationalism has taken on characteristics peculiar to each of these sites only gets us started. That fact becomes an intrinsic part of each story without explaining how any of those stories relate to one another. How far can nationalism be stretched to cover these highly varied stories? On the one hand, nationalism's adaptability has been one of its greatest assets. As we track that variety globally, it is as if we were discovering nationalism afresh over and over again. On the other hand, when we try to make nationalism good for everything, it becomes good for nothing. Hence, one of our primary challenges is to recognize what, in an infinite universe of events, nationalism can and cannot explain. Coming full circle, how do those inherent limitations help us understand nationalism's remarkable success among some people under some circumstances, its ambiguous effect at other times and places, and its patent failure at still others?

Think of what follows as a grid. Chapters cut across the account, breaking it horizontally by time and place; common problems integrate it vertically. Chapter 1 discusses the meaning of nationalism and sets the terms for the chapters following. Because Europeans and their kin abroad more or less monopolized nationalism until the First World War, chapters 2 and 3 focus exclusively on that story. Migration was the motive force behind its origins (chapter 2). Related movements, democracy and socialism, and related developments—in state building, in race theories, in church ambitions, and in linguistic innovations—were the shaping influences in its history before the war (chapter 3). Case studies of Irish, German, and Jewish nationalism that illustrate these trends carry us overseas to the United States, where people had remarkable freedom to participate as they wished in migration-inspired movements. Chapter 4 explains America's place in this transatlantic history, with emphasis on its liberal government, its cultural diversity, and its white racism. Two world wars wound the United States tightly into the final phase of nationalism's Europe-centered story, one that actually ended on another continent with the founding of Israel (chapter 5).

Meanwhile nationalism was spreading worldwide. Chapter 6 addresses this diffusion, largely during the first two-thirds of the twentieth century, through three of the most significant ways nationalism expressed itself outside Western society: state-dominated nationalism, with Japan, Turkey, and Mexico as case studies; the pan movements, with Pan-Africanism the primary illustration; and anticolonial-postcolonial nationalism, with Nigeria as one example. India's history highlights the difficulty of extracting nationalism's thread from any of these tangled skeins. Chapter 7 demonstrates how during the 1960s and 1970s nationalism throughout the world—including Europe once again—became integrated into a genuinely global process, only to find itself competing at a disadvantage with god-driven and gun-driven alternatives that one way or another outbade it. At the turn of the twenty-first century nationalism worldwide was clearly in decline, with its greatest strength in Western society's well-established liberal states. Canada's recent history illustrates that proposition. Finally, chapter 8 returns to the challenges of understanding that underlie this study and invites a reassessment of nationalism in light of its history, our history, and everybody's prospects. My hope is not that you will come to like nationalism—I am not its advocate—but that you will come to see it as so thoroughly human that no simple judgment does it justice.

# Acknowledgments

A grant from the Spencer Foundation enabled me to begin this project; four weeks at the Rockefeller Foundation's Bellagio Center encouraged me to rethink it. Throughout its development, the College of Arts and Sciences at Northwestern University provided unusually generous support, as it has throughout almost all of my career. The Northwestern University library fed my insatiable appetite for published materials. I am especially grateful to James McMahon, Catherine Feeney, Sharon Smith, and the staff of the interlibrary loan division.

I owe an immense debt to colleagues who helped me identify useful readings: James T. Campbell, Jonathon Glassman, Peter Hayes, T. W. Heyck, John R. McLane, Edward Muir, Carl Petry, Conrad Totman, and Ivor Wilks. Unlike the skeptic who promised to bury me with my notes, many friends kept the faith, alternately prodding and cheering me on: Margaret Lavinia Anderson, Herbert and Barbara Bass, Daniel and Naomi Feldman, Patricia Albjerg Graham, Barbara Heldt, Peter Parish, Gerry Smith, and Clarence Ver Steeg. Josef Barton, the master of the positive response, listened patiently to my original, ill-formulated hypotheses, advised me on readings in a breathtaking variety of fields, and offered suggestions to the very end. A friend indeed. James J. Sheehan gave the manuscript a careful, critical reading to my great benefit.

For the settings in which I could explore aspects of my work, I am particularly grateful to Willi Paul Adams, Tony Badger, Tom Bender, Christopher Beneke, Ellen DuBois, Mary Furner, Robert J. Norrell, and—again—Peggy Anderson and Peter Parish. Special thanks to those critics whose rejection of my scholarly judgments obliged me to reconsider them: Joyce Appleby, John Ashworth, Drew Gilpin Faust, Daniel Walker Howe, John H. M. Laslett, Daniel T. Rodgers, and the persevering Betty Wood, who has been nudging me leftward for fifteen years. In these discussions, Robin Einhorn made the single most arresting observation: that I had returned to the theme of community unraveling that marked the start of my career. I still do not know what to make of that insight.

I apply some ideas from chapter 1 to a different end in "Humanizing Nationalism," *World Policy Journal* 13 (Winter 1996/97): 81–88; and I turn material from Chapter 4 to a different intellectual purpose in "Framing United States History," in *Rethinking American History in a Global Age*, Thomas Bender (ed.), forthcoming.

Not a person who knows me would wonder for a second to whom this book is dedicated. In this project, as in everything else, Penny has made the difference.

# WHO
# WE ARE

# CHAPTER 1

## Thinking about Nationalism

How did educated Westerners come to make enemies of an inspiration that has changed the lives of billions? It was not always so. At the turn of the twentieth century the philosopher William James judged "the attempt of a people long enslaved to attain the possession of itself, to organize its laws and government, to be free to follow its internal destinies, according to its own ideals . . . the sacredest thing in this great human world."[1] Championing just such causes made Woodrow Wilson a global hero. But disillusionment after the First World War turned to revulsion after the Second, and at midcentury Western intellectuals dug in to battle the nationalist spirit.

What took the urgency from their campaign was a widespread belief that once Europe's colonies were freed nationalism would die of its own accord, and in place of its divisiveness, a new transnational connectedness would have its day. At least in the United States no generation was so thoroughly indoctrinated in universalist values as the one coming of age around midcentury. Scholars and scientists buried the idea of race. Humanities courses taught a core of eternal values; studies comparing religions declared their underlying agreement. If before the war educated Americans had routinely assumed human differences—the stairsteps from barbarism to civilization in *National Geographic*—after the war they routinely assumed human unity. From the bipartisan statesman Wendell Willkie's vision of *One World* to the hugely popular photographic exhibit *The Family of Man*, American public life celebrated the essential sameness of the human condition everywhere.

The magic wand most often expected to make nationalism disappear was modernization, a marvelously capacious concept that bundled Western society's major trends in science and technology, liberty and democracy, production and distribution, organization and education, into a single historical force and set it on a path of inevitable worldwide dominance. Some merged modernization with the triumph of capitalism; some considered it the flowering of the Enlightenment; others dated it from the Renaissance. In all cases, however, modernization was the juggernaut of progress. Whether nationalism represented a phase in modernization or a primitive opposition to it, it would pass. No one could "deny," Harvard's Rupert Emerson thought, "that the nation and the nation-state are anachronisms in the atomic age."[2] Or in the political scientist Alfred Cobban's version: "Self-determination is [now] an irrelevant conception."[3] If nationalism resisted, it would become the raccoon on the highway, squared against the truck's onrushing headlights.

But nationalism refused to go away. As this infuriatingly persistent anomaly, it became a convenient dumping bin for the frustrations that educated Westerners felt in a fractured world. Nothing so thoroughly affronted the universalist values that the champions of human rights and of law and order alike used to measure the health of the world. It accumulated modifiers: atavistic, fanatic, xenophobic, blind, bloody. . . . Nationalists never smiled; nobody smiled at them. The more intense the nationalism, the worse for everybody else. Who ever heard of a caring nationalism?

Democrats and socialists—followers of nationalism's two great competitors in modern times—explain nationalism to us. Even as they argue fiercely, socialists and democrats show respect for one another, but almost none for nationalism. For one thing, democracy and socialism come with impressive bodies of systematic thought, the stuff that Western intellectuals bite and chew. Nationalism, on the other hand, has inspired no theories worthy of the name. Even more significant, socialism and democracy have impressive universalist dimensions. Both like the panoramic worldview; both hope to inherit the earth. Nationalism, by contrast, is brazenly particular. If a few people long ago made gestures toward an ideal world of nations, contemporary nationalists have no interest in that kind of big picture. They care about the cause at hand. In the end, nationalists themselves have virtually no voice in Western circles. It is as if we read only Iranian scholarship on United States history.

To no surprise, then, Western intellectuals seldom have anything favorable to say about nationalism. First of all, they tell us, it is flimsy. Leaders invent it and followers imagine it. In one of history's truly monumental tricks, according to this line of reasoning, millions upon millions spread over continents and centuries have denied what was really happening to them in order to chase after fantasies.

Moreover, these millions have been as desperate as they have been deluded. Nationalism feasts on damaged psyches. According to Karl Popper, the high priest of philosophical rationalism, "Nationalism appeals to our tribal instincts, to passion and to prejudice, and to our nostalgic desire to be relieved from the strain of individual responsibility."[4] *Escape from Freedom*, in Erich Fromm's haunting phrase. Nationalism, declares Tom Nairn, an expert on its role in the United Kingdom, is "the pathology of modern developmental history" with a "built-in capacity for descent into dementia."[5] Desperate people are dangerous people, easy prey to the peddlers of modern society's most vicious nostrums. For

George Mosse, a specialist on Nazi Germany, racism is nothing more than "a heightened nationalism"; in the same spirit, the journalist Michael Ignatieff equates "European racism" with something he calls "white ethnic nationalism."[6]

Above all, nationalism is the voodoo doll that absorbs the sins of the world's states—that is, those sovereignties dividing up most of the earth's land and purporting to govern its people, bounded unit by bounded unit. Thanks to a general confusion of nation with state, we usually treat the omnipresent state and *nation-state* as interchangeable terms and with that sleight of hand make nationalism available to take the blame for sundry state actions. Proponents of democracy and socialism bridle at distorted uses of their own value systems: hollow constitutions and rigged elections posing as democracy, secret police and dictatorial rule posing as socialism. When it comes to the uses of nationalism, however, anything goes. Law-abiding states seek peace and order; nationalist ones wreak havoc. Good states further the general welfare; nationalist ones persecute minorities and squander resources. The more of a bad thing we find in a state, the more nationalist we say it is.

Indeed, nationalism subverts sound states like Canada and Belgium, then proliferates rickety ones that crowd each other like shacks in a slum. Balkanization is our byword for what nationalism has wrought. With the Balkans themselves in mind Misha Glenny writes in the *New Yorker*: "[too many people are scrambling to establish nation-states on too small a patch of land."[7] The situation in Africa and Asia is even worse. "In the third world," Arthur Schlesinger, Jr., a bellwether of liberalism, declares, "nationalism, having overthrown Western colonialism, launches a horde of new states, large and micro, often at each other's throats."[8] It's a jungle out there.

Most damning of all, nationalism takes the blame for the state's militarism. Advocates of democracy and socialism recognize that something in their own value systems—democracy's or socialism's better self, as it were—pulls against state aggression; but nationalism, with scarcely an advocate, seems to have no better self: It *is* state aggression. "I make no secret of my belief that nationalism"—its lifelong student Boyd Shafer has concluded—". . . leads to war and destruction."[9] More succinctly, the scholar Mark Beissinger writes: "In an age of mass politics all interstate wars are nationalist wars."[10]

By demonizing nationalism we avoid reckoning with it. Let's step back and start over. *Nationalism is the desire among people who believe they share a common ancestry and a common destiny to live under their own government on land sacred to their history.* Nationalism expresses an aspiration with a political objective. Behind that aspiration lies a sense of kinship that is simultaneously fictional and real—that is, culturally created, as all kin systems are, yet based in some measure on an overlapping of customs, histories, and genealogies. In each of the three primary contexts for nationalist movements during the nineteenth and twentieth centuries—people in migration, people in fear of cultural disintegration, and people in search of freedom—kinship holds out the prospect of a closer connection, a deeper trust, a surer protection than alternative ties seem capable of providing.

There is nothing inherently violent in a movement based on kinship. The people in one house are no more a family if they blow up the house next door. It is simply absurd to blame nationalism indiscriminately for the terrorism and thuggery let loose in the modern world, as if it were responsible for—say—China's Cultural Revolution or Argentina's military brutality. Nationalism is no more militaristic than Frederick the Great was nationalistic.

The scope of a nationalist movement is determined by the people who join it, wherever they may be. Its sacred land, as much a beacon as a location, may or may not have fixed boundaries. Nationalism gives people a way of thinking about a place. In the literal, not the invidious sense, it is Janus-faced, always looking both backward and forward. Anatole France encapsulated it nicely: "A nation is a communion of memories and hopes." Partisan nationalists are no more selective about what they remember than professional historians, even if they use quite different criteria. Nor are they more dreamily optimistic about the future than enthusiasts for democracy or socialism. In the philosopher Anthony Birch's useful distinction, "People are not conservative nationalists or liberal nationalists; they are nationalists who may happen also to be either conservatives or liberals."[11]

In a tough environment of competing loyalties—religious, civic, and occupational among others—nationalism has been strikingly versatile. Sometimes the nation acquires the attributes of an organic being that "can be said to have a soul, spirit, and personality."[12] In crisis, it can be transmuted into an immortal force, the phoenix that rises from defeat over and over to fight again. In fact, disaster may be construed as an essential preliminary to the ultimate triumph. Where a people's primary need is to find a source of integration, nationalism can provide it; where their primary need is to draw a line of separation, nationalism can do that, too. Change, change, change: Belying nationalism's own dogmatism, permeability and adaptability rank among its greatest strengths.

Appropriately, nationalism's relations with the state have been shifting and elusive. States, hovering like crows over the nests that nationalists make, have also played on the sentiments of ancestry, destiny, and sacred soil. Try though they might, however, they have rarely inspired feelings of kin-connectedness, the core around which cultures of nationalism have developed. If the forefathers in the Gettysburg Address are the forefathers of its readers, it may rouse nationalist sentiments among them; but if thoughts of forefathers send people's minds to the four winds, nationalism will follow after them, no matter how dedicated and obedient citizens of the United States they may be.

The more common state role is its attempt to swallow kin-based groups inside a civic whole. Aggressive states, seeking to stamp their values on a dissident population, trigger the nationalism of cultural survival. Contrary to common wisdom, nationalism does not shape militarism; militarism shapes nationalism. The weaponry of the modern state, spread promiscuously, has influenced cultural clashes much as it has domestic conflicts: With guns, people shoot. Much of what passes for nationalism's intractability is better understood as a defense in the face of the state's capacity to kill. Almost all the great massacres of modern times have been state inspired, state directed, or at least state supported. States, not nations, generate the miserable millions of stateless people.

Curiously, the state is most deadly to nationalism when nationalism triumphs. If a nationalist movement succeeds in forming a state, it almost always dissolves in the process. As the anthropologist Richard Handler has explained it, the nationalist vision is incompatible with the exercise of state power. By its nature, the day-to-day affairs of organized government shatter nationalism's promise of a harmonious whole: Bureaucracy trumps unity. Phrased another way, an institutionalized nationalist movement is a contradiction in terms. Where "[c]ompeting groups all proclaim their paramount concern with the 'national interest' . . . nationalism as a specific form of politics becomes meaningless," writes the historian John Breuilly. "Nationalism remains distinctive only for so long as it is unsuccessful."[13] If nations were the organic beings their champions sometimes claim, we might call this the larva's paradox. But that image misses nationalism's blindly aspiring nature: how its very ambition obscures the deadliness of the goal. Instead we will call this the Icarus Effect.

In the end, nationalism and the state have innumerable overlaps and fundamental differences. States, for example, often seek to expand their domains, but nationalism, coveting a homogeneous community, stands at odds with imperialism. Hannah Arendt, no friend of nationalism, considered the nation "least suited for unlimited growth because the genuine consent at its base cannot be stretched indefinitely."[14] As Alfred Cobban noted, the more that minorities within a multiethnic state support its imperialist ambitions, the weaker their drives for self-determination tend to be. It is no surprise, therefore, that under scrutiny the vaunted nation-state practically vanishes. One estimate counts "1,500 nations, 150 states, and 15 nation states."[15] Walker Connor, a leading scholar in this field, considers 12 of the 132 two states that he has examined to be full-fledged nation-states. Another respected scholar, Will Kymlicka, qualifies only 3 out of 184. The philosopher Michael Oakeshott has dismissed the entire crop: "No European state (let alone an imitation European state elsewhere in the world) has ever come within measurable distance of being a 'nation state.'"[16]

Once we disengage nationalism from the crimes of the state, the rest of the charge against it looks quite provincial. We like our own commitments and priorities, our own myths and modes of violence, and we hunker down in defense of what the geopolitician Samuel Huntington calls our civilization. When dissidents in the hills of Sierra Leone hack off the hands and feet of hapless passersby, it is the work of African savages; when American land mines blow far more limbs to kingdom come, it is an unavoidable consequence of military necessity. No punishment is too severe for guerrilla fighters who bomb civilian sites. But what of pilots who bomb civilian refugees? The government says it is sorry. Big power, big price. Not many Americans volunteer to die for the sins of their president. Yet not many complain when United States policy forces hundreds of thousands of Iraqi civilians to die—or at least suffer mightily—for Saddam Hussein's.

By cool Western standards nationalists care too much, and they care about the wrong things. Ethnic pride may pass, but ethnic passion definitely not. Nationalism in action is just another form of holy war, the social theorist Benjamin Barber tells us. Among competing loyalties in modern times, nationalism is as likely as any other to provide an integrated framework for everyday life. To sophisticated members of the wealthiest societies in the history of the world, people who wear many hats in their many lives at work, at home, and at play, the prospect of any integrating framework sounds suffocating. We seem incapable of recognizing social and psychological creativity in a reconceived sense of kinship.

Our universalism is another form of provincialism. Even the most widely cited declarations of human rights originate somewhere, not everywhere. American universalism, to no surprise, highlights American values—constitutionalism, a merit system, religious pluralism, a consumer culture's standard of living, and the like—which its advocates then declare absolute and timeless. There seems to be no room for an alternative measure of right and wrong, one, for example, from the perspective of a Peruvian peasant or a Sudanese herdsman who might judge Americans, squandering incredible quantities of natural resources at irreversible cost to the environment, the globe's greatest violators of human rights.

Indulging the strange conceit that we are smarter than the rest of the earth's population, Western intellectuals reserve the right to decide what is best for them. The logic of modernization presses the case for bigger, faster, richer, smoother. A strong pull toward smaller units, however popular, seems perverse. On the eve of Czechoslovakia's dissolution, America's cosmopolitan press predicted the rapid impoverishment of those purblind, seceding Slovaks. In fact, both Czechs and Slovaks have profited. Even educated Westerners, who are sure that the world's ethnic hostilities flare only because unscrupulous leaders manipulate impressionable masses, routinely flunk the factual tests. Now let me see, did Serbs massacre Croats during the Second World War, or was it vice versa? Why would Hutu hack the bodies of all those Tutsi who never did anything to them? Answers that elude us are chiseled in other people's collective memories.

What a world universalized according to Western standards might look like is by no means clear. No leader in the West advocates a world without boundaries where people come and go, live and work, erect governments and institute law as they choose.

Contrary to the social philosopher Liah Greenfeld's assertions—"[a] nation coextensive with humanity is in no way a contradiction in terms"—the universal nation is in every way a contradiction in terms.[17] Even as an imagining, the sociologist Anthony Smith reminds us, a "global culture answers no living needs."[18] In its vastness it offers us no way of situating or identifying ourselves.

We need a fresh start. Let's begin with three propositions. First, the world has been, is now, and will be into the foreseeable future crosshatched with divisions. Second, nationalism has been one, but only one of the modern world's major divisions. Others include language, religion, and race, each of which has sometimes been allied with nationalism and sometimes been at odds with it. Third, with one of these related divisions, the state, nationalism has repeatedly made a Faustian bargain, trading its soul for its own fulfillment as a state.

On these terms, comfortable Westerners have excellent reasons to dislike nationalism. It is disruptive. It has no affinity for democracy: National self-determination specifies an outcome, not the process that gets people there. It shows scant tolerance for self-conscious minorities in its midst. "In the logic of nationalism, a nation cannot contain within itself another nation."[19] In power, nationalists threaten to initiate an Onion Effect. Peeling off the authority that has been oppressing one ethnic group may free it to oppress other ethnic groups, who in turn try to peel off the layer constricting them, and so on. In Sri Lanka, Tamil, who comprise 20 percent of the population, seek a state of their own, Eelam, which if it came into being would contain minorities constituting 20 percent of Eelam's population.

But we cannot understand nationalism, let alone judge it, if we measure it against our universalist standards. Nationalism is just one of many divisions that stand impervious to that deeply flawed Western concept. Better we set it against alternative divisions. Would we prefer separations dictated by race? or by religion?

With these cautions in mind, let us proceed to the history of nationalism, which thrusts three questions to the forefront. First, *where* does nationalism appear? As its cultural contexts changed, so did nationalism. Although this variable should alert us in particular to the dramatic differences between nationalism's Western varieties and its many guises elsewhere in the world, geography was not destiny. Western-style nationalism and the state associated with it had an easier passage into Japan than into Bulgaria. Second, *when* does nationalism arrive? Copying from one another, nationalists developed movements that had specific times stamped all over them. By the same token, the particular range of problems and possibilities that roughly common circumstances set before an array of nationalist movements—the centralization of European state power around the turn of the twentieth century, for example, or the anticolonial prospects around midcentury or the proliferation of deadly weapons late in the century—fixed them just as firmly in time. Third, *why* nationalism? What has given nationalism its powerful appeal for some people sometimes?

Nationalism, which looks like a major problem to us, arrived during the nineteenth century as the solution to an even more fundamental problem: How could people sort themselves in societies where the traditional ways no longer worked? Rather than a gigantic fraud perpetrated time and again on the mindless masses, nationalism thrived because it addressed basic human needs. Examining the nature of those needs in nationalism's original home, Europe, is the first step in our inquiry.

CHAPTER 2

## European Origins

During the long nineteenth century from the French Revolution to the First World War, nationalism was a monopoly of European societies. The very few exceptions, notably Japan, only highlighted the rule. Otherwise, nationalism outside Europe remained the province of tiny elites, borrowing heavily from Western ideas, who could not or did not want to spark popular interest. On the other side of the Great War, when nationalist movements did spread globally, Europe generated no new ones. As old ones revived or remade themselves, they were playing out stories already underway. The nineteenth century in Europe, in other words, marked out a distinct period in the history of nationalism.

Before the French Revolution, the overwhelming majority of Europeans lived within systems that the German historian Peter Blickle has called *Kommunalismus*: local land- and town-based hierarchies that invested their primary energies in self-perpetuation. By no means static, they showed remarkable resilience in the face of one assault after another from the Four Horsemen. Europe's rulers occasionally dissolved some of those communities and certainly milked all of them for whatever they could get; but they did not upend the system itself. Fundamental changes came only when the strains of maintaining those communities burst manageable bounds.

The primary source of those pressures was a demographic revolution that doubled Europe's population between the mid-eighteenth and the late nineteenth centuries. After centuries of erratic ups and downs in total population, Europe's disease pool stabilized, protecting the young in particular against epidemic disaster. Even though Europe's food resources diversified, increasing caloric intakes and thereby enabling more people to survive on the same land, population pressures continued to mount, with the overflow pouring out of those swollen villages in search of work, often to live and die in the cities. Then in a second phase of this demographic revolution, sanitized water and improved sewage systems significantly lessened urban death rates. As city populations soared, consolidated farms with seasonal labor fed them, sending even more villagers on the move. Increasingly during the nineteenth century the inertia of European society kept people in motion, not in place.

Even if, as Charles Tilly claims, "the *pace* of migration changed much less than its *character*," the consequences transformed European society.[1] Instead of swinging out year after year to work and return, work and return, ever larger percentages kept going. Millions of villagers remade themselves into city dwellers. Others— about 65 million between 1800 and 1914—crossed the Atlantic on journeys that had no predictable pattern or predetermined end. Migrants relocated over and over again. Millions who thought they would return to Europe never did; many others who thought they would never return did. Once cheap transportation allowed it, some shuttled back and forth. At the peaks of migration between 1870 and 1914, the effect was "one of a swarming or churning of people back and forth across the Atlantic."[2]

It would be a grave error to picture these basic changes as wholesale human disaster. Nothing persuasive argued that the old system of quasi serfdom and hovering catastrophe was somehow more natural, as Pierre Nora would have it, or more humane, as Louis Dumont claims, or that migration produced massive anomie, as intellectuals since Emile Durkheim have assumed. Working people always had hard lives. While population pressures drove some of them out of their communities, others left willingly enough in search of opportunities. In fact, what stands out is a remarkable adaptability, particularly among families.

As more and more matters central to community life fell beyond local control, families took increasing authority upon themselves. What David Sabean has said of the Neckarhausen peasantry of the early nineteenth century applied equally in the Irish countryside and the Russian ghettoes: "As a large part of the village became dependent on wages [from outside sources], kinship became more rather than less important."[3] Especially in migration, chains of kin were indispensable, relaying news, job prospects, and remittances back and forth along the lines of movement. Along these same lines, people with ties to the same locality or region stood in as relatives, uniting the kin of tradition with adopted kin in an expandable weave of obligation and affection. Need generated hope. It did not require much of a stretch for migrants to assume wider and wider cirlces of people whose cultural profile gave them special attributes not just of familiarity but more important of trust.

From adoptive kin into fictive kin, from bonding with chance acquaintances to sensing bonds with similar people wherever they were: That marked the path from family to ethnicity and eventually to nationalism. History did its part, verifying a common ancestry among these culturally linked strangers and sanctifying soil that the sacrifice of those ancestors had made the heritage of all succeeding generations. Assigning a unique meaning to one set of customs created the semblance of a single people with a code for distinguishing insiders from outsiders and for connecting insiders with invisible yet powerful ties of understanding.

These fictive kin composites, or ethnic groups, were not like an extended family; they were extended families, culturally constructed—as all kin systems were—in response to the challenges of migration. Ethnicity turned into nationalism when cultural consciousness acquired a political objective. Ethnicity and nationalism, in other words, solved problems that migration posed. In a mobile world, as families inherited the authority of traditional communities, they passed authority along to ethnic communities, some of which aspired to govern themselves. Eventually they spun a circle: Extended kin sustained migration, migration underwrote ethnicity and nationalism, ethnicity and nationalism glorified the grand fictive family.

In broad terms, the new ethnic consciousness and its expression as nationalism followed in the wake of a boom in population that rumbled from the British Isles eastward into the Germanic center of the continent, swung north into Scandanavia and south into the Italian peninsula, then doubled back into pockets of Western and Central Europe that it had missed, and finally swept across Eastern Europe from the far tip of the Baltic Sea through the Balkans. What mattered was not the soaring populations themselves but the migration they triggered. Extensive migration from any source was usually sufficient. England, with a precocious national consciousness already congealing before the French Revolution, experienced an equally early swirl of migration during the eighteenth century, some to its factories and cities and some abroad. Nationalism in Ireland, ballooning with people who went on the move in search of work, followed soon after. In Norway, the birthrate rose sharply around midcentury, and as those children were reaching adulthood, a half century of heavy emigration commenced. Norwegian nationalism tagged immediately behind. The bulge struck Italy first in the north, where nationalism originated, then in stages down the boot, with migration and nationalism picking up the pace together. Doubling back, pressures in rural Wales sent waves of migrants into the English and American labor pools during the 1860s and 1870s, and by the 1880s its politics resounded with a new Welsh consciousness. Then between the 1880s and the First World War, exploding populations, rising outmigrations, emerging nationalisms, and hardening differences blanketed the European domains of the Austrian-Hungarian, Russian, and Ottoman Empires.

As impressive as the relation between migration and the arrival of nationalism was in nineteenth-century Europe, in the end it served as the backdrop for what was a highly textured, case-by-case process. Migration, even on a large scale, did not cause nationalism in the sense of creating it. There had been great migrations earlier and there would be great migrations later that produced no nationalist movements. Nor did it help to picture nationalism rising out of migration. In a sense it did, but so did other movements. Migration generated the needs—the context and the incentive—and nationalism, which was then hammered into many shapes by the distinctive circumstances of each setting, provided one popular way of addressing them. A few examples highlight European nationalism's variety.

Basque nationalism, a latecomer in Western Europe that first flourished in the 1890s, expressed a mixture of concerns about both outmigration and immigration. Spanning France and Spain but far stronger in Spain, where bitterness over losing out in the long, vicious Carlist Wars gave nationalists common memories, the movement grew in a climate of anxiety over the thinning of Basque ranks at home and the prospect of their inundation by invading outsiders. Here nationalism served as a bastion of defense, relying on Euskara, a language almost incomprehensible to outsiders, as the sine qua non of the true Basque. In line with other nationalist movements built primarily on fears, this one was deeply reactionary.

A new sense of jeopardy also precipitated Danish nationalism. A surge of population during the second half of the long nineteenth century, doubling the number of Danes in their core territory and propelling them out of traditional villages into towns and cities there and abroad, prepared the way; a disastrous defeat in 1864 at the hands of Prussia, with the consequent loss of Schleswig and Holstein, brought it into the open. After 1871, Bismarck's new state set about transforming the Schleswig Danes into Germans. Indeed it looked as if Germany might just swallow the whole of Denmark in another bite. Against this background of jeopardy and anger, a cultural revival and a theme of reunion, appealing to Danes everywhere provided the substance for a nationalist movement that dominated public life by the end of the century.

As the Danes' story illustrated, aspirations fueled the most energetic nationalist movements. The contrast between rising and shrinking expectations was particularly revealing in the case of the Swedes and Norwegians, whose demographic histories were strikingly similar. With population pressures rising on the same schedule, the two Scandanavian peoples migrated in successive waves after 1866, 1880, and 1900, totalling for both of them an impressive 20 percent of the home population. For both groups, the Lutheran church reinforced the chains of migration; in both instances, those chains ran primarily between the home country and the United States. Despite these almost identical elements, however, the commentator who observed in 1902 that "the Norwegians are more Norwegian than the Swedes are Swedish" caught wind of the critical difference.[4]

National consciousness among Swedes was a relatively quiet matter. Perhaps its sharpest expression came just before the Great War when Russia threatened to swallow up those Swedes who lived in Finland. Norwegians, on their part, labored mightily to give themselves a distinctive stamp. First they wrestled their culture away from their onetime rulers, the Danes. Then they fought among themselves over the form a distinctive Norwegian language should take. Should it be the academic Bokmål or the vernacular-driven Landsmål. Almost by definition, popular nationalism promoted the latter. By the 1870s Norwegian nationalism was in full swing, with no abatement until the eve of the First World War. What accounted for the difference between the two people was simple enough. The Swedes had a well-established state; the Norwegians did not. Swedes found glory in the past, before they had slipped to the standing of a minor power. Norwegians saw glory in their future.

Ethnicity knew no bounds. Although its reach did not have to span great distances, nothing inhibited it from doing so. In the nineteenth century, ethnicity generated identities in motion, flowing across boundaries as migrants did. Appropriately, Swedish and Norwegian nationalism manifested the same characteristics on both sides of the Atlantic: sedate Swedes, energized Norwegians. Where Swedes in the United States honored the memory of empire by naming institutions after Gustav Adolph, Norwegian Americans apotheosized the eleventh-century martyr Saint Olaf, whom Danes and traitors, it was said, had assassinated. The Sons of Norway appeared in 1895, then the Daughters of Norway in 1897. The use of Norwegian picked up at the turn of the century, church collaboration with German Lutherans weakened, and an American-based campaign to celebrate everybody's ancestral province had its moment of popularity. Norwegian flags cropped up across Minnesota, North Dakota, and Wisconsin. In 1905, as Norway officially separated from Sweden, cheers for independence boomed across the Midwest, with the echoes resonating for years afterward. By contrast, Swedish Americans, looking on as another piece of empire disappeared, emphasized the American side of their identity. Some even suggested that the really bright future of the Swedish nation lay in the United States.

Wars created another set of special cases. One way or another, war affected almost every nationalist movement in Europe. In a few instances, it was even possible to argue that war precipitated nationalism. The most persuasive cases in point materialized during the First World War, when the vicissitudes of battle and the dreams of self-determination opened a door to people who had given no signs of trying to push it open themselves. Among Slovaks, Ukrainians, and Lithuanians, for example, there was no nationalism that could claim a popular base until the opportunities or vicissitudes of war generated one. Yet even then war's specific influence was difficult to isolate. These people, as well as the Estonians, Letts, and Romanians for whom a similar case might be made, had just recently experienced bursts in population and migration. Under the circumstances, their nationalism constituted less of an exception than a variation.

Migration, in other words, worked in a combination of influences. Situation by situation, it was migration-and-something-else that generated popular nationalism. One of the most significant of these additional factors was the degree of elasticity in an ethnic group's family-kin relations: By and large, the more flexible—the more amoebic—those structures, the more extensive the mobilization and the more expansive the vision of its nationalist movement. After midcentury, an open, inclusive approach to adoptive kinship stirred a nationalism among northern Italians that stretched easily across the ocean. Down the boot, on the other hand, migrating Sicilians, with a tightly woven, place-bound kin structure that riveted loyalties to their villages of origin, were slow to develop even a Sicilian consciousness, let alone an Italian one. As another example, the Dutch, leaving in waves between the middle and the end of the century, by and large came in family units to fixed American destinations: minimal movement, inturning kinship, no nationalism worth mentioning.

The most important of all the related factors shaping nationalism was the modern state, never far from the center in any of these movements. Long before Randolph Bourne's famous barb, war proved to be the health of the state, which came bristling and snorting out of Europe's bloody seventeenth century. Those best geared for war—first Britain, then Napoleonic France, then Germany—served as Europe's models for modernity. From the beginning the modern state bent every effort to absorb loyalties that would otherwise have gone elsewhere—to church, to locality, to occupation, to kin. As a matter of course, the loyalties that migration was inspiring became fair game.

One of the modern state's most notable functions was to facilitate the free flow of people within its boundaries. In fact, the essence of a full-fledged state citizenship, as distinct from an earlier citizenship derived from a town or district, was its uniform applicability throughout the state's domain. States benefited, and citizens benefited. For those on the move, the trappings of patriotism satisfied important ongoing needs: An official language, official holidays, even an official hierarchy served as a common currency easing the transition from one place and one job to the next. A common understanding of history, a celebration of the state government, could make a critical difference in easing transitions from one place and one job to the next. Migrants who left the state's jurisdiction, however, lost standing and risked disappearing from consciousness entirely. Hence where the state dominated nationalism's development, emigrants had no influence. They were now outsiders, sometimes even deserters. In these cases, it was massive internal migration that gave nationalism its popular base. In an early example, eighteenth-century English nationalism could incorporate those Scots who chose to join but not the North American colonists, whose impressive reservoir of loyalty to England was squandered after 1763 by a government in London that simply could not imagine a single imperial body of citizens.

Where nationalism evolved apart from—or in spite of—the state, its scope stretched this way and that to cover fictive kin as they moved. Nationalism's remarkable plasticity reflected the fact that the migration stirring it was itself a fluid process rather than a departure from one point and relocation in another. It was not that this protean nationalism lost its sense of home: Deep attachments to a place did not require living there. Indeed, many migrants first discovered their home by leaving it, by making it something other than the only thing. A malleable, expansive nationalism thrived best where new obligations in new territories did not compete directly with it. In this regard the United States, overwhelmingly the favorite destination for Europeans who crossed the ocean, stood out in the nineteenth century as unusually permissive toward white immigrants. While the territory of the United States became a critical site for nineteenth-century nationalism, the government of the United States was rarely a critical influence in its development.

Schematically that is how nationalism originated. What an emphasis on its common characteristics obscures, of course, are the twists and turns it took in various settings. Now let us see how patterns of kinship, relations to the state, and the meaning of a homeland actually worked themselves out in three quite different movements: Irish nationalism, German nationalism, Jewish nationalism.

If European nationalism had been a function of modernization, the Irish, stuck early in the nineteenth century in the throes of a bloated peasant economy, would have dragged in much later, perhaps near the turn of the twentieth century. On the contrary, they pioneered in mobilizing and sustaining popular support behind a nationalist movement.

Demographics set the calender for Irish nationalism. Nowhere in the Western world "in any half-century," the historian Kenneth Connell estimated, "has the number of births so vastly exceeded the number of deaths as in Ireland before the Famine."[5] Women were often married by sixteen, men usually by twenty, and the children, no longer swept away by disease, came tumbling after. Between 1780 and 1840, Ireland's population more than doubled. Decade by decade, more people crowded into the same spaces.

Although potato production improved the caloric return per acre, enabling more people to retain a marginal attachment to the land, relentless population pressures pushed increasing numbers out. Quantities of them roamed Ireland. An expanding flow of emigrants sought work in England, another stream sought opportunities in America. Some ranged as far as Australia.

Whether the nineteenth-century Catholic Irish inherited an unusually flexible kinship system or devised one to suit necessity remains a question, but the outcome—an extraordinarily successful adaptation to migration—is not. They forged links in their migration chains easily and used them heavily. Even those who left home individually soon reconnected with groups: "[A] lone emigrant was almost unknown."[6] At home, kinship defined mutual obligations; abroad, mutual obligations created kin equivalents. At home, "friends" actually were relatives; abroad, friends virtually became relatives. By contrast to their Protestant Irish counterparts, Catholic emigrants also maintained strong commitments to the kin who stayed behind. At the height of the Famine, which killed a million and sent nearly two million to North America, three out of four emigrants had their passage paid by people already on the other side of the Atlantic. An astonishing statistic under any circumstances, it revealed how early and how thoroughly these transatlantic networks blanketed Ireland. Out of these experiences in migration, Irish kinship, according to Conrad Arensberg, can best be understood as "a system of potentialities. It is expansive, rather than restrictive. . . . Thus [an Irishman] embraces ever wider numbers of his contemporaries." What happened abroad reverberated among kin back home; what mattered at home radiated out to those abroad. "The behaviours and sentiments of kinship 'travel' with them."[7]

If large-scale migration explained the timing of Irish nationalism, the British presence explained its force. During Britain's prolonged conflict with the Catholic giants of the continent, the Act of Union in 1801 drew Ireland tighter under its rule. The systematic, dogmatic governance of the early nineteenth century, including Britain's imposition of the English language, squeezed Ireland tighter still. An abiding hatred of Britain defined Irish nationalism everywhere. Charismatic Daniel O'Connell, who dominated Irish nationalism for approximately a quarter century, brought these feelings into focus. In fact, before his emergence in the late teens, Irish nationalism scarcely existed. Henry Grattan and Robert Emmet, whose isolated, dramatic challenges to British rule around the turn of the nineteenth century made them nationalist martyrs in retrospect, had taken guidance from the Declaration of Independence and the Rights of Man: They were far more republican revolutionaries than Irish nationalists. What the eloquent O'Connell did in league with a network of priests was weave the cause into the one institution large numbers of Irish could claim as their own, the Catholic Church. In the process they energized a genuinely popular movement, a nationalism grounded in the lives of Irish peasants before a continental movement had anything resembling this kind of broad-based constituency.

In 1825, with the introduction of "Catholic rent"—a penny a month to the priest for O'Connell's campaigns—Irish nationalism added a second innovation: a contribution of money to clamp their hearts to the cause. For the very poor, the last penny went to the first love. Within a few years, presumably docile tenants were voting in legions for the man their landlords most feared. By embedding nationalism in the church, however, O'Connell had difficulty keeping his constituents' eyes on British power generally rather than on Catholic disabilities in particular. Many parishioners probably felt no need to try. In any case, all his years of campaigning netted substantial benefits for the church but nothing in the way of self-government.

No sooner did a weary O'Connell, threatened by jail, finally give up than the Famine commenced. Between 1845 and 1855, Ireland's population fell from 8.5 to 6 million. This terrible Malthusian moment transformed Irish culture. The birthrate plummeted.

In place of the traditional early marriage, post-Famine Irish either delayed or avoided it: By 1900, 20 percent of the women and 25 percent of the men over forty were single. Yet illegitimacy remained "astonishingly low for a people marrying so little and late."[8] The customary division of land among heirs ended. By maintaining the integrity of each plot, families sent a regular flow of young people on the road. Between the Famine and the First World War, about 3.5 million Irish landed in North America. Ireland's population continued to decline: under 5 million by the early twentieth century; then by the 1920s half the pre-Famine number, coming full circle back to the level of 1780 when the surge began.

Irish life, in other words, pivoted on the Famine. Nationalism might well have been one of its casualties, obliging the Irish at some later time to start over again. What sustained it were their flexible chains of fictive kin. While the Irish in Ireland buried the dead, nationalism survived by shifting its center of gravity across the Atlantic. In the years of O'Connell's ascendancy, the Irish in America had played only a minor role, cheering his cause and contributing money to it but otherwise simply watching from abroad. Now, as they took the initiative, they gave Irish nationalism a distinctive stamp: secular, public, and violent.

By and large, the Irish escaping famine did not bring strong church discipline with them; "In fact, many were ignorant of basic Christian beliefs."[9] Even though Roman Catholic churches mushroomed along with immigration, they never matched their authority in Ireland. A variety of public figures—in the broad sense, politicians—seized that authority in America. If as some experts claim the crucial fact about the modern Balkans is that they missed the Enlightenment, one of the critical clues to modern Ireland is that the Enlightenment only brushed the top of its Catholic culture. In the United States, however, the brash liberalism of its remarkably open public sphere affected almost all institutions that came near it. Irish American politicians, glad for the church's help, did not need it to survive. Political newspapers, which cropped up wherever Irish Americans congregated, assumed many of the tasks of instructing the public, and the church, to stay in the discussion, funded periodicals of its own, with revealingly secular names like *Freemen's Journal*, the most important of the lot. Organizations ranging from sports clubs to mutual aid societies constituted another means for mobilizing opinions. At least at the level of rhetoric, nationalism permeated all these arenas. Wherever Irish Americans gathered, calls for Irish freedom echoed off the walls. Visitor after visitor commented on it. Typically one expressed astonishment at "the existence, three thousand miles away, of a people numerous, comfortable and influential, animated by a spirit of nationality beyond all belief."[10] Charles Parnell, the great nationalist icon of the late nineteenth century, thought they were more self-consciously Irish than Ireland's Irish.

Around midcentury they were certainly more violent. For the Irish in Ireland, working through the Famine meant setting its horrors behind them and making new lives. For Irish Americans, however, the Famine was a memory to keep at white heat, a hatred for the British to sear over and over again into their collective consciousness. Those feelings fueled their nationalism. Its characteristic expression was Fenianism—an attempt to inspire a general uprising with dramatic acts of violence—a style that flaired for only a second in Ireland but continued to smolder, then periodically burst into flames, in the United States. The American Fenians' abortive invasions of Canada in 1866 and 1870 were cases in point. If in one sense they were opéra bouffe, the cheers greeting them spoke to a stubborn streak of bloodymindedness among Irish Americans. Of course it mattered that Irish American violence carried almost no penalties in the United States, that talk was indeed cheap there, and that the sheer size of the nationalist pool in America swelled the ranks for all points of view. As the number of Irish declined at home, the proportion abroad rose steeply. Depending on the formula for calculation, by 1920 somewhere between three and six times more people could claim to be Irish in the United States than on the home island.

By the time nationalism revived in Ireland, it was a thoroughly transatlantic movement, including noisy branches in Canada, New Zealand, and Australia as well as in the United States. In 1879 after prison terms in Britain, Michael Davitt and John Devoy, two members of the Irish Republican Brotherhood (or Fenians), founded the Irish National Land League in America, where within three years about fifteen hundred branches with perhaps a half-million members were supporting rent wars throughout the Irish countryside. By then the British home secretary had no difficulty identifying "an Irish nation in the United States, equally hostile, with plenty of money, absolutely beyond our reach and yet within ten days' sail of our shores."[11] During the 1880s, Charles Parnell funded his campaign for Home Rule with American money. Michael Davitt stayed long enough to join Henry George's 1886 mayoral campaign in New York City; John Devoy remained in America, and much later dickered with the German ambassador to Washington over a secret alliance against the British during the First World War. In time, Fenian became a shining badge of honor in Ireland, one that would be pinned posthumously to the hero of the Easter Rebellion, Patrick Pearse, himself a member of the IRB's Irish branch. Perhaps half of Ireland's nationalist leaders lived for a substantial period abroad. The crucial fact was that the Irish generated nationalism wherever they congregated. What did it matter who was in Ireland, who was in America, and who shuttled between them? Leaders and followers lived everywhere along the serpentine lines of migration.

If Irish nationalism followed people wherever they went, German nationalism stayed home. Nowhere in Europe did nationalism march more closely to the beat of the state. Although German writers, beginning with Johann Gottfried von Herder, pioneered the idea of nationalism, its realization in their midst seemed remote early in the nineteenth century. A scattering of liberals did keep alive the dream of some kind of united Germany, but their failures both of imagination and of strategy during the revolution of 1848 bankrupted their cause. Popular nationalism was not an issue. As one historian has summarized it, until well after midcentury "nationalism was a minority movement, deeply divided and with only a marginal impact on German life."[12] Towns stood guard against little states and little states kept watch on the bigger ones, crisscrossing the German-speaking lands into a mosaic of jurisdictions and traditions. Though Vienna was decaying as an imperial center, it remained the most important German city, and the government's erratic policy toward this pieced and parceled north generally served the status quo.

Nevertheless, combining many small units into a large one was the story of both nation-building and state-building everywhere. Within the German lands, site of the Reformation and source of the Counter-Reformation's bloodiest struggles, religion more than politics—or religion as politics—accounted for the special resistance to unification. In the nineteenth century, as both Catholic and Protestant migrants infiltrated states that had once been enemy territory and hence lived increasingly side by side, they identified themselves not by their common territory but still through their deep devotional differences. They had moved without budging. German nationalism, largely a Protestant impulse, had to reckon with the consequences. It was no longer possible to create a Protestant Germany without Catholics. Was it possible to create one with them?

Prussia begged the question by hammering out a state instead. In Carl Becker's witty summary, Bismarck united Germany by dividing it into three parts. Two quick wars—one crushing Austria in 1866, the other humiliating France in 1870—secured the new state, essentially an institutionalization of Prussia's dominance across the heart of German-speaking Europe. France licked its wounds, and Austria turned its attention south and east. Nationalist sentiment grew in the wake of these victories. Urban middle-class talk of a united Germany—vague even by the permissive standards of mid-nineteenth-century nationalism—picked up with the creation of a North German Confederation in 1866, but popular nationalism, in effect, dated from the French capitulation at Sedan. Triumph over the old enemy gave a national sheen to the new German Empire. Hence as Bismarck set to the task of forcing Catholic citizens into this Germany's mold, two matters besides its essentially Protestant nature became clear: The state's centrality in the entire process merged nationalism with patriotism, then encased the combination inside German territory.

Statistically, Germans had as much incentive as the Irish to stretch conceptions of kinship to cover migrants in Eastern Europe and North America. Their population boom started early in the nineteenth century. In Prussia alone, it rose around 70 percent between 1815 and 1860. In the south and west, Germans experienced their version of Ireland's great famine, initiating the first large wave of emigrants to the United States in 1846. When a second wave rose after the American Civil War, its sources were already shifting to the northeast, which dominated the last wave ending in 1893. By then the territory contained within the new German Reich had contributed to a nineteenth-century outflow of well over 4 million.

Culture and politics combined to minimize migration's impact on nineteenth-century German nationalism. Nothing abroad encouraged Catholic and Protestant Germans to consider themselves branches of a single family. Moreover, Lutheran emigrants who did feel drawn into a German nationalist movement found themselves dismissed back home. Where the state controlled the making of the nation, emigrants counted themselves out. To matter, they needed to live in Germany. For those Germans whose nationalism derived from language and culture, the Bismarckian solution did not cover nearly enough Germans; for those who placed the accent on Protestantism, it had too many Germans; but for the large proportion who let the state define their nation, only citizens of the new Germany were truly Germans. In fact, Bismarckian policy did not reach out, it drove out. Migration's relation to nationalism always had two sides: gathering in dispersed kin and excluding unwanted aliens. During the late 1880s, Germany expelled tens of thousands of Polish speakers, pressuring others to follow.

As if they heard the doors closing behind them, emigrating Germans, who began arriving in quantity around midcentury, concentrated on life in America. Proudly German in culture, they constructed inturning little societies around church, language, customs, and celebrations. There they prospered in groups: German families embedded in German communities situated once and for all in America. The more binding the cultural cement, the more self-sufficient their social environment became; the more self-sufficient their environment, the more distant they grew from Germany. Even as the initial communities eroded, people moving on looked back to those settlements, not to Germany, as the home they had left. The percentage of naturalized citizens climbed, ties across the Atlantic slipped away, return rates stayed very low. Although there might be thrills in visiting and in indulging a moment of German immersion, these people knew that they belonged somewhere else.

German Americans never lost an awareness of events abroad, of course. The Franco-Prussian War and unification were certainly occasions for celebration. Especially in America's industrial cities, where transoceanic connections tended to be considerably stronger among German Americans, debating European trends fit into everyday life. Here, however, it was socialism, not nationalism, that maintained the best communications and framed the hottest discussions, and throughout the formation of imperial Germany, socialists and nationalists were snapping at each other's throats. Hence with the outbreak of the First World War, while the sympathies of German Americans went with the Central Powers, they were little more than a remote cheering section. It was simply too late for German officialdom, which had dismissed nineteenth-century emigrants as deserters, to expect any more from them. Perhaps beady-eyed American patriots would have gone hunting for spies among people with German backgrounds no matter what. As it was, the superpatriots misread cultural consciousness as nationalist commitment—a major error in the case of German Americans, where the two orientations worked at odds. In retrospect, it is obvious that the spy chasers picked the wrong group: There was much more going on among the nationalist-driven, British-hating Irish Americans.

The movement of people that did spur German nationalism was migration inside the Reich itself. After a rocky quarter century of internal conflict and confusion, a state-based and state-bounded nation began to congeal in the 1890s, as the flow from the farms and towns into Germany's industries and cities picked up and emigration declined to a trickle. With Bismarck's Kulturkampf against Catholicism abandoned, the emphasis shifted from the conflict over cultures to the definition of citizens: what were their rights and responsibilities and how should they fulfill their obligations to the state, matters that bonded Germans inside the Reich with one another and sealed them even more tightly from outsiders. On the eve of the Great War, "few German speakers in the German Empire thought of Germany as anything other than the territory of the Empire, and of themselves as anything other than national members of that state."[13]


If the state threatened to swallow German nationalism, it threatened to elude Jewish nationalism altogether. Like Irish nationalism, it grew out of large-scale, transoceanic migration and sought to gather in Jews wherever they had gone, but unlike the movement among the Irish—or for that matter any other European movement—it spent years debating where on earth it should come to rest.

Zionism materialized in the context of many East European nationalist movements. Late in the nineteenth century, the Jewish population there soared along with the populations of neighboring East European peoples, and the scramble to make limited resources cover more and more people resulted in immiserization and neoserfdom all around. Communities everywhere cracked at the seams under these pressures, sending sundry people throughout the entire region on the move. As for the Jews in particular, between 1882 and 1914 roughly 2.5 million left the Pale—about one-third of its total population. Yet in a sense nothing changed there. With population increasing 50 percent between 1882 and 1914, emigration simply siphoned off the surplus: There were as many Jews in Russia after the mass exodus as before.

In many ways, Zionism looked like the nationalism developing around it. Early in the 1880s, proto-Zionists gave old experiences new meanings and new experiences collective meanings with a traditional ring. Migrations spurred by specific regional causes were pictured in the universal context of Jews wandering in exile for two thousand years; ritual expressions of a return to Jerusalem conjured prospects of an actual return. The most creative of these voices for a new Jewish consciousness, Asher Ginzberg—better known by his pseudonym Ahad Ha'am—founded B'nei Moshe in 1889 to promote Hebrew as the foundation for a grand spiritual and cultural revival. Hence when Theodor Herzl issued his dramatic warning in 1896 of the Jews' false faith in assimilation, advocated a separate homeland, and called up the World Zionist Organization to achieve it, he could draw together many scattered pieces awaiting a full-fledged nationalist movement.

Although Herzl was a cosmopolitan Viennese out of Paris, his primary audience did not lie in Western Europe, where a small, stable Jewish population contributed only occasional converts to Zionism. The people who heard him shared Eastern Europe's shtetl culture, seething with movement and sustaining chains of migration that almost always bypassed Western Europe for the

United States. With strong community and family traditions and a long familiarity with catch-as-catch-can survival, shtetl life proved to be excellent preparation for stretching family networks, elaborating systems of mutual support, and reconceiving kinship to cover countless thousands of strangers—the essentials for an expansive, inclusive nationalism.

Rising anti-Semitism gave Zionism its urgency. In 1893, three years before Herzl published his clarion call, *The Jewish State*, Karl Lueger raised political anti-Semitism to a new level with the formation of the Christian Social Party, based in Herzl's Vienna. Throughout Zionism's emergence, anti-Semitism was heating up across the Western world, even in Britain, a pioneer in Jewish emancipation. In retrospect, Zionist myths attributed its appearance—in effect, the necessity of Zionism—to these fresh waves of anti-Semitic violence that drove shtetl Jews in search of a real home and frightened intellectual Jews into imagining one for them. Pogroms in 1881, followed a year later by draconian imperial restrictions, did pose immediate threats to Jews in the Russian Pale. As brutal as those actions were, however, they did not set the pace of migration. Rates of departure from swollen but peaceful Austrian Galicia, Albert Lindemann has pointed out, matched those from violence-ridden Russia: "Economic factors were almost certainly more important than political ones."[14] Despite the special viciousness accompanying its birth, in other words, Zionism nicely illustrated the standard sequence: population explosion, migration, nationalism.

The extraordinary feature of Zionism was its free-floating quality. What kind of space did it seek for Jews? If it only wanted a safe place, it was not nationalism; it was a refuge movement. The former did not automatically recommend a barren piece of Turkish territory. The Russian Leo Pinsker, whose *Auto-Emancipation* (1882) initiated debate on the issue, had safety on his mind, and a barren piece of Turkish territory around Jerusalem, however sanctified, did not recommend itself. Although Herzl showed a greater appreciation for the uniqueness of Palestine, he kept his mind open to all kinds of alternatives—Argentina, Mesopotamia, in desperation Uganda—and after his death in 1904, other Zionists such as the writer Israel Zangwill continued to scan the globe for a Jewish haven.

Under Herzl's successor, the cosmopolitan East European Chaim Weizmann, Zionism's most enduring leader, the movement did come to focus on a Jewish holy land. Nevertheless, under the best of circumstances Palestine was a peculiar base. Unlike other nationalist homelands, it contributed no substantial constituency of its own to the movement. As late as the Second World War, less than half a million Jews lived there. The Zionist organization was equally adrift—now meeting in this city and now in that, now headquartered in Europe and now in the United States, but never rooted in Palestine. Even if Zionists could agree on the boundaries of their holy land and the rights of people other than Jews to live there, what role would it play in Jewish life: the ultimate haven? the symbol of freedom? the site of pilgrimages? Contrary to the belief that Yahweh had already marked out the story of the Jews, Zionism as much as any nationalist movement was obliged to make it up as it went along.

Vagueness at its core affected everything else about Zionism. Ahad Ha'am, whose mission was to give Jewishness substance through a Hebrew-based culture, had little patience with these geographical preoccupations. Ardor for Palestine, he feared, would drain energies from the primary objectives: Jewishness now, a homeland in all good time. After all, he pointed out, Palestine was already occupied. Herzl on his part had little interest in the cultural revival among East European Jews. The Jewishness he prized was scarcely distinguishable from the virtues that cultivated Westerners of all sorts valued—cooperation, for instance, or charity. He concentrated on a place: land in the forefront, Jewishness in the shadows. Because the wealthy Jews on whom most Zionist enterprises more or less relied lined up behind Herzl, Weizmann, who considered a heightened Jewishness and a relentless pursuit of the Palestinian homeland two sides of the same coin, had a devil of a time keeping his politics and his appeals for money aligned with his vision.

The problems of a Jewish homeland and a Jewish culture, in turn, overlapped with a final source of controversy: the problem of Judaism. Some Zionists anticipated reestablishing a traditional community under Judaic law that citizenship in a Western European state had all but eliminated among emancipated Jews. Many more Zionists wanted a secular state, sometimes more socialist than Jewish. Even more envisaged a spiritually elevated but not a theocratic Palestinian homeland. Although these differences shot to the top of the agenda only when someone in power sat hard on one end of the seesaw, they added another element of diversity to a movement that always seemed on the verge of splintering.

One puzzle in the study of Zionism is why this spindly movement survived at all, an outcome for which the tenacious Weizmann deserved special credit. An even more interesting puzzle is why it did not grow into a robust mass movement. The answer lay in the United States, which the great migration out of Eastern Europe made a home for Jews second only to the Pale. By all odds, New York City in particular—destination, way station, nerve center for Jews in motion—should have been a flaming center of Zionism. What the Irish, 20 percent of its population in 1860, had once been to New York City, 1.5 million Jews—more than 30 percent of its population—were by 1920. That concentration, in combination with the migrants' transoceanic ties, adaptable communities, and tenacious traditions of uniqueness, gave Jews in America just the resources that a thriving nationalist movement—Irish nationalism, for example—required. Despite it all, Zionism fared poorly in the United States. Critically weak at the American end of the migration chain, the movement never managed to compensate in some other way.

The explanation was revealed by the light that the American

experience cast on the three controversies circling Zionism: the problem of a Jewish home, the problem of Jewishness, and the problem of Judaism. Early in the twentieth century, Jews in America broadcast the message that they had solved Herzl's problem. Measured against their past, the meanness and the jeopardy they experienced in the United States—probably similar to what the Irish had once met—seemed little short of a miracle. They had families, homes, and synogogues, money to spend and freedom to explore, an openness to life that no one in the Pale could have dreamed of enjoying. In cities with many cultures and none in charge, Jewishness transmuted into another kind of hyphenate Americanism. To become American, in other words, meant to remain Jewish—that is, Jewish in whatever ways other Jews recognized. Judaism was subsumed under Jewishness: Create temples that suited this ever-fluid, remarkably safe environment. The result was a distinctively American Reform Judaism: long on moral responsibility and short on ritual observance, a center of service and support rather than keeper of the ancient law, and a link to wider communities—Gentile as well as Jewish—rather than a community unto itself. Families, taking authority from the synogogue into the home, increasingly decided how their religion would be observed.

In the tradition of mobile Jews restructuring their lives again and again as the context changed, this vigorous culture gave cohesion and identity to millions of Jewish Americans whose fortunes—as individuals, as a community—had by all the standard criteria improved astonishingly through migration. What could Zionism, a wandering minstrel of a movement, offer them? A place of refuge, a means of expressing Jewishness, a way of preserving Judaism were simply not on their agenda; they concentrated on fighting for more in America. Even at the level of philanthropy, the response among recent migrants to the hardships in their communities of origin was to bring more people to America. Unlike Irish American nationalism, American Zionism had no real focus.

If Jewish Americans hated Russia as much as the Irish Americans hated Britain, so what? They had no desire whatsoever to rule the Pale. Although Jewish Americanness—here and glad of it!—did show a resemblance to German Americanness—here and that's it!—the critical difference in their larger stories was that German nationalism cut ties with emigrants whereas Zionism desperately needed to connect with Jews on the move. In effect, Zionism dangled, an East European movement left holding its end of the migration chain.

What these Irish, German, and Jewish examples illustrate are the protean, transatlantic qualities that shaped European nationalism's beginnings. Nevertheless, they leave nationalism too isolated within Western society and too frozen in time. Now we must pick up the stories of other powerful movements that interacted with nationalism, and the changes—in some cases profound ones—that all of these movements experienced in the course of the long nineteenth century.

CHAPTER 3

## Changing Contexts

In two fundamental ways, the company nationalism kept shaped its history. One of these crucial contexts linked nationalism with the other great popular movements of the nineteenth century, socialism and democracy. A second context interwove changes in nationalism with changes in the other major dividers in nineteenth-century Europe: language, race, religion, and above all the state. In both cases, these interrelationships became tighter and their consequences deeper in the four decades that led up to the outbreak of the Great War in 1914. During those years, the course of socialism, nationalism, and democracy, the trio of movements that was now dominating European public policy, entwined like vines on a trellis. Following much the same chronology, Europe's primary dividers crowded around nationalism to form increasingly complex composites that seemed on the verge of dividing the continent into exclusive compartments of culture and territory. Together, these two processes tell a story of rising expectations, accelerating competition, and hardening differences that eventually transformed Europe.

The breakup of communalism, sweeping west to east across Europe, inspired all three of Europe's great nineteenth-century movements: socialism (the collective management of common resources to ensure equitable rewards for work); democracy (responsible government with popular elections and the peaceful transfer of offices); and nationalism (the right of a people claiming common ancestry to control their own destiny on their own land). Especially after 1870, the timing of the arrival of these movements' and their interaction mapped European history as effectively as any alternative guidelines.

The same broad transformation powered each of the three movements. As populations ballooned and local opportunities shrank, more villagers and townspeople had to go farther in order to find work, and when they did, they more often received wages in return. Goods made by wage earners undercut those made by local artisans and cottagers, sending still more people out to work for wages. Meanwhile, consolidated landholdings and urban pressures to produce more food more cheaply turned more and more peasants into wage earners. Although migrants overseas sometimes reversed the trend by founding new agricultural communities, nothing eased the pace in Europe, where more people continued to crowd their working lives into the same spaces.

As local cultures of work, revolving around land, household, and artisanal skills, shriveled, standards of living did not necessarily fall: Some people did better, some worse. Winners and losers alike, however, increasingly lost control over the terms of their labor, widening the gap between what they did today and what they could plan for the future and sending more and more of them in search of an elusive security. The more they moved from job to job, the more their work seemed like a game rigged against them. Publicists and officials representing the men who employed them sought to atomize wage earners, use the threat of starvation as their basic incentive, and restrict charity to keeping the worthy poor alive for future labor. Even if these mobile workers improved their lot, it was evident enough that they were being used by others in ways and toward ends beyond their control: They were a class set apart by the nature of their work.

Class replaced an outworn local identity with a portable one ready for the new working world. Wherever wage earners went, they found others in a similar situation, people on the loose whose livelihood depended on the unfathomable twists and turns of a hostile system. Especially for those who saw no way out of the working class, socialism went directly and dramatically to the heart of their situation: It promised an entirely new system built specifically around working people's needs. In none of its many variations did socialism offer an escape from work, only fairness at work. Socialism, in sum, was a system of work for workers, with as much protection against the hazards of chance as nineteenth-century radicals could imagine.

Local public life in communal societies, ascribing rights and responsibilities in a hierarchy of familiars, also unraveled under the pulls of migration. People's standing rarely moved with them; a society of strangers required new rules. The formal solution was a new citizenship, a single one mandated across a state's entire jurisdiction to replace many varieties of citizenship in myriad local units. In practice, however, uniformity evolved slowly and unevenly. Because those of highest prestige—people of rank and wealth—were the least likely to migrate, the emerging modern state continued to draw its resources through them, and the traditional hierarchies they capped, as long as it could. Well into the nineteenth century the inertia of vested rights kept the meaning of citizenship mired in a confusion of distinctions relating to property, status, birthplace, and jurisdiction. Even states otherwise responsive to modernizing changes accommodated to this crazy quilt of embedded localism, customary privilege, and favored forms of property, as the British Poor Laws and the constitutions of the United States and Prussia demonstrated.

Although it took time to work out the effects, the drastic

changes accompanying the French Revolution and the Napoleonic Empire did channel Europe's development toward uniform state citizenship. Before the Revolutionary era, the French state itself relied on "provincial estates, municipalities, chartered guilds, military governors who often held their offices hereditarily, courts whose judges owned their offices, religious institutions that exercised great independence, and thousands of proud nobles who clung jealously to their own particular privileges," along with a bevy of moneylenders and tax farmers.[1] Where Napoléon's France ruled, it destroyed the legal basis for this kind of hierarchical, haphazard conduct of state affairs. Attempts to patch up the Humpty-Dumpty of Europe's anciens régimes after 1815 might have turned out better if the relentless flows of population had not subtly, systematically eroded every effort. Following Napoléon, it no longer made sense to hire armies; nor were either local quotas or British press gangs a reliable alternative. The state's pool of young men, available wherever and however often they moved within the state, were the soldiers of the future. Much the same applied to the problem of taxing and extracting labor from a mobile population, too elusive a target for tax farmers and local grandees but manageable enough on a statewide basis. As traditional communities shrank in significance, in other words, the new citizenship both facilitated migrants' adjustment and the state's mobilization of resources. Lesser states then mimicked larger ones: Every ruler aspired to a scientific mastery of his domain.

Systematizing citizenship did not popularize it. For the right to live somewhere under the state's laws, citizens traded the state's right to levy taxes, extract labor, and exact services. It was a bad bargain: These streamlined new regimes consistently took more out of people's hides than the cumbrous old ones had. But citizenship also held within it the dream of an open public life where participation affirmed each person's humanity: liberty, equality, fraternity, as the eloquent, if gendered revolutionary slogan expressed it. It was this thrilling prospect that democracy promised to achieve. People who ruled themselves would have the power to secure their own rights and guarantee the justice of their own government.

In sum, three sequences marked out solutions to the fundamental problems that mass migration created. One ran from family life to ethnicity to nationalism, one from working life to class to socialism, and one from public life to citizenship to democracy. Each, in other words, gave priority to one of the three critical issues that community breakdown raised. All three were complicated processes: It was a long, winding road from families under stress to nationalism, from job grievances to socialism, or from overtaxed townsmen to democracy. Of course, not all expressions of ethnicity were nationalistic, not all class schemes socialistic, and not all forms of citizenship democratic. Nevertheless in the nineteenth century other variations increasingly orbited these dynamic centers.

Democracy, socialism, and nationalism were holistic visions: We the People, Working People, My People. Each purported to be a total solution. Nationalism, with its own version of political self-determination, also envisaged an economy of trust among kindred folk. Socialism, metaphorically a league of brothers and sisters, also pictured honest governance emerging naturally out of economic justice. Democracy's promise to free citizens for their own pursuits doubled as a vision of economic opportunity and family independence. Each of the three carried within it the radical potential of a new equality—at the ballot box, among laboring comrades, in a conclave of kin—and the engine in each case was migration. "Modern society is not mobile because it is egalitarian"—in Ernest Gellner's neat summary—"it is egalitarian because it is mobile."[2] All three affirmed both the personal worth and collective power of their members: New individual identities provided new means for concerted action. In each area, action itself was a triumph. The experience of asserting rights generated rights. Each of the three addressed pressing concrete needs by grandly enlarging the scope within which they could be met and by turning the very elements of crisis in civic, work, and family life into solutions. Atomization became freedom. Alienation became strength. Strangers became kin. As the three of them were rendering old social arrangements obsolete, each claimed to be preserving the best of the past: the spirit of the town meeting, the personal connection between workers and tools, the mutual assistance of family life. In fact, each cultivated a fantasy of Edenic roots: the myth of the social contract, the innocence of honest workers, the ur-connectedness of the first kin.

Each had distinctive weaknesses and strengths. Socialism, the most abstract in its reasoning, dealt most effectively with survival issues like food, shelter, and health. Democracy, with the thinnest provisions for mutual support, compensated by best expressing individual aspirations. Nationalism, the least articulated, issued the most open invitation to membership: no citizens' rights to win, no class loyalty to prove. Kinship, the claim went, explained itself. In the nationalist fold, there were no orphans, no bastards, no families without heirs.

As the three movements came alive in the wake of the Napoleonic Empire, all of them revealed a primary tension between their universalistic and particularistic aspirations. On the one hand, leaders in each case declared their cause the true heir of the French Revolution's vision of an emancipated humanity. Their version of socialism or democracy or nationalism, they claimed, could encompass the entire civilized—that is, white Christian—world, and they proceeded to act on that belief with extraordinary, sometimes suicidal optimism. Whatever else the era of French-generated turmoil contributed, it smashed assumptions about the inevitability of traditional ways and fed dreams of fashioning new societies. Early in the nineteenth century, socialism, nationalism, and democracy all reflected that heady faith. At the same time, each movement spawned diverse, quite separate experiments that in some instances were also mutually exclusive.

Before midcentury, socialism especially manifested those fragmenting characteristics.

For sheer variety neither democracy nor nationalism came close
to matching early nineteenth-century socialism. France was particularly fertile ground, ranging from the detailed comprehensive
schemes of Henri de Saint-Simon and Charles Fourier to the vague
destructive ambitions of Auguste Blanqui. Cooperative production, illustrated by Louis Blanc's workshops on one side of the
English Channel and Robert Owen's factories on the other, was a
natural area of exploration in a movement predicated on the
alienating, unjust nature of wage work. Most famously as the
Rochdale Plan, projects for the cooperative distribution of goods
also surfaced on both sides of the Channel. Moreover, socialism
tinged many activities that it did not dominate. During the 1830s
and 1840s, for example, socialist visions slipped in and out of the
working men and land-reform campaigns in the northeastern
cities of the United States. Early in the nineteenth century some
Methodist working people in Britain were influenced by socialist
ideas, which around midcentury were also inspiring the Anglican
Charles Kingsley's Christian Socialism.

Some of these experiments, notably the Owenite and Fourierite
communities, responded directly to the failure of traditional communities by creating new ones. Owen's paternalistic factory villages functioned like surrogate kin networks, assuming collective
responsibility for the children and the disabled. Nevertheless,
these self-contained ventures, too, envisaged changing the civilized world. They presented themselves as "patent office models
of the good society," communities designed to resolve basic issues
of work and justice so persuasively that, their founders anticipated, they would attract an ever widening circle of converts.[3] In a
fateful error, however, they waited for the world to come to them.
Where people were in motion, success depended on messages—
hopes, strategies, goals—that moved right along with potential recruits. Because early socialist communities self-consciously set out

to make a fresh start from first principles, a number of innovators took the seemingly vacant spaces in America as an ideal location to begin over again. Isolation in a vast country of mobile people was doubly disastrous. Unwilling or unable to float their ideas on the currents of migration, these test cases just dwindled and disappeared. In the face of early socialism's immobility, the decision of its challenger Karl Marx to focus on the propertyless wage earner—the quintessential worker on the move—was a stroke of genius.

What the irresistible model was to early socialism, the dramatic gesture was to early nationalism. On the twin assumptions that each people had a spirit of its own and that each spirit could give birth to a distinctive nation—assumptions that derived from the innovative nationalist theory of Johann Gottfried Herder—champions of early nationalism looked for the way to bring their people alive. Nationhood in this scheme of things was natural, and hence peaceful. "I am convinced," wrote Alexis de Tocqueville, with the price of the French Revolution in mind, "that the interests of the human race are better served by giving every man a particular fatherland than by trying to inflame his passions for the whole of humanity."[4] During the first half of the nineteenth century, nationalism's inherent thrust drove it toward freedom—freedom from the tyranny of an imperial power, the tyranny of superstition, the tyranny of an alien culture. A spark might ignite a nation. No need to worry in advance about boundaries, even in as ambiguous a case as Germany's: The very act of creation would clarify the nation.

In the most famous of early nationalism's sacrifice missions, Prince Alexander Ipsilandis in 1821 led his Sacred Battalion of utterly unprepared, outmanned youth against the Ottoman army to die for Greek liberty, and within a decade there was an independent state of Greece. Early nationalists drew a straight line between those two points. A quarter century after the prince's suicidial gallantry, the martyrs of Young Ireland stood up to die with the same hopes. Leaders simply had to find the lever, the crucial latch opening the door to a nation's realization. Hence the extraordinary perseverance of some leaders whose failures merely sent them searching over and over again for the real key. In years of exile, Guiseppe Mazzini expected that at the right moment he would land on Italian soil, plant his flag, and precipitate the nation. With only a little more attention to the logistics of his enterprise, Mazzini's friend Lajos Kossuth rode the revolutionary hopes of 1848 and 1849 in pursuit of roughly the same vision in Hungary. Unlike early socialism, where theory clashed with theory, advocates of early nationalism cheered one another's efforts as encouragement for their own. "I believe [nationality] to be the ruling principle of the future," wrote Mazzini. "I feel ready to welcome, without any fear, any change in the European map which will arise from the spontaneous general manifestation of a whole people's mind."[5]

Early democracy showed the least variety of the three. As a way of exercising citizenship, it had the most intimate ties to a state. Nationalism moved with a people and socialism with an ideology; but democracy stayed home to mobilize citizens. Although it would be a mistake to overemphasize those differences—neither English nor German nationalism exported well, many microexperiments in socialism never budged an inch, and democratic aspirations floated freely on the breezes of hope—there were far fewer models for democracy before the mid–nineteenth century than for either socialism or nationalism. In fact, only two had wide currency: French Revolutionary democracy, and the democracy in America that took its name from Andrew Jackson and found its publicist in Alexis de Tocqueville.

France and the United States shared important characteristics. In a century of long-range, long-term outmigrations, neither could reasonably be defined as an emigrant country. Population growth, which never skyrocketed in France, was already tapering off by the 1820s, a half century before any of its continental neighbors, and the expansion that did occur was largely absorbed in a countryside of small-scale peasant proprietors and in its many centers of small-scale manufacturing. The United States was the great recipient of other countries' exploding populations. Appropriately, neither generated a major movement that transformed migrating family members into the fictive kin of a French or an American nation. In fact, both made their primary contribution to nationalism by encouraging other people's: France by stirring new national consciousness at the point of a revolutionary bayonet, the United States by making room for the mobile partisans of Europe's many nationalist movements. Rather than exemplifying nationalism, both illustrated how another common denominator, citizenship, might give scattered people a sense of unity.

Revolutionary France could lay claim to inventing modern citizenship, by which people gave services to and received benefits from a central administration representing all of them as an integrated civic body. The democratic meaning of this citizenship derived from the revolutionary catchwords liberty, equality, fraternity: uniform standing before a code of law, regular participation in the selection of governors, and a collective commitment to the common welfare. If the Jacobin moment in the early 1790s was as ambiguous as it was brief, the dreams it let loose had remarkable staying power. The Revolution's armies, continuing a tradition of French cultural leadership and carrying the authority of actual citizens in arms, spread subversion wherever they went. Even in the reactionary years after Napoléon's exile, widespread hopes remained that another French uprising would ignite democratic revolutions throughout Europe.

Only with the eclipse of France's prospects after 1815 did a second democratic model attract serious European attention. The events around the American Revolution, radical in their own right as affronts to customary authority, positioned the United States to claim the mantle, a half century later, of the Western world's sole functioning democracy. America's source of distinction doubled as its source of cohesion in two ways. First, it was an additive democracy in which every vote counted as one more piece of the civic whole. The few bring only their limited wisdom to public life, explained George Bancroft, the troubadour of American democracy; the many contribute that much more, and ad infinitum: As the pool expanded, so did the people's wisdom. That kind of democracy invited both a boundless growth and an instant assimilation of new voters. Second, it was a mobile democracy that white men could exercise with equal ease wherever they went. The incessant politics that filled nineteenth-century America's public spaces looked very similar everywhere, and hence the strikingly frequent elections carried much the same meaning wherever they occurred: regular, repeated affirmation of the voters' freedom, their equality, and their membership in a collective governing body.

Nevertheless, the French ideal exercised a much greater influence than the American experience. Through midcentury, democracy in Europe remained an aspiration, for which France's revolutionary model—broad brushed, exciting, infinitely applicable—was wonderfully suited. American democracy, on the contrary, was a place-bound operating system, one that virtually every early nineteenth-century commentator, European or American, treated as unique to that country: Outsiders could only look. Two characteristics in particular—the abundance of farmland and the invisibility of government—seemed to prove the irrelevance of the American experience for Europe. However fragile France's democratic legacy, France itself was quintessentially European. It gave educated continentals a common language and a cultural frame of reference, it exemplified systematic central government, and it merged patriotism with military glory, attributes that Europeans readily understood. If this country at the pivot of their universe turned democratic, the rest of Europe might well follow after.

The crucial partner in the development of democracy, nationalism, and socialism alike was the modern state. In fact, none of these movements made sense without it. Democracy, a way of exercising citizenship, presupposed the existence of a state. Nationalism reached for the equivalent of a state of its own. Even socialism, ostensibly boundaryless, accommodated to the state's jurisdiction and eventually competed for its power.

At the same time, these systems of loyalty were constructed along conflicting lines. If, in Cynthia Enloe's phrasing, the state was "a vertical creature of authority," each of these movements was "a horizontal creature of identity," a way of visualizing connections laterally, not hierarchically.[6] In each case, the state was its natural predator, ambitious to devour all other loyalties for its own purposes. It set out to overwhelm democracy's suspicion of arbitrary power with a glorification of itself right or wrong; to replace nationalism's mutual assistance among kin with patriotism's rituals of duty and obedience; and to sacrifice the class needs of working people to the state's preoccupation with production and warfare. Eventually champions of the state would claim that it replicated on a grand scale what its mobile citizens once derived from communities: Now, it was said, the state provided them with identity, welfare, and opportunity. Quite rightly, advocates of democracy, socialism, and nationalism all associated the European state of the early nineteenth century with autocracy and repression; just as sensibly, the state on its part outlawed those movements as subversive. And in fact each was a wild card, capable of dramatic surges beyond the state's control. At the radical end of the spectrum, each movement did wish the state away: nationalism through a general will, socialism through a classless order, democracy through a self-regulating liberty. None of the three could live with the state, none could live without it: That was the standing contradiction of the new order.


The half century after 1870 was a grand era of European state building, when central governments everywhere amassed power, systematized administration, and mobilized re-sources. As they did, they fundamentally altered the terms within which the movements for socialism, democracy, and nationalism pursued their objectives. In all cases, the initiative lay with the state. Democrats, nationalists, and socialists certainly were not pressing central governments to expand; all three fought them in the name of the people's freedom. Nevertheless, by the end of the nineteenth century whether in emulation, in defense, or simply in escalating ambitions, tougher, harder nationalist, socialist, and democratic movements were growing throughout Europe along-side its expanding states. One way or another, all three interlaced their future with some version of the big state, even though the builders and keepers of the state—Bismarck and Cavour were ex-emplary—had no affection whatsoever for these movements.

For one thing, all three now acquired large, sustained follow-ings. Even in Western and Central Europe where nationalism, so-cialism, and democracy already made a significant difference before midcentury, those movements were eruptive and epi-sodic—at times popular, as the turmoil extending from Britain to Hungary demonstrated between 1847 and 1849, but even then fleeting. In Slavic Europe, there were no popular movements at all before midcentury, just isolated elites talking among themselves about ideas coming from the West. Then the greatest waves of nineteenth-century migration commenced, rising across the conti-nent and pouring into cities on both sides of the Atlantic. After 1870 more and more people listened to the great trio's messages, joined their campaigns, and stuck with their causes.

The momentum of these movements inspired similar policies in all three. Whether out of concern for the chronic dependence—or the threatening independence—of their followers, leaders every-where set about consolidating with a will. As they organized, they preached discipline. Where democracy, socialism, and nationalism had once been open and malleable, their counterparts at the end of the century were increasingly articulated, bureaucratic, and self-protective. Continental political parties, characteristically personalized and ephemeral as late as the 1880s, systematized around a corps of insiders. To be partisan was to follow the agenda. Champions of labor, once eager to fan the sparks from workplace grievances, instead formed trade unions to channel discontent and decide in their members' behalf. Faith in the spontaneous nationalist uprising waned: Plotting gave way to planning, gesturing to staging.

The Iron Law of Oligarchy, Robert Michels's uncanny insight into modern organizations, captured the basic changes in all three realms. Over and over again, power was siphoned to the top where small groups competed for the right to define goals and set strategy. Nothing mattered more to the leadership than maintaining the organization. The nature of the struggle left no option, the new logic insisted: Power had to be met with power. As the standard metaphor went, generals marshaled their troops for battle, loyal soldiers manned their posts. Movements lost their voluntary qualities. The Italian nationalist Guiseppe Verdi caught the new spirit in the scene from *Nabucco* (March 1842) where the Israelites—not from any claims of justice but strictly from arguments of necessity—banish Ishmael forever for breaking their code. The socialist commandment was no longer to identify one's comrades; it was never to desert them. People were not asked to choose loyalties, only to declare them.

A fine line separated mobilization from distrust. Given the "hard, continuous, repeated, creative ideological and political labor" these movements required, little wonder their leaders fought to preserve the results.[7] Nevertheless, discipline became an obsession. Socialist and democratic leaders expressed deep doubts about the ability of the very poor to get in line, let alone stay there. Marxists, now the predominant socialists, scorned a lumpenproletariat and its wildcat initiatives; middle-class democrats, now party men, feared the street politics that were once their great hope. Like strikes and elections, nationalist rallies were carefully designed activities. The more leaders thought of themselves as the movement's experts, the less they trusted ordinary followers. What could the average mind know of scientific materialism, administrative government, or cultural purification? In each of the three movements, continuing resistance to these trends in the name of a freer spirit only sharpened the urge at the top to tighten control.

By the 1890s each movement had its distinctive look. Across Europe working people's institutions congealed in class frameworks, to the consternation of vested interests everywhere. Democratic movements rallied behind responsible government and universal suffrage—sometimes just for males, sometimes for all adults. Nationalism, the first of the three to abandon its universalistic rhetoric, claimed not just the superiority but increasingly the separateness of each culture. To organize the fragmentary experiences of mobile people, each movement created its own narrative: democracy's whiggish tale of progressively evolving liberty and law; the socialist dialectic with its ultimate resolution in favor of the working class; the nationalist's drama of a folk on the verge of reclaiming its culture and homeland.

Necessarily the three movements interacted. Who could say where the disruption of civic life ended and the redefinition of work life began, or where needs at work separated from needs in the family? When a parent could no longer pass profitable skills to an offspring, an entire fabric unraveled. Hence it is not surprising that movements sometimes collaborated. Drives for union rights and universal suffrage moved side by side in Britain, Germany, and Sweden. Democratic champions in Flanders threw their weight behind Flemish autonomy, in Denmark behind Danish irredentism, and in Norway behind independence. Visualizing a future for the heterogeneous Austro-Hungarian empire, Karl Renner and Otto Bauer proposed a socialist state where citizens would have the freedom of a distinctive national identity without the need for territorial exclusiveness. In general, a widely perceived threat to the nation rallied democrats and socialists alike.

In those prewar years of jostling and maneuvering, however, it was easy to mistake collaboration for communion. Implicit in much of their cooperation was the sense of a zero-sum competition, one that the record often supported. In Britain democrats did absorb their socialist allies, just as in Germany socialists did the same to their democratic allies. In Sweden, with its muted nationalism, socialism flourished as it did not in Norway, where a vigorous nationalism tended to veil class differences. Hence, when victory seemed at a movement's fingertips, the urge to eliminate the competition had some basis. Following different logics, they pulled in different directions. Nationalism's responsiveness to kin interests looked like a corrupting nepotism to ideological socialists and meritocratic democrats. Neither a nation's autonomy nor the socialists' collective ownership could survive on democracy's teeter-totter of winning and losing. On the eve of the First World War, dreams of simply swallowing the alternatives ran through all three movements. American democrats pictured nations and classes dissolving in secret-ballot elections. Nationalists in northern Italy expected their victory to destroy socialism and erase democracy. Revolutionary socialists thought of nationalism and democracy purely as facilitators for the proletarian triumph that would render both obsolete.

The more intimate a movement's relations with the state, the stronger the impulse toward control. Beginning in the 1870s, the democrats in charge of the Third Republic used the state's schools and its army to indoctrinate everybody inside the boundaries of France as citizen-patriots and in the process trivialize attachments to region, ethnic community, union, and church alike. Shifting the basis of citizenship from bloodline to residence underlined the centrality of the state in crafting French unity. After 1881, with the examples of France and Germany before them, state-based nationalists mounted aggressive Russification campaigns against minorities in the tzar's empire. Serbia's iron-fisted nationalism, which materialized in the 1870s along with the autocratic Serbian state, simply merged its ambitions with those of the state: "to . . .

unite [within a Greater Serbia] all the Serbian people living under Ottoman and Habsburg rule."[8]

Phrased another way, competition mattered. Where none of the three movements could dominate the other two and, even more important, where none of them could merge with the state, a greater openness—a stronger check on autocracy and aggression, a higher likelihood of accommodation—almost always followed. Turning just to nationalism, this rule of competition applied equally to its relations with the other great dividers of the nineteenth century: language, race, and religion. The more these powerful sources of separation crisscrossed one another, the less any one of them could dictate the terms of division in Europe. By the same token, each one that coincided with nationalism raised its walls and thickened its gates to the outside world. A layering of all three atop nationalism made it a formidable fortress indeed.

Language always carried power. Skill in Latin and French helped to define the top of Europe's hierarchies well into the nineteenth century. Imperial centers ruled in the language of their choice, and subjects ignored that fact at their peril. The more systematically those centers tried to govern, the more insistently they imposed that choice. In the 1770s, to consolidate power at home and integrate a widespread empire, the court in Copenhagen insisted upon the use of a standard Danish wherever it ruled. Two decades later Jacobins in Paris mandated one French idiom throughout the republic. During the middle of the nineteenth century, an independent Greece, which Europe's great powers had carved out of the Ottoman Empire, consolidated its authority by replacing a Babel of dialects with a standardized modern Greek. In the second half of the nineteenth century, as states grew more and more ambitious, this trend accelerated. The newly created Italy set out to superimpose a single language across the mutually incomprehensible vernaculars that its subjects spoke—more or less the same goal that the newly energized Third Republic pursued in France. After 1867, rulers in the Hungarian portion of the Hapsburg Empire forced Magyar on its diverse population, most of whom spoke a Slavic language with entirely different linguistic roots.

At the receiving end, nationalist movements rose to resist. Macedonian nationalism—battling Serbs, Bulgarians, and Greeks on several fronts—developed late in the nineteenth century around the right to use its own language. When Albanians, caught in an even more complicated and bloody crossfire of Turks, Greeks, and Slavs, struggled to do the same, they only managed as late as 1908 to settle on an alphabet. In 1911 Breton nationalism with its own political party—Fédération Régionaliste de Bretagne—materialized in reaction to a mandated Parisian French. Nevertheless, simply imposing an alien language rarely triggered a full-scale nationalist movement. For centuries people rooted in their communities had learned just enough of a conqueror's language to make exchanges, evade rules, and get work. Among themselves, they used their own language. Now, however, the stakes were increasing as people moved. When perennially mobile people mingled, the question of whose language would dominate turned into a constantly changing contest with big winners and big losers, one that affected merchants and bankers and clerks as much as farm laborers and factory workers. Late in the nineteenth century, as Catalonia industrialized inside traditionalist Spain, a cross-class movement with Catalan at its core emerged to secure the gains for the home folk—that is, for the fictive kin of modern nationalism. At about the same time, Flemish speakers, who had been pushing out of their swollen villages since midcentury and mixing at a disadvantage with the wealthier, French-speaking Walloons, mounted a campaign to make Flemish the official language in their part of a divided Belgium. Though a linguistic line had run through Belgium's territory since medieval times, new pressures from migration demanded new solutions.

Many of these linguistic movements had longer histories. American missionaries, of all people, had helped a tiny band of Bulgarians compile their first dictionary in the 1840s, decades before there was any hint of a popular nationalist movement. At about the same time, a bilingual Flemish elite had tried futilely to interest their indifferent Walloon superiors in making all Belgium bilingual. A generation later the introduction of penny-press newspapers marked another way station in these language campaigns. Flemish nationalism, for example, grew much more assertive with the publication of the first cheap Flemish newspaper in 1870. Still, the crucial matter was who paid attention. Where elites marched to their own beat, nobody followed. Establishing a learned Bokmål around midcentury did nothing to inspire Norwegian nationalism. Nationalist newspapers survived in Belgium when there were enough receptive Flemings loose in the cities to buy them.

Widely circulating newspapers also told nationalists in one movement what nationalists elsewhere were doing. As one example, Ahad Ha'am, the inspiration behind modernizing Hebrew as the language of the Jews, taught himself several languages, read avidly, and knew exactly what was going on in the nationalist movements around him. By the 1890s the passion for a distinctive language seemed to infect every nationalist movement. Douglas Hyde led the movement to exhume Gaelic for Irish nationalism. Serbs and Croats, whose leaders only a few years earlier had agreed upon a language in common, now did their best to extend the linguistic distance between them. Much of this was admittedly symbolic. Although Basque nationalism—also dating from the 1890s—set great store by the distinctiveness of Euskara, it was a language that even most of its followers found too difficult to use. A similar fate befell Gaelic, which precious few Irish still spoke. Nevertheless, if it played only a ceremonial role, ceremonies were important.

Race, the second of the great dividers running alongside nationalism, has come to have such horrific implications that it is hard now to reclaim its nineteenth-century uses. Nevertheless, just as language could be a device either to build communities or to annihilate them, so race could justify human diversity as well as human destruction. Like nationalism, it took on a modern meaning with the Enlightenment, when a deepening awareness of the globe's many cultures rendered obsolete the time-honored, Christian-centered dichotomy of civilized us and barbaric them. But unlike nationalism, innovative ideas about race did not grew out of local needs; they filled intellectual space that the shrinking relevance of Christian explanations left vacant.

Race, the new idiom for conceptualizing a varied world, was not itself an explanation of anything, only a vocabulary common to a great range of explanations. Throughout the long nineteenth century, nothing discouraged Europeans from giving race multiple, fluid meanings. During the first half, it seldom rose above a manner of speaking, a way of remarking on cultural differences within Europe and of restating routine beliefs about Europe's superiority to the rest of the world. Once inside that Eurocentric framework, race often had quite optimistic connotations. A biblical faith in the single origin of all humankind gave the world's current diversity a sense of contingency: From one, many had come; from the many of today, other outcomes always remained possible. Even theorists of Aryan and Anglo-Saxon superiority commonly believed in the inheritance of acquired characteristics: What you learned, you passed on to the next generation. In a progressive universe, therefore, backward cultures/races were almost certainly changing for the better.

The great exception covered the population of sub-Sahara Africa. In the discourse of the philosophes as well as the prejudices of the marketplace, African blacks were already singled out by the eighteenth century as the lowest of the low. To an old identification as natural slaves, Europeans added the curse of science—both pre-Darwinian and post-Darwinian—that one way or another consigned black people to the bottom of the human scale.

These beliefs hardened considerably in the second half of the nineteenth century. More and more intellectuals attacked monogenesis: White and black, they insisted, must have been different from the very beginning. Even those who retained the faith in monogenesis increasingly abandoned its egalitarian implications. So many centuries of divergence, Europeans argued, had made these inequalities permanent. Or perhaps black Africans were not really humans after all. When skeletal evidence could not establish an evolutionary connection between the gorilla and the human, for example, there was a strong tendency, in the historian George Stocking's telling phrase, "to throw living savage races into the fossil gap."[9]

Although color-coded racism had devastating consequences abroad, it had little influence on the perception of race differences at home: Black savages were far away, other people were here. In Europe race remained a rough synonym for culture. Intellectuals of various persuasions—Karl Marx and Joseph Ernest Renan, for example—construed it that way. So did many government officials. Apparently the Greek government convinced a substantial number of the country's ethnic minorities that assimilation would make them members of the Greek race. Sundry people who married the migrating Irish were welcomed into the Irish race. In this spirit, the historian Henri Pirenne argued that from years of interaction several peoples had come together to form a distinctive Belgian race.

Even where a science of race contributed to the hardening of exclusionary attitudes, it tended to reinforce predilections rather than freeze people in preassigned categories. Hence Count de Gobineau, the mid-nineteenth-century theorist who has been called the godfather of Europe's worst racism, discarded theories of a biologically pure race as irrelevant and considered some intermixture the best for all parties. As rigid a nationalism as the Basque variant used race to denote its unique culture, not a biologically differentiated people. Eugenics, the hardest edge of biological determinism on the eve of the Great War, enjoyed its greatest success across the Atlantic in the United States. In Europe, in other words, the strong forces of racism went into imperialism, the weak ones into nationalism. Of the layers that other dividers placed atop European nationalism before the First World War, race was the least burdensome.

Europe's Jews, commonly called a race and increasingly at risk late in the century, might well have disagreed. Of course anti-Semitism, gouging a channel through centuries of Christian history, was nothing new. It may be an idle question but it is not an idle consideration whether medieval Crusaders, provided the means, would have killed all the Jews in the world. Against that background Jews were the greatest single beneficiaries of the Enlightenment theories of racial variety. Though observant Jews remained a strange lot apart in the new dispensation, they were not necessarily evil or even inferior. During much of the nineteenth century, the trends ran toward greater openness, with age-old anti-Jewish restrictions falling throughout Western and Central Europe. Indeed, one of the rationales behind the Hebrew-based cultural revival late in the century was a fear that spreading tolerance might achieve what centuries of persecution had failed to accomplish: the disappearance of a distinctive Jewish people.

As nationalism hardened, anti-Semitism also spread and deepened. Intimations in the 1870s rose in volume during the 1880s, not only in the Pale but also in the heart of cosmopolitan Europe. Karl Lueger's anti-Semitic political party in Vienna was soon joined by French conservatives who used the Dreyfus affair to attack Jews generally. For those hostile to a multitude of anonymous migrants, Jews—part of the flow, of course—were the quintessential wandering strangers. Although the numbers were scarcely significant, Jewish migration into London's East End triggered the British Aliens Act of 1905, limiting the rights of Jews even if they did become naturalized citizens. By then, a systematic and aggressive anti-Semitism was operating in a stretch of countries that ranged from Greece and Romania through Poland into Finland.

Nevertheless, the old and the new wove together in complicated ways. Jews continued to find homes and hopes in Lueger's Vienna. The brief Dreyfus affair went up in smoke after 1900. As assimilated Hungarians, Jews participated in the campaigns to Magyarize Slavic and German peasants. Although race was now competing with class for working people's loyalties, as Marx's onetime colleague Moses Hess noted, nothing kept Jews from playing a prominent role in the socialist politics of early twentieth-century Europe.

In fact, it was rarely clear how to factor concepts of race into this rising anti-Semitism. Christianity, its traditional source, remained dominant, a fact that underlined the special significance of religion in changing nationalism's fortunes throughout Europe. In general, the more seriously a church took its role as a universal institution, the more likely it would muster power against nationalism. For deeply committed Roman Catholic clergy in Spain, France, and Italy, nationalism was a deadly secular enemy. Early in twentieth century, when Spanish nationalists set out to overcome the church's repressive, antimodernist record, the Roman Catholic hierarchy bested them by channeling popular energies back into the church. At the end of the nineteenth century, French Catholics countered the Paris-centered civic integration of the Third Republic with a Rome-centered movement for moral purification. An unforgiving pope treated the loss of his domain to Italian unification as a mortal sin. Add to that impressive record of resistance along Europe's Mediterranean flank the collapse of Bismarck's Kulturkampf in the new Germany, and the strength of a militant Roman Catholicism as a counter to European nationalism becomes clear.

Not surprisingly, where a church did join its mission to the nation's cause, it, more than any other additional influence, toughened prewar nationalism. Despite the efforts of the patriarchate in

Constantinople to keep Greek Orthodoxy true to its universal claims and hence aloof from all nationalist movements, the church divided against itself, with the Bulgarian and Greek branches reinforcing rather than tempering those warring loyalties. Eastern Orthodox clergy in Serbia, viewing the new state as the church's champion against Ottoman tyranny, threw themselves unreservedly behind the national cause. At the other end of the spectrum, ambivalent religious establishments opened the way for other influences. Unresolved rabbinical disputes over the meaning—indeed, the wisdom—of Jewish nationalism left secular Zionists in charge of the movement. Although the pietistic, Rome-bound Irish Catholic church never repudiated Irish nationalism, its suspicions of a secular leadership kept the church at the edges of the movement after 1870. In early twentieth-century Poland, it required aggressive Lutherans on one side and aggressive Eastern Orthodox on the other to pressure a reluctant Roman Catholic clergy at long last into an alliance with secular nationalists.

The best way to highlight the changes in European nationalism after 1870 is to look first at what those movements shared, then at what differentiated them. One way or another, all of them participated in the hardening process that began in the 1870s and intensified in the 1890s. As Eric Hobsbawm has demonstrated with particular clarity, the stakes of success increased dramatically. Movements that had once sought autonomy now demanded independence; movements that had once sought independence sometime in the future demanded it now. Movements otherwise as different as Norwegian and Macedonian nationalism showed the effects of that acceleration. Little wonder that *self-determination*, a term that might have meant many things, became a synonym for independence in the 1910s. Nationalists paid attention to one another, then proceeded to copy one another. Hence, *when* a movement arrived—that is, what characteristics predominated in the nationalist causes around it—had a good deal to do with the kind of movement it would be. Basque nationalism, appearing in the

1890s, was born hard. Zionism, organizing around the turn of the century, was born oligarchic.

The differences among Europe's movements spread them across a spectrum that set nationalism in competition with other loyalties at one end and surrounded it with reinforcing passions at the other. In Bohemia, for example, the presence of a vigorous socialist movement and the absence of both a firm religious connection and an exclusionary linguistic turn kept Czech nationalism notably mild. In Spain—where socialism and democracy reinforced regionalism, the church dug in its heels in opposition, and factions squabbled over their cultural heritage—no popular nationalism ever appeared. In Greece, on the contrary, the inconsequence of socialism and democracy, a fervent commitment from the Orthodox hierarchy, demands for linguistic and cultural homogeneity, and a dark strain of racism heated its nationalism to a point where only the state's chronic military limitations held it in check.[10] Subtract some racism, add an effective army, and the same summary applied to Serbia.

As the Balkan cases illustrated, wherever nationalism disappeared inside state patriotism, the mongrel results bristled with aggressive, coercive qualities. Each of the major dividers influencing nationalism had the mark of the state stamped on it. It was state power that transformed the French and Hungarian drives for linguistic and cultural homogeneity into juggernauts. It was the state, in pursuit of its imperial dreams, that turned racism into a scientifically embellished justification for mass brutality. It was the state that gave clerical megalomania the muscle to act out its fantasies. Because Eastern European nationalism arrived late, because it was rarely accompanied by strong socialist and democratic movements, and because partisan churches exercised unusually strong influence on it, there is some truth to the customary wisdom that as nationalism shifted from Western to Eastern Europe it grew harsher and more rigid. Nevertheless, the larger truth is that nationalism everywhere in Europe was becoming more oligarchic, more exclusive, more violent. Antipopulist trends, ambitions to eliminate socialism and democracy, companion movements for linguistic, racial, and religious monopolies, and above all militarizing states that costumed themselves as champions of the nation characterized nationalism throughout Europe on the eve of the Great War.

# CHAPTER 4

## The Case of the United States

As an extension of Europe, the settlements that became the United States shared in the transformation that accompanied migration. On both sides of the Atlantic, democracy, socialism, and nationalism developed on roughly the same schedule; none had meaning without reference to the other two. In America as in Europe, the degree to which each in the trio was absorbed into a central state—and the degree to which nationalism especially was layered by influences from religion, race, and language—best accounted for any of the three movements' softness or hardness, its tendency toward accommodation on one hand or exclusion on the other.

American society's origins as a European outpost, however, gave it a distinctive stamp. Like the rest of the European settlements in the Western Hemisphere, the colonies in North America were places of exploitation where overflows from Europe came to better themselves. The standard fabric of European restraints did not hold there. As a matter of course, settlers in the British colonies from Massachusetts to Georgia expected and were expected to ride roughshod over anyone who stood in the way. Slaughtering the indigenous people who had not died from Europe's diseases was sufficiently routine to eliminate almost all of them from the North American coast by the mid-eighteenth century. Importing blacks to North America meant, in effect, a shifting of labor from possible colonial locations on the African side of the ocean to already lucrative ones on the western side, no different in kind from the later entrepreneurial shuttling of slaves between the West Indies and the North American mainland. In Europe's outposts, whites used other people as they saw fit.

During the eighteenth century European elites simultaneously condoned and despised these activities. Almost no one at home doubted the right of Europeans to squeeze profits out of the hides of colonial laborers, but like caste stigmas in other cultures it dirtied and degraded the ones who did it. While its colonies served European civilization, they were not strictly a part of it. However much some whites in North America wanted to be accepted as full-fledged Englishmen, they harbored no illusions about the logic of life in those colonies, and they took the tough-minded materialism of Europe's colonial periphery into their revolution against British rule. Southern planters never lost focus on their interests: Prosperous colonials in one setting, they expected to be more prosperous still in the next. Even those North American revolutionaries who, like their European counterparts, were disgusted by black exploitation as a way of life occupied shaky ground: They too were scrambling, ambitious colonials who gambled that independence would benefit their enterprises. Against this background of ruthless colonialism, the United States Constitution was an astonishing accomplishment.

Recognizing, then, that American society lay simultaneously inside and outside the European experience—integral to its migratory flows, off the scale of its everyday morality—two characteristics marked out the special path that the United States would take: the weakness of its central government and the importance of a white-black axis in defining its social boundaries. Because transplanted exploiters had largely set their own terms in the mainland colonies, revolutionary Americans inherited small governments and proceeded to consolidate that heritage. Heavily dependent on black labor at the time of the Revolution, whites built slavery into their federal government, opened appropriate new territory for its expansion, and released other whites from even roughly comparable dependent labor. Freedom was as clear—and as complicated—as the difference between black and white. Along these broad guidelines, the rest of the American story unfolded. Democracy, flooding into the spaces that small government left, moved hand in glove with race. Nationalism in America only made sense in the framework these characteristics dominated.

No country in the world was more inviting to mobile white people than the nineteenth-century United States. Land was cheap, agriculture varied, and short-term labor usually in demand. To take advantage of its extraordinary opportunities, old settlers and newcomers alike moved and moved and moved again. In a country where the challenge was not to dismantle but to create a social order, these persistently migrating whites seemed forever in the midst of remaking the identities that in Europe's traditional order community life had once provided. In this sense, nineteenth-century American society was a quintessential expression of the Western world's transforming process.

In this sprawling country the three great innovations for a society in motion—nationalism, socialism, and democracy—operated to a striking degree apart. A society without a core, America provided ample room for all kinds of communal experiments and ethnic assertions that neither intruded on one another's space nor involved themselves with democratic government—which rarely paid them mind in any case. For socialism, permissiveness in a diffuse, opportunistic society was the kindness that killed. To begin with, early socialism asked people to stay put and follow its rules, a disastrous strategy in fluid nineteenth-century America. Not until the beginning of the twentieth century did socialists learn how to float their cause on a sea of mobile people. Even more crippling, the unprecedented and exhilarating assumption among white men that they could control their own working lives undermined any movement that required them to think of themselves as pawns in a capitalist game. During the 1820s, as the supply of land and the demand for labor exploded, already teetering schemes of dependent labor collapsed: Servants walked away from their indentures, apprentices stood up and negotiated the terms of their work. Wage work seemed no more than a way station to a farm or shop of one's own. Although it would be foolish to ignore the hardships trailing many of these laborers on the move, it would be far worse to underestimate the revolutionary impact of America's self-directed work in a transatlantic world where the overwhelming majority of adults remained dependent on someone above them. The centuries-old connection between property and independence snapped. No property, no will of one's own, the traditional logic went. But men who took charge of their own working lives acquired independence as a gift of adulthood. Keeping socialism alive in America required regular transatlantic infusions of people who brought their commitments with them.

In one sense, a mixed migrating population had even more devastating effects on nationalism, a way of thinking that could not begin to encase America's diversity. English-Americans, the closest approximation to a dominant ethnic group, had no ready means of distinguishing themselves from their transatlantic parent. In any case as the century progressed, they lived cheek by jowl with more and more people making deeper commitments to a wider variety of other loyalties. In different settings—New Zealand and portions of Canada, for example—the counterparts to these English Americans had a chance of defining their countries as poor-relation British; in the United States they could only build cultural bunkers for themselves. No powerful enemy except possibly Britain itself hovered close enough for long enough to force a new collective identity on America's diverse population. A generalized American Protestantism never transcended the multiple denominations and sects into which it splintered, and claims otherwise, such as the Benevolent Empire's evangelical collaboration of the 1820s and 1830s, expired with few regrets. What was left? A thin history on occupied land and an official language that increasing numbers of migrants considered optional. Rather than treasure their past, European visitors were quick to notice, Americans cited statistics: the extent of their country, the size of the harvest, the rate of a city's growth. American society provided no basis, that is, for nationalism as a comprehensive, unifying movement. If George Washington was the father of his country, he had no children. Uncle Sam was no one's relative.

What undid socialism and nationalism prepared the way for democracy, which swept across an expanding America early in the nineteenth century. The impressive popular energies released by revolutionary committees in the 1770s, public rallies in the 1780s, and republican clubs in the 1790s rattled the rafters of America's eighteenth-century hierarchies but did not topple them. The first political parties took direction from a handful of leaders with no taste for popular initiatives. In party matters if not in street manners, they expected and for a time got obedience from ordinary citizens. Then after the War of 1812, flourishing enterprise and accelerating migration shattered those hierarchies. In their place, white men assumed the right to rule themselves. Nobody waited for permission; everybody validated himself. Nobody ruled anybody else; everybody ruled together. "The great principle," the respected democratic spokesman Stephen A. Douglas told the white men of the Midwest, "is the right of every community to judge and decide for itself whether a thing is right or wrong, whether it would be good or evil for them to adopt it."[1] Where such standard eighteenth-century measures in public life as wealth, learning, and family no longer applied, the American democrat was an endlessly replicable type.

The obverse side of strong citizens was weak government. Until the Civil War, the central government had little to do, and by and large did it with little aptitude. It collected a few indirect taxes and underfinanced a few transportation projects. It gave away resources. It embarrassed itself in the second war with Great Britain and fared better against Mexico only because there really was no Mexican state in 1847. American federalism parceled responsibilites down the line until it reached local government, which often passed them on to private groups.

Two corollaries to a weak government were particularly significant for America's democracy. First, it mattered profoundly what government did not do: It did not lay heavy taxes to support a military establishment, it did not monitor dissenters or deviants, and it did not homogenize the laws and their administration. In a country of farmers—sitting ducks whenever the state's rulers went hunting for greater revenue—the lower the taxes, the greater the freedom. The state police systems that guarded the establishments of Europe had no counterpart in the United States. At the worst moments of war-charged persecution late in the 1790s, the government brought only fourteen indictments under the Sedition Act, which quickly disappeared in the new century, along with the few prison sentences it had produced.

Diversifying the laws state by state, then locality by locality, was the context for a second crucial attribute of America's democratic government: its proximity—its familiarity—to ordinary citizens. If, as Yaron Ezrahi argues, modern democracy relies "on the idea that politics is transparent, that political agents, political actions, and political power can be viewed," then early nineteenth-century America pioneered the principle for the Western world.[2] Americans, Alexis de Tocqueville reported, "strip off as much as possible all that covers [their government]; they rid themselves of whatever separates them from it, they remove whatever conceals it from sight, in order to view it more closely and in the broad light of day."[3] In the 1820s and 1830s, it was the imagined dangers of secrecy above all else that justified the political attacks on Catholics and Masons. In 1858 Abraham Lincoln, rather than dispute the logic behind the crucial *Dred Scott* decision, chose to attack it as the product of a conspiracy linking Presidents Pierce and Buchanan ("Franklin and James") and Chief Justice Taney ("Roger").

In fact, the system worked remarkably well. As visitor after visitor discovered early in the nineteenth century, constitutional federalism was the pride of educated Americans everywhere, and as these travelers then reported in dry detail on their return, mastering its intricacies was the qualifying quiz for any outsider who would explain America. Weak government did not produce weak attachments. Nothing indicates that the intensity of white men's loyalties to American democracy suffered in comparison with any European alternative. Indeed, transatlantic migrants, glad to leave the burden of Europe's governments behind them, continually reinvigorated American democracy with their own thrill at self-rule. In general, the less their government did, the better most Americans liked it: Denying power to a distant government reaffirmed it among themselves. George Washington, a peerless hero on two continents, gained fame above all for leaving office and returning home. Until the Civil War, civil society functioned quite well without a clear connection of any sort between good citizenship and state service.

The results might have been chaos. Without the discipline of a common danger, loyalties dispersed—into the voluntary associations that captured Tocqueville's attention, among levels of government, and along myriad channels of cultural and religious identification. Political parties did little to compensate. Earlier, in a spirit of hierarchy, a political leader presumed to represent the interests of all decent people below him, whether they had voted for him or even had the right to vote at all. "We are all Republicans," the incoming president Thomas Jefferson could say in a gesture of inclusiveness. By the early nineteenth century, however, a new partisanship made each elected official the representative only of those who belonged to his party, perhaps only of those who had voted for him and hence had earned his attention. Precisely that assumption justified Southern secession when Northern votes for a Northern party elected the Republican Lincoln.

What did hold white Americans together was their common citizenship. If the Revolution, which after all was fought over citizenship ("Liberty"), prepared the way, it was the Constitution that riveted a single, countrywide citizenship in place. It worked miracles. Despite the latitude that the several states still enjoyed in setting their own terms, citizens moved across the face of the United States year after year with an ease that gave substance to an American identity. Western territories filled up with people who did not have to put their citizenship on the line to get there, as many a European expatriate was forced to do. The package of rights associated with citizenship lay at the heart of the widely articulated sentiment of Americans as a free people in a free country. Historians with a parsing sensibility who count out the meaning of nineteenth-century politics in spoonfuls of power and patronage miss the critical point. Standing upright as everybody's equal in American public life, wherever citizens happened to be, was itself a revolutionary declaration, a ringing affirmation of personal worth and collective identity that retained its power no matter how many times it was repeated.

Phrased another way, affirming the equality of white men affirmed their place in a collective process. As these gambling, questing nineteenth-century whites with their multiple interests had no difficulty understanding, "Democracy involves more than participation in political processes: it is a way of constituting power. . . . Power is not merely something to be shared, but something to be used collaboratively in order to initiate, to invent, to bring about."[4] Commitments that looked helter-skelter from one vantage point reinforced America's unity from another. The very act of mobilizing power made white men colleagues in their competition for it. Hence the force behind the theory of an additive democracy, in which everybody's participation always mattered. What the British commentator James Bryce thought of as ridicule—"two men are wiser than one, one hundred than ninety-nine, thirty million than twenty-nine million"—did indeed capture an essential nineteenth-century American truth.[5] Each vote contributed value in its own right: It gave weight to the people's authority, it dignified civic life, it rounded out a public decision.

Mobility, the challenge democracy set out to meet, turned out to be one of its greatest assets in unifying American society. Child-rearing in a mobile society prepared the young to pack a handful of immutable truths in their knapsacks and go out into the world. They left home as a matter of course, astonished European visitors reported: Adulthood automatically made white men everybody else's equal. Democracy's first principles slipped easily into their bags. People on the move—carrying with them the Ten Commandments and the party platform, as it were—fell naturally into cooperation with others who brought along the same principles. It was as if all white men, upon becoming adults in America, picked up a citizen's ticket that was good for admission to public life wherever they might go. With them went the words! words! words! of nineteenth-century democratic discourse, moving along America's world-renowned transportation network, its criss-crossed lecture circuits, and its patronage-driven postal service, the most important and remarkably unobtrusive exception to the rule of an inconsequential central state.

Whatever cohesion nineteenth-century Americans enjoyed, in other words, derived from democracy: an expanding body of equal male citizens who were committed to governing themselves inside a loose constitutional federalism. On a countrywide scale, democracy not only swamped the alternatives, socialism and nationalism; it actually replaced them. In particular, it was the proxy

American nationalism, one that perversely seemed to thrive on the country's ethnic heterogeneity. During the heart of the nineteenth century—1815 to 1875—as greater and greater varieties of people came to live in the United States, it remained impressively free of ethnic repression and exclusion. That openness, moreover, was a self-conscious matter, a repeatedly debated and reaffirmed public policy. In retrospect, it might seem that citizenship was given away for a pittance, with voting cheapened even further through the participation of resident aliens. In fact, before the twentieth century, precisely these practices constituted assimilation: not cultural homogenization but civic action. Neither poor immigrants nor elite European observers had difficulty recognizing the astonishing outcome of America's population mix. At midcentury, the Scot Alexander Mackay, an otherwise hostile critic of democracy, tipped his hat to American politics: "In one sense, truly, you have a congress of nations in this Congress of the United States." Inside America's governing system, he continued, you have an extraordinary sample of human types "with all their diversified habits, predilections, histories, creeds, and traditions; you have the representatives of almost every country in Europe living together, not a paralytic life, but a life of constant industry and active competition, and regulating their [own] political existence."[6]

Eventually American and European commentators alike accepted democracy as the inevitable outcome of historical forces that could only have come together in the United States. America, it seemed, had created democracy. Except as a tautology—it occurred where it occurred—those claims missed the most crucial element of all: America's integration in a transatlantic world. Democracy was the solution that whites of European background gave to problems of European origin, to the challenges that overflowing populations carried across the Atlantic and into the North American interior. What is most impressive about the creation of democracy in America is that it came in tandem with solutions to a second Europe-derived problem: How could the benefits of America, the colonial outpost, be translated into the benefits of the United States, the independent country? As other whites who wrestled with this question in other colonial settings were to discover over and over again, race was the heart of the matter. Slavery was no more an anomaly in the land of democracy than democracy was an anomaly in the land of slavery.

In post-Enlightenment Europe, race was a progressive idea. In place of a severe Christian ethnocentrism, a world of races opened the possibility of recognizing differences without condemning them. By shifting the terms of discussion from who should control and who should obey to various people's rights, race as a concept facilitated the critical change in Western Europe from slavery's routine acceptance in the mid-eighteenth century to its general delegitimation in the nineteenth. In sharp contrast to these benign uses on the European continent, however, race justified a broad range of rapacious, exclusionary practices at the many colonial sites that Europeans established around the globe. There, ironically, it was Christianity that from time to time put a brake on the crudest horrors of colonial racism. The United States inherited the colonial version of race, with only a small measure of Enlightenment leavening.

In colonial settings around the world, race was color coded. Because basic privileges were at issue, what mattered was not the actual "unbroken stream of [skin] color [ranging from light cream to near black that] . . . changes with changes in light . . . clothing, and surroundings" but colonist white or something else.[7] For the governing whites who drew that line, skin color served quite well as a sorting device in the United States, despite murky borderlands where only arbitrary rules could settle the disputed cases. The purpose of the line was to define issues of life, liberty, and property. As at other colonial sites, Europeans and their progeny in America set out to seize what they could get, murdering indigenous people of color and destroying their habitat as they went. Blacks served as replacement labor. So, in effect, did white immigrants, whose single most important task was to get to and stay on the right side of the exploiter-exploited line.

Again in common with other colonial experiences, this pattern of bloodshed and brutalization reinforced white Americans' faith in violence as a means of resolving problems. Early white settlements in North America were the objects as well as the agents of warfare, with European armies and navies battling over and around them during the seventeenth and eighteenth centuries. White men maimed and murdered one another settling personal disputes. In cities, towns, and countryside alike, mobs, militia, and ad hoc armies took it upon themselves to settle public disputes. Early in the nineteenth century abolitionists tried to bracket the horrors of slavery as a unique kind of violence producing equally unique effects on the slaveowner's character. In fact, colonies everywhere were built around the ordinariness of using and taking lives. A callousness about death spread generally. Work in the coal mines and on the railroads of the United States generated death rates about three times higher than in Britain. European visitors were appalled by the indifference. "The stabbing of a man in the streets, or the falling of a man into the river, even when attended with instant death, does not excite so much sensation . . . [as] the death of a dog would do in the streets of any town in England," one concluded.[8] "If [during construction] some men were killed," Count Francesco Arese reported to his fellow Italians, "'No matter!', a very common phrase in America."[9]

Nevertheless, abolitionists grasped an essential truth: Only people of color were constantly at risk against their will. White Americans who placed the sanctity of property at the heart of their legal system counted on that same system to ratify their seizure of colored people's property—sometimes systematically en masse, sometimes individually at random. Undermining the incentives to plan, labor, and save, whites condemned people of color for their laziness, improvidence, and criminality. Shiftless people of color, whites concluded, did not have the capacity to benefit from self-directed work: They had to be directed by whites. In the 1890s, Frederick Jackson Turner took the essential elements in this story and turned them into the sources of American democracy. Released from European restraints, white Americans tested their mettle in a rush across the continent, generating their fundamental values at the cutting edge of the colonial encounter, then turning their newfound strength of character to the process of further exploitation. In one sense, Turner's fable of a democracy renewed time and again on successive frontiers neatly met the challenge of transforming the problems of mobility into their own solution: the good society always in the making among good people always on the move. Yet as he cleansed a multitude of sins, he could not hide the intrinsic connection between his democracy and America's colonial rationale. In Turner's scheme, *where* the process occurred—vast spaces awaiting white enterprise—determined *what* it created. American democracy belonged exclusively in America: Its frontiers—its colonial sites—were not for export.

What gave some cohesion to the many different experiences of people of color in America was the axial relationship of white to black, the contrast that to European as well as American whites seemed the starkest. The lighter people of color appeared to white eyes, the lower the barriers to their acceptance in white society. Rates of intermarriage were a rough gauge: highest between red and white, substantial between brown and white, tiny between black and white. With enough white in a red-white mix, children became white, something that could rarely be said of black-white offspring. People of largely Spanish ancestry from Latin America found far easier acceptance among whites in the United States than did those of largely indigenous descent.

As the lot of African Americans shifted, so by and large did the lot of other white-defined races. It mattered above all how whites institutionalized their treatment of African Americans. Until the

Civil War, slavery set standards for race relations of all kinds. The rights of so-called free blacks measured up from slavery, not down from white freedom. Under President Andrew Jackson, at a moment when slavery had virtually no challengers in the federal government, a particularly vicious round of Indian removal drove the major tribes of the southern United States out of their homelands. As the Compromise of 1850 nestled slavery into federal law, rampaging whites, with an abandon unusual even for them, set about robbing, killing, and enslaving the indigeneous people of California. Civil War and Reconstruction changed matters all around. Ending slavery elevated all blacks; enscribing their freedom in amendments to the Constitution raised expectations of a uniform citizenship; opening the possibility of federal enforcement loosened the vice of racism generally. As blacks acquired new rights in Northern states and struggled for places in Southern states, white brutality against California's natives abated and treaties with Plains tribes, especially one in 1868 with the Lakota Sioux, hinted at a rising standard of white justice.

Because nineteenth century Europeans felt free to eliminate indigenous people wherever they went, the reputation of white Americans did not suffer particularly for doing the same. Black slavery, however, did set the United States apart. Eighteen thirty-one—the year of white fright over Nat Turner's Rebellion in South Carolina and also of a major slave uprising in Jamaica—marked a fork in the road. Whites in the American South responded by tightening the noose; the British government, on its part, cut the Gordian knot. With the French in their wake the British moved expeditiously to end slavery in the West Indies and in the process isolated the United States, the world's most thriving colonial site, as the institution's only powerful defender.

Early in the nineteenth century, spokesmen for European states and nations alike claimed a uniqueness that doubled as moral superiority. It was this patriotic self-image even more than economic self-interest that powered the European drives for abolition. White

Americans had no trouble understanding that impulse. Champions of Revolutionary America, an instant curiosity in the late eighteenth century, had pioneered this kind of self-promotion at least a quarter century before it became standard European practice, and black slavery handicapped them from the outset. Jefferson and his colleagues were no fools in blaming *their* colonial masters for foisting slaves on America's reluctant colonials. By the 1820s, however, the debate over the institution's meaning had shifted from its contamination of whites to its abuse of blacks. A sea change in values had swept the Western world, investing individuals with an integrity that slavery seemed fundamentally to violate: the right to make choices about both earthly and eternal life; the right to protect the body from arbitrary pain and mutilating punishment; the right to a moral family life. What became the standard antislavery imagery of slavery—the chained legs, the scarred backs, the women and children at auction—flaunted each of those principles. As the extraordinary success of *Uncle Tom's Cabin* on two continents attested, by midcentury large numbers of white Americans outside of the slave South shared those values. More than guilt by association alienated them. Their culture of self-directed work was itself new enough, challenging enough, to raise serious questions about which of the two labor systems, living side by side, would survive. Lincoln's House Divided speech in 1858 played on just those anxieties: "[T]his government cannot endure permanently half slave and half free. . . . Have we no tendency to . . . [make slavery] alike lawful in all the States, old as well as new—North as well as South?"[10]

Sectional crisis threw up for grabs the critical qualities setting the United States apart. In the Western world's premier colonial site, the two primary ways of exploiting people of color now stood at loggerheads: The staple-producing Southerners relied on the labor of black slaves, other whites pushing westward relied on native peoples' land. Northern whites denied Southern whites the security that their slave system required; Southern whites paralyzed the westward expansion that Northern whites considered their god-given right.

Secession in 1860–61 eliminated America's other distinctive characteristic: its cohesion through a white man's democracy. If the process of democratic decisions—winners took office, losers tried again, ad infinitum—was America's only effective cement, the country came unglued with the election of 1860. In the United States it was majority rule or no rule: Eleven Southern states stopped democracy's perpetual motion machine. Little wonder that countless Northerners who despised the victorious Republicans and distrusted President-Elect Lincoln did not hesitate to brand the secessionists traitors. The unity that depended on citizenship, unlike the unity of a class or a fictive family, required a definite jurisdiction within which citizens could act collectively. Beyond the Constitution nothing bounded America: no borders of a common language, no history of imperial glories, no religious divide or military threat. By abandoning the Constitution, secession dissolved a distinctive America. Reconstructing it began with secession itself, and among people as violent as these, war was a natural way to start.

In forming their own confederacy, some leaders in the seceding states thought of themselves as the triumphant champions of Southern nationalism, a claim just plausible enough to require closer examination. A nationalist movement had been picking up momentum in the South for three decades before the Civil War, with race its crucial element. First, its advocates set about constructing a white society. No person of color had standing in a white court, a vote in a white election, or a right to a white education. Southern migrants, tying Southeast to Southwest with chains of kin, took those values with them wherever they went. Nevertheless, the more Southern nationalism relied on whiteness, the more difficult it was to distinguish Southern from Northern whites, who almost always segregated blacks and who shared essentially the same history and political tradition. As a white enterprise,

Southern nationalism sounded like a family squabble: the South with few European immigrants was purer than the North, Southerners were the true heirs of the Revolution, only Southerners understood the Constitution, and so forth. Sometimes unintentionally, historians have exposed the flimsiness of the case by reminding us that a knighted Brit, Sir Walter Scott, was this nationalism's indispensable author and that a paean to state particularism, "Maryland, My Maryland," was its finest lyric expression.

A second use of race, the slave system, served better. Decade by decade, slavery indeed widened the distance between the South and the rest of Western society and gave some white visionaries intimations of a unique Southern destiny. Through the kind of transforming stroke so dear to early nationalism, they pictured independence releasing a purely Southern, slave-based white freedom. Unlike other slaveholders in the Western Hemisphere, aspiring Southern nationalists never looked for the exit, for an acceptable escape from slavery into another social system. On the contrary, they exulted in slavery. Turning their moral isolation to advantage, they sought to create a body of true believers. Blacks were natural slaves, whites natural masters; free blacks were an anomaly, antislavery whites an anathema. By these lights migrants from Europe, bringing Western society's repudiation of slavery with them, actually were a threat to the white South, even if almost none went there.

Gambling everything on slavery and losing, this venture in nationalism collapsed completely with a war-imposed abolition. There was no safety net, no fallback position in case slavery failed. As the former Confederacy was drawn into the mainstream of Western society, slavery lost virtually all its Southern defenders, too. It would be decades before any public figure seriously tried to glorify its memory. In a final salvage operation, some whites rummaged for a distinctive South in the rubble of the Lost Cause, which yielded them heroism but no nationalism. With neither a past nor a future the Confederate warriors could only offer an existential moment of glory. By focusing obsessively on the field of battle, it walled off the rest of Southern society, including, of course, its slavery. In the end, it was a celebration of men who had fought for independence by people who no longer sought independence. Robert E. Lee doubled as the great Confederate hero and the great Anglo-Saxon hero, the best of the South and the best of America.

It was an ending appropriate to the beginning. As the historian David Potter explained many years ago, territorial loyalties in America's federal system tended to run along a line from locality to state to something beyond until they were blocked. In shifting and uncoordinated ways, more and more whites in the antebellum South hit their limits short of a union of all the states. Before the Civil War the American way permitted a great deal of sliding up and down the federal scale. Abruptly, secession forced an either-or choice. Reconstruction, in turn, continued this reliance on force as it remade the Constitution. It was the Compromise of 1877, closing out Reconstruction, that allowed white men in the former Confederacy once again to play the accordian of expanding and contracting loyalties. As they reclaimed the right to determine their own political rules, state by state, they were no longer obliged to choose between clear-cut alternatives: *Maybe* replaced *either-or*. Nor did hate stop old enemies from functioning together inside a loosely structured democracy. Southern whites' attachments once again slid up and down the federal scale. What all the bloodshed had settled was the issue of secession: Southern nationalism was no longer an option.

The nationalism that did thrive in America derived from ethnicity: an "extended analogue of kinship" that presupposed a common ancestry and common cultural code among a people sufficiently widespread to remove the possibility that they would view their connection as self-evident.[11] Many other identities competed with ethnicity, and many times they won. Nevertheless, ethnicity proved to be an exceptionally resilient form of consciousness. In an American environment of shifting choices and changing needs, nobody's path had a clear, determinate destination; ethnicity adapted itself to all kinds of journeys. It is always in process; it never ossifies. Ethnicity's meaning lies as much in what it is becoming as in what it has been. It is not like a body part that the analyst's X ray can spot and study. It is not something we find in other people; it is something those people find in themselves. Nor in a simple sense is ethnicity perishable, lost forever once it has slipped from sight. Over and over again when an ethnic consciousness has been given up for dead, it actually lies latent, capable of a sudden revival. In Walker Connor's phrasing, a man "can shed all of the overt cultural manifestations customarily attributed to his ethnic group and yet maintain his fundamental identity as a member."[12] Ethnicity, Cynthia Enloe concludes, is "a much *sparer* phenomenon" than scholars have traditionally assumed.[13]

Among the people in nineteenth-century America who traced their ancestry to Europe, ethnicity was inherently hyphenate, an ongoing transatlantic negotiation among people in the midst of change. Appropriate to its protean nature, ethnicity by itself left ample room for many different formulations to suit many different situations. However, one of its common expressions in nineteenth-century America, nationalism, narrowed that range of choices. For one thing, nationalism named people's identities: Italian, Polish, Japanese, and so forth. For another, it wove those identities into a state, either the creation of one that did not exist or the completion of one that did. As a consequence, nationalism weighted the scales toward the homeland end of the migration chain. Being Irish in Boston did not necessarily have much to do with Ireland; being an Irish nationalist there did. Better focused and less personalized, nationalism was a limited subset of ethnicity: no nationalism without ethnic identifications but many ethnic identifications without nationalism.

At the same time, nationalism did not in some simple sense lie at the extreme end of an ethnic spectrum. The intensity of ethnic feelings did not predict the likelihood of an intense nationalism, or in fact nationalism of any kind. America's late nineteenth-century Chinatowns, though models of ethnic strength, gave rise to no nationalism worth mentioning. Nor did the frequency of visits to the migrants' land of origin or even the probability of resettling there. Return rates were exceptionally high among nationalist south Slavs and exceptionally low among nationalist Norwegians and Irish. Nor, finally, was deepening oppression a good indicator of which ethnicity would turn into nationalism. If that had been the case, Amerindian nationalist movements would have ripped through nineteenth-century America.

Mirroring influences that shaped nationalism in Europe, the major variables affecting nationalism in America were the state and the family. Where a well-established state existed in their land of origin, migrants had little incentive to channel ethnicity into nationalism, as Swedish Americans demonstrated. What generated nationalism was a state's insecurity, its struggle to define itself, or best of all its absence—that is, a people's unfulfilled desire to create a state of their own. Moreover, where the state dominated the process of forging a nation, it more or less bounded the nation as well. England was a case in point. Beyond its borders, nationalism had little meaning. At best, the English abroad were a cheering section; at worst, they lost membership entirely.

Families underwrote nationalism by reconceiving themselves in migration: extending, expanding, transmuting kin connections to suit their world in flux. Italian Americans, as Michaela di Leonardo describes them, illustrate the process: "While they emphasize blood ties in ideology, in reality they use fictive kinship to sanction the intimate nonkin ties they form."[14] Appropriately, Italian nationalism had a long, vigorous life in America, fading only with the Second World War. By contrast, the more families migrated as units and relocated in a close community of comparable families, the less they needed to stretch and strain. In the prewar years, Jewish consciousness flourished in urban America but Jewish nationalism did not.

Family structure held the crucial clue to why, despite their impeccable credentials, Native Americans mounted no nationalist movements during the nineteenth century. At a glance it seems incredible that they did not. Their tribes, after all, were kin networks with deep historical and ancestral roots in sacred soil where, their chiefs insisted, they wished only to govern themselves in peace. By the end of the eighteenth century, a number of Amerindian leaders at the Atlantic end of the continent, paying attention to how whites did their business, had worked out the rudiments of the red people's separate origins, their spiritual distinctiveness, and their right to specific areas of land. Early in the nineteenth century a major group of Cherokee developed a sophisticated protonationalist scheme of language, law, and group identity. After the fashion of white nationalists, resourceful Lakota Sioux invented traditions when they needed them. The charge that Native American cultures were simply too porous to sustain an exclusive nationalist consciousness had no justification. Amerindians drew cultural lines as they needed them, creating outsiders who fell beyond the protection of moral restraint and devastating them accordingly.

What they did not have was an expansive sense of fictive kinship. Kin connections remained literal and articulated, not soft and amoebic. Although tribes adopted new members through marriage, that process strengthened the home base without extending the tribal reach outward. Members who left the tribal kin to marry—and as the law allowed it, a substantial proportion did—remained on the outside. Hence it mattered very much that nineteenth-century law blocked a reciprocal movement between white and red societies: Amerindians could abandon their tribes to become United States citizens but whites could not abandon their United States citizenship to become tribal members. The native people's own pull toward the center made it exceedingly difficult for spiritual and cultural revivals to grow into nationalist movements. With only momentary exceptions, their efforts at revitalization turned inward rather than stretching outward; they were purifying rather than mobilizing; they subdivided kin into smaller groups rather than uniting them into larger families. These precise, particular identities, remarkably enduring in the face of monstrous white attacks, set barriers that nationalism could not penetrate.

The state that mattered the most to nationalism's history in nineteenth-century America was the United States itself, whose modest objectives allowed a great variety of movements to flourish within its borders. Perhaps most important, it did not compete with hyphenate nationalism by attempting to mobilize an American nationalism of its own. Phrases such as Manifest Destiny that have sometimes had a nationalist ring to twentieth-century historians gave expression in the nineteenth century to countless private initiatives but only rarely and awkwardly to public policy. As whites slashed through native territories, federal forces generally moved in their wake. The army's task, by and large, was to kill or contain Indians who tried to reoccupy their land. The Mexican War nicely illustrated the fumbling nature of nineteenth-century federal leadership, even at the height of what came to be called Manifest Destiny.

A brazenly partisan war, it was never meant to mobilize an American people—reasonable enough by the rules of nineteenth-century American politics but equally indicative of the government's chronic inability to sustain an expansionist policy. Even as the Democratic party's war, what was striking about it was not the Polk administration's gobbling of foreign territory but its limited greed. At least twice the extent of territory that the United States did seize lay open for the taking. The Mexican state, claiming a large domain it had never governed, let warring elites with their sometime armies so thoroughly exhaust civil society that ambitious Europeans would soon accept an invitation to rule the country. The question that invading this rickety structure raised was how much of a fragmenting country should the United States keep. The answer was not very adventurous: In effect, fill out the most obvious spaces on the way to the Pacific. Not until the end of the century did the federal government set more expansive goals.

Anti-Catholicism suggested another strategy for mobilizing an American nation. There were European precedents dating at least from the Treaty of Westphalia in 1648, and there were Protestant migrants ranging from Pennsylvania Germans to Minnesota Scandanavians who might well have picked up on those precedents. Nevertheless, the new United States set out on a different course. Following France's indispensable aid to the American Revolution, in what one historian has called "a tremendous cultural shift," restrictions singling out Catholics disappeared.[15] In fact, during the French Revolution, Jacobin atheists roused greater public anger in the United States than France's counterrevolutionary Catholics. Around the middle of the nineteenth century, a flood of Catholic migrants from Ireland and Germany renewed old hostilities on a new basis. Now the issue was American democracy's civic morality. Could the alcohol-soaked minions of the pope and his priestly hierarchy share in the process of self-government, anti-Catholic publicists asked? However widespread these prejudices and however mean their day-to-day expressions, organized anti-Catholicism, peaking in the prohibition and Know Nothing movements of the 1850s, proved to be so much sound and fury. Its scattered, fleeting political successes had no lasting consequences. Attacks on Midwestern parochial schools late in the century drew Lutherans and Catholics together, and those on Catholics as aliens rallied immigrants of all kinds to a common cause. Fractured and mutually suspicious Protestants never mustered the political power to persecute; Catholics free from persecution had at least as much trouble maintaining a collective religious consciousness of their own. The long tradition of equating America with a vague Prot-estantism, irritating but not threatening to other religions, was about as much as these episodic outcries ever netted.

Even in civic life, the one realm that did hold promise of uniting Americans, the United States set a bare minimum of requirements. Not only was an American citizenship optional for European immi-grants, but those who opted for it found themselves obligated to little more than perpetuating the frame of government. The clearest translation of that came with the Civil War, when entire groups took on a reflected legitimacy from their soldiers. Civil War service, for example, did wonders for the reputation of German Americans and a good deal for Irish Americans, too, despite their prominence in the antidraft riots of 1863. Those migrants who fulfilled their civic obligations to the United States also sustained their transoceanic connections to a nation without any sense of conflict. Different loyalties came out of different pots: public obligations from one, ethnic-nationalist attachments from another. "Is the Irish-American less of an American because he gathers money to help his struggling brethren in the Green Isle?" a Zionist asked rhetorically at the turn of the century.[16] Millions of migrating Poles created what one nine-teenth-century wit called the "fourth partition" in industrial Amer-ica, "giving allegiance to the government under whose jurisdiction they live, but remembering their origin and . . . conscientiously paying back what they owe their nation."[17] Carl Schurz, the most widely respected German American of the nineteenth century, used much the same language: "[H]owever warm their affection for their native land, [German Americans] have never permitted that affec-tion to interfere with their duties as American citizens."[18] What the United States required bore no relationship to what nationalism required. The United States, on the contrary, made room for a multitude of nations.

In sum, almost nothing kept ethnic groups from working out their own version of nationalism at their own pace. Extending local and regional attachments into an Italian consciousness occurred at about the same time and rate on both sides of the Atlantic. The Polish in America were as slow to mobilize a popular nationalism as the Polish in Eastern Europe. When Irish American Fenians tried to invigorate their nationalist movement in the summer of 1866 by invading Canada, it took the inspired incompetence of their private army to force a response from Washington. Their ranks riddled with spies, their supplies limited to their guns and gear, and their strategy gone with the wind, Fenian irregulars stalked the New York–Canadian border until finally the government sent General George Meade, the hero of Gettysburg, to round them up, whereupon the good general, realizing that many of them were Union veterans, bought the bedraggled outlaws railroad tickets home. They had paid their dues as American citizens; the rest was more or less their business. Scarcely deterred, the Fenians recruited another ragtag army for another abortive invasion in 1870.

A final factor keeping nineteenth-century American society open to all kinds of ethnic and nationalist expressions was the geographical diffusion of its many peoples. Because Congress refused to grant large tracts of land by immigrant nationality, none of them founded a state or anything like it of their own. White migrants collected in ethnic settlements then left them, gained control of a city government then lost it, dominated a local labor market then shared it, all in fluid ways that reflected a mobile, heterogeneous society of residential mixing, marketplace competition, and petty capitalist bargain-and-sale where nobody's monopoly held for long. What seemed to outsiders like exceptions to the principle of diffusion— Midwestern domains of Germans and Norwegians, urban enclaves of Italians and Poles—roused some antagonism. Moreover, a scattering of peoples diminished the effects of another kind of abrasion: white ethnic group facing white ethnic group at a boundary. Even in the major cities, such face-offs were almost always passing phenomena with constantly changing casts of characters. Here, too, ethnic identities were much more matters of choice than of necessity.

It was the genius of the Mormons to violate all of the basic principles governing ethnic behavior as they risked America's most curious and creative venture in domestic nationalism, one that in its thoroughness actually anticipated the characteristics of late nineteenth-century European nationalism. Appropriately, migration and Mormonism were practically synonyms: New England to New York to Ohio to the Missouri-Illinois border to Utah for its expanding core of converts; then the harvests that missionaries drew from Europe and America into Mormon land. To families separated but not shattered in migration and to chains of kin glad for additional support, Mormonism offered a great deal. Not only did the living church approximate a grand extended family, with members greeting one another as brothers and sisters, fathers, mothers, sons, and daughters; but the dead, who might otherwise never experience the eternal bliss of such a recently revealed religion, were also eligible for conversion, preparing long ancestral lines to march together in a heavenly procession. As the Mormon church developed, moreover, it strove for the self-sufficiency of an idealized farm family that grew, processed, and manufactured whatever it needed, setting aside enough to care in hard times for all fictive kin, young and old.

Leaders strictly disciplined the Mormon's grand family-hierarchy. Faith in the divine origin of the tablets that the movement's prophet, Joseph Smith, turned from memory into the *Book of Mormon* (1829) and of further revelations that became additional sacred texts served not simply as the acid test of belonging but also as the authoritative history that nationalist movements everywhere required. They were picking up a thread, Mormons learned, that original Christians had once carried but that over centuries of complicated wanderings and fallings away had been lost. That history, moreover, established the Mormons' right to their sacred land—roughly, the territory of the United States. In the Mormon narrative, Native Americans played a critical role as the surviving Lost Tribes of Israel, a people once uniquely blessed, now uniquely cursed, but soon to be redeemed. As heirs to these people's initial grace and agents of their ultimate salvation, Mormons acquired a divine right to the soil where they alone could link past to future in God's plan for human kind. In general, however, people of color did not fare well in the holy plan. Not only were blacks headed for hell once Brigham Young, Smith's successor, officially banned them from the church; a Mormon's price for miscegenation, Young declared, was instant death. Native Americans escaped ostracism only because their color, it was believed, expressed God's punishment, and redemption would make them white again.

Together, Smith and Young fashioned a model of adaptation. Responding to the same flow of experiences that inspired transatlantic nationalism, they resolved much the same set of challenges that nationalism addressed: reconceiving the network of fictive kin, bounding the grand family in ways that reflected the participants' communal values, giving them a common history and a common destiny, and binding the sacred with the secular in a single cause. Completing the nationalist agenda, Smith, before his murder in 1844, and Young, after the trek to Utah, unquestionably wanted to establish an independent state. The fact that Smith scanned sites from Oregon to Texas underlined the marvelous flexibility that a claim to much of a continent built into the Mormon imagination. *"The whole of America is Zion itself."* Smith declared in the year of his death.[19] In the end, Utah was just fine as sacred ground. Little wonder Mormonism was such an astonishing success, both in recruiting and cementing members to the movement.

But why was the movement trailed by a pattern of violence unusual even for the United States? Founded by a mere handful in 1830, the church was already at war with its neighbors in 1833, driven at gun point from Missouri in 1838 and from Illinois in 1845, then geared to battle federal troops off and on in Utah for three decades. The Mormons counted their dead, including the prophet himself, the way another church might tally the comings and goings of its temporary members. The argument that their

leaders consciously provoked these attacks in order to tighten loyalties inside a beleaguered church makes no more sense than a
blanket charge that committed leaders of all sorts—say, democrats
in a totalitarian state—court martyrdom by meeting oppression
with a deepened resolve. Sending the bullets, not receiving them,
requires the explanation.

Resolving that problem requires the elimination of a second
confusion, this one a flattering image of Mormonism as the all-
American nineteenth-century religion: a down-home addition to
this country's flourishing denominationalism, a quintessential version of intrepid pioneers moving west in search of freedom, an
exemplification of such basic American values as initiative, hard
work, and godliness. "Mormonism," the twentieth-century philosopher Ralph Barton Perry concluded, "was a sort of Americanism
in miniature."[20] On the contrary, Mormonism, atypical in all essential respects, stretched an elastic American tolerance for religious
differences to the limit. Secretive and totalistic, it aspired to be a
theocracy. It remade the Bible, restructured the trinity, reconstrued death, redefined the Last Judgment, and reconstructed marriage to accommodate plural wives. If, as some modern commentators claim, Smith and Young built Mormonism on practical,
commonsense principles, they certainly fooled most of their fellow Americans.

Nevertheless, other groups pushed the boundaries of acceptability, including marriage mores, without getting shot for it. What
distinguished the Mormon challenge was its frontal assault on the
basic sources of American cohesion, a democratic process within
the sovereign United States. Viewed from a distance, the Mormons
looked like an unusually promising batch of settlers: law-abiding,
church-going, industrious, and solvent. Close up, however, it did
not take long to discover how appearances could deceive. The
Mormons did not just covet land; they claimed it as a divinely
sanctioned transfer from owners whom Smith called "your enemies." They did not just work that land as a unit; they voted as a

unit. They did not just seek land in large contiguous blocks; they sought to govern themselves in their own domain. And more of them came.

In Jackson County, Missouri, outsiders quickly picked up on Smith's ambition for an imperium *in imperio* and, with characteristic nineteenth-century American problem-solving flair, went after the Mormons with rifles. Everywhere the dialectic repeated itself. As a religious colony that held promise of rewarding its friends at the polls, the Mormons won a special charter from Illinois in 1841. Among their immediate neighbors, however, it was no secret that Smith sought the closest thing he could get to an independent state: For obscure reasons, he even decided to run for president of the United States. The one certain thing about the colony's politics was that Mormons voted as they were told. It certainly did not ease local tensions to discover that church leaders officered a militia, four thousand strong in 1844, in which every able-bodied man served—a defensive move perhaps, but by the same token a bristling show of Mormon defiance. And still more converts came.

In the Utah chapter of Mormon resistance, the facade of mere piety and industriousness did not hold for long. With surprising deliberateness, all things considered, the postwar federal government gradually increased pressure on the Mormons in Utah Territory with an eye fixed on the important stakes. The horror of polygamy might get the headlines, but the struggle over sovereignty dictated the terms. The church had to relinquish its claims to govern: disband its army and its ruling political party, abide by the United States courts and a sparse band of additional federal officials. Accepting these simple but central principles, the Mormons cleared the way for the state of Utah in 1896 and simultaneously abandoned its dreams of independence.

At least in the years after Smith's death, the Mormons' drive for statehood did not really qualify as a nationalist movement, even by the loose standards of the nineteenth century. It was an authoritarian religion that used nationalist tactics without any intrinsic need for nationalist goals. Once assured of their security within the United States, Mormons not only abandoned nationalist ambitions but outdid their fellow citizens in loyalty to the new government. An independent state had not been a need in itself, only a device—no matter who governed it or what its principles—to maintain the health of the church.

During the 1880s and 1890s, as nationalist movements and state mobilizations were hardening throughout the Western world, some Americans did yearn to make a nation of their own country. Contrary to later myths, the Civil War strengthened regional far more than comprehensive loyalties. *Union* referred to a constitutional doctrine, to the winning side in the war, not to the whole United States. The war not only burned a North-South consciousness into American minds; it stirred and legitimized regionalism in a variety of other settings. The West acquired a cowboys-and-Indians identity. From Longfellow and Emerson back through their Puritan ancestors, loyalists in the Northeast celebrated a distinctive New England culture. Even an amorphous Middle West of neat farms and settled small-town ways had its promoters. As America's analogue to Europe's contemporary nationalist literature, writers such as Joel Chandler Harris, Sarah Orne Jewett, and Bret Harte generated local color fiction that separated rather than joined the particular parts of the United States. Hence the spreading concern about an American patriotism after 1890 represented a self-conscious reach to another level of loyalty. Fourth of July festivities grew more regularized and commodified; flag ceremonies—some fixed by law—ritualized moments of unity; and a romantic militarism, replete with bands, uniforms, and tales of valor, invoked the traditional duty that male citizens owed their country. At the end of the century these new patriots rallied along with other new imperialists behind a United States war for empire.

By the late nineteenth century, transatlantic norms equated a successful state with a unifying culture, and the prerequisite, according to this consensus, was a single language. In that spirit, there were drives around 1890 in Wisconsin and Illinois to mandate English as the language of public education, paralleling campaigns in Europe to impose a uniform French throughout France, to Magyarize the Hungarian empire, and to systematize languages in virtually all aspiring nations. Before the turn of the century, merit examinations at all levels of government were in English. By 1906 some knowledge of it was required to acquire citizenship.

These so-called Americanizers were not chasing phantoms. As the heaviest waves of nineteenth-century European migration brought people from almost every corner of the Western world, it was by no means clear whether American democracy could function without a common language, a common culture, and a common commitment, and it was perfectly reasonable to raise these questions as matters of public policy. In America's diversified occupational marketplace, moreover, English was the language of opportunity, especially in managing the critical passage between blue-collar and the rapidly expanding range of white-collar jobs. An English-language high school education, now standard in middle-class America, marked the ladder upward. Nevertheless, what stood out in these Americanizing campaigns was not their rationality but their partisanship.

The motive force behind them were well-placed, well-educated, and often well-heeled citizens who sought toward the end of the nineteenth century to make an English American ethnicity double as American nationality. From an elite circle of Northeastern colleges and clubs emanated new truths that located the origins of American values in a distant Anglo-Saxon past, merged Americans and English into a single race, and, contrary to the prevailing wisdom before the 1870s and after the 1920s, declared the essential unity of the British and American constitutions, rooting both in Magna Carta. For the first time, English literature took its place at the core of the college curriculum, institutionalizing a particular definition of literacy for the educated American. The source of this aggrandizing Englishness, of course, was the same heightening of ethnic and nationalist consciousness that rose simultaneously all across Europe. Equally obvious, it was the unique positioning of English Americans that allowed them, and no other group in poly-ethnic America, to lay transcendent claim to the entire culture. Although just enough high government officials shared those English American biases to give the contemporary diplomatic rapprochement of Great Britain and the United States an aura of naturalness, millions of other Americans were not fooled. "Americans," a Polish priest snorted. These pretenders were just "English-Americans. . . . There is no such thing as an American nation. . . . Poles form a nation, but the United States is a country, under one government, inhabited by representatives of different nations."[21] As if to flaunt the truth of the priest's assertion, more languages expressing a wider range of intense ethnicities sounded every year in America's cities. By European standards, America's spotty patriotism, tentative militarism, and splintered nationalism seemed feeble indeed.

What did stand out was American racism. Around 1880, a new round of it struck people of color with increasing severity, this time sweeping Chinese and Japanese along with western Amerindians and the bulk of American blacks into a comprehensive pattern of institutionalized racism. Of course that story had a larger context: Racism followed roughly the same trajectory in both Europe and the United States. The counterpart to America's experimental years after the Civil War had been the accelerating emancipation of European Jews around midcentury. Then beginning in the 1880s, racism hardened everywhere. Cross-class anti-Semitism spread across both Europe and the United States. However white

Americans and Europeans had differed over slavery, they never wavered in a common conviction that dark people, especially the irredeemably barbaric black Africans, were inherently inferior. Appropriately, racism acquired a new viciousness on a similar schedule throughout the white world. As Jim Crow settled into the American South, colonial rulers rigidified the separation of races throughout sub-Sahara Africa. Indeed, white savagery there exceeded anything in the United States. At the turn of the century, not a single prominent European spoke up in behalf of the African's full humanity.

Between 1880 and the First World War, in other words, trends on both sides of the Atlantic revealed the same components: intensified ethnicity and nationalism, mobilized patriotism, sharpened racial-cultural division. The mix, however, was quite different in the United States. First of all, what Europe divided, America combined. Europeans, who integrated race differences among whites into their lives, exported white racism thousands of miles away. The United States, on the contrary, was home to both. Second, the American state, unlike most of its European counterparts, did very little to define or encourage patriotism. In general, except in enforcing the hard new lines of white racism, the American state remained much weaker than roughly comparable European states. Third, both the rationale behind white racism and the structures expressing it were far better developed—more elaborate, more articulated—than in Europe. As Americans institutionalized it, white racism came to cover everything from education to consumption to manners. At the same time, as if to provide a balance, white-on-white racism took significantly softer, vaguer forms in the United States.

Before the war, race permeated American public discussions. Even the most innovative white reformers and scholars—Mary Ovington White of the new National Association for the Advancement of Colored People, the liberal anthropologist Franz Boas—used the term as a matter of course to sort out the world's variety.

When whites applied it to other whites, however, it merely labeled. Though a soft biological mist might surround those discussions, race rarely added any meaning of its own. Sometimes a mix of European prejudices and American color-consciousness put a group—Sicilians, for example—in limbo, but limbo was a waiting area, not a fixed category. A number of observers believed that simply living in America changed a group's racial characteristics. Even in the hands of the chauvinistic educator Ellwood Cubberley, the substance of "our American race" boiled down to "the Anglo-Saxon conception of righteousness, law and order, and popular government," values that in theory anyone could learn.[22]

This American take on race—fuzzy and permeable among whites, stark and hard between whites and people of color—framed the arrival of the United States as a dominant force in twentieth-century world affairs. A number of whites, especially recent immigrants, then embellished this basic division with subdivisions of their own. On the one hand, new arrivals who brought a European disdain for black Africans to a country where whiteness counted above everything else had no trouble joining the white racist crowd. On the other hand, their ethnic identities, deepening in the years before the Great War, simultaneously denied white unity. This was their form of double consciousness—or at least double vision. Yes, they were white, but they were white Irish Americans, white Polish Americans, white Italian Americans, and nothing less. Oriented toward Europe, many of them were nationalists; oriented where they were, many were American patriots. Until the war scarcely anyone seriously challenged their right to look in both directions at the same time.

CHAPTER 5

## Climax in Europe

Between the 1870s and the 1940s, European states old and new, large and small, used the appeals of nationalism to mobilize power, only to unleash destructive forces on one another that crippled the continent and simultaneously released drives for freedom on a global scale. Before 1914, however, these consequences would have been hard to predict. In the three decades prior to the Great War, the major European states expanded as they centralized, adding 10 million square miles to their colonial empires and sucking an ever larger proportion of the world's resources into their urban-industrial systems. Where nationalist, democratic, or socialist movements had not yet materialized, they had at least made cameo appearances as far east as Russia. Competition and collaboration among them intensified throughout Europe.

In one sense the war changed everything. What opened in 1914 with a sense of apocalyptic anticipation ended four years later in a spirit of chaotic weariness, with only dim ideas of what winning, apart from a stop to the fighting, might mean in people's everyday lives. In place of the prewar's tight interplay among socialism, democracy, and nationalism, one of the three swept away the others to establish itself as the single, orthodox truth in almost all postwar states. That triumph of democracy or nationalism or socialism became proxy for the meaning of the war, sanctifying its horrors and even in a number of cases promising to turn battlefield defeat into ultimate victory. Now it was winner take all, losers take the blame. By the 1930s, the trend in Europe was running strongly in favor of the state's appropriation of nationalism and its elimination of democracy and socialism.

In another sense, however, the war scarcely changed anything. The next two decades were Europe's golden age of state arrogance, more flourishing than ever now that states had spread throughout Eastern Europe. Symbols and rituals of state loyalty trailed citizens from their school days to their graves. It became routine to hound minority cultures on the assumption that under enough pressure they would simply disappear. Because a sense of danger proved to be the state's most effective recruiter, its patriotic messages concentrated on the military, relating the memory of past glories to the perception of contemporary threats. So Europe's states, stumbling to their feet after the First World War, rode the whirlwind to the Second, this one sufficiently calamitous to bring an entire system of unregulated state sovereignty down around them. Nationalism, the facade behind which a large majority of those proud states had acted, plummeted into disrepute, and the European states themselves, divided and subordinated, fell under the wing—or thumb—of a postwar superpower.

The most important change in Europe's state system during the first two decades of the twentieth century was the arrival of the United States as a powerful and integral participant. Between 1894, when Frederick Jackson Turner described American democracy as exclusively American, and 1917, when Woodrow Wilson offered it to the world, the United States government came out of hiding, never to return. As the world's most vibrant center of capitalism, it finally shed the old image—not the heritage, of course, but the reputation—of colonial outpost and replaced it with one of commercial-industrial pacesetter. Beginning in the 1890s, as mobilizations of power picked up speed in Europe, the United States raced alongside. It seized its own empire, gobbled its own lion's share of global resources, and underwent its own centralizing process, both in business and in government. By the turn of the century, socialism, democracy, and nationalism jostled one another in America, too. It was the Great War, however, that took the United States to the head of the table of great powers, and Woodrow Wilson led it there.

Not much prepared Wilson for the job. Although American politicians had often spoken out on world affairs, almost no one pictured the government acting on those sentiments. In 1913 it was still possible for the newly inaugurated president to assume that foreign affairs would be restricted largely to the Caribbean. If they did range farther afield, "the main task of diplomacy" in Wilson's eyes, his biographer tells us, "was the simple one of translating [American] ideals into a larger program of action."[1] When entanglements in the Great War and then America's entry into it exploded those expectations, Wilson voiced the widespread hope that this terrible conflict would answer once and for all certain fundamental questions about the world's future.

Even before the war, the pressures of competition among socialism, nationalism, and democracy had heightened anticipation in all three movements for a final day of reckoning: a time of clearing the field and settling scores, a time of ultimate fulfillment. Like rumblings before the big quake, revolutionary uprisings were already spreading around the periphery of the Western world: in Russia and Turkey during the first decade of the century, in China and Mexico at the beginning of the second. Between 1912 and 1914 two Balkan wars kept observers edgy. Once the seriousness of wholesale European war settled into people's consciousness, the assumption that old systems could not survive it, that a new world would have to emerge from it, flourished: Now was socialism's—or nationalism's—or democracy's—time.

At the center of Wilson's vision of the new world stood self-determination, a grandly suggestive, inherently imprecise slogan that gave aspirants of all persuasions hope that theirs would be the victorious cause. If people really did control their own destinies, they would choose socialism, one camp believed. Nationalists construed self-determination as nothing less than the fulfillment of their movements, precisely what they dreamed of achieving. Because Wilson himself coupled self-determination with democracy, it was easy enough to believe that here lay the actual heart of the matter. Many white Americans saw no conflict between democracy and nationalism. After all, the United States was the original champion of the right to form an independent government in the face of an imposed tyranny, and as if in echo of that assertion, nationalists of all kinds in the United States equated the American Revolution with the cause of freedom in their country of origin. In liberal circles the leading opponents of nationalism in Central and Eastern Europe were already archetypal villains. The Austro-Hungarian and Ottoman Empires were no better than "racial tyrannies," declared Theodore Roosevelt for one: "Neither democracy nor civilization is safe while these two states exist in their present form."[2]

The socialists' moment of glory came in 1917 with the Bolshevik Revolution in Russia, followed immediately after the war with the prospect of a revolutionary socialism rolling into the heart of Central Europe. Nationalists looked like even bigger winners: Latvia, Lithuania, and Estonia along the Baltic, a resurrected Poland, new creations of Czechoslovakia and Yugoslavia, and myriad boundary adjustments for Italy and the Balkan states. At a glance, it was democracy that had the least to show for its efforts. But appearances were indeed deceptive. Bolshevism's boundaries were pushed back and sealed at the Russian border. Perhaps a quarter of the population inside Central and Eastern Europe's reconstructed states were ethnic minorities, many of them frustrated nationalists. Although these states, under duress, promised to honor all their citizens' rights, those guarantees covered only individuals, not minority populations, and in any case no one held the ruling governments to account. Moreover, by some people's reckoning, democrats had reason to take hope from the postwar settlements.

For Wilson—an English American with a deep suspicion of America's multiple ethnic passions and a political scientist with a firm commitment to executive leadership—state governments, not nationalist ambitions, framed the solutions to self-determination. Vague assumptions about cultural-racial affinities—birds of a feather flock together—deceived even educated observers into expecting a more or less natural gravitation of people into their separate national camps. If state and national boundaries could not be made to match exactly, approximations would do. Who got precisely what territory mattered considerably less in the Wilsonian scheme than how that territory was governed, above all whether it operated under constitutional law with elected governments and secure property rights. Language, Wilson's favorite divider, was an erratic measure of ethnicity but a sensible prerequisite for electoral politics. Scattered minorities in Europe, like scattered minorities in the United States, would adapt to a just government, he thought. Hence the plebiscites that Wilson envisaged settling which of two states would control ethnically mixed territories were really a citizenry's choice between the better of two governments. Finally, self-determination's limited scope was no drawback. Neither Wilson nor his circle of admirers gave serious thought to the colonies of Asia and Africa, let alone the so-called backward countries in the Caribbean, joining the self-governing nations. The readiness rule—when they are ready we will give them rights—already used to disfranchise American blacks, applied even more forcefully to people of color around the world.

For the thinness of his democratic criteria, the thickness of his racist hide, and above all the destructiveness of his fragmenting vision, Wilson has been vilified in the best scholarly circles ever since. In that spirit, the historian Eric Hobsbawm accuses Wilson of releasing the demon of "ethnic-linguistic nation states" and thereby causing "a disaster [that] can still be seen in the Europe of the 1990s."[3] In a number of respects, these criticisms lead to a dead end. For one thing, Wilson had little appreciation of ethnicity and less of the nationalism it inspired. Like Hobsbawm and his intellectual companions, he gave priority to states over nations, and he pictured a common language among white people under-writing a state's civic culture, not its ethnic homogeneity. Self-determination would make states into colleagues: There was no useful "distinction . . . between nationalism and internationalism," he thought. The one flowed into the other, as the League of Na-tions would demonstrate.[4] Wilson may have been a naive univer-salist, but he was no ethnic atomizer.

It is not clear what Wilson's critics imagine as the correct alter-native. Nostalgia for the old empires and skepticism about all peo-ple's ability to rule themselves do little to settle policy issues. Not even the Metternich of their dreams could have put the imperial Humpty-Dumpties together again. Would an Austrian-Hungarian confederation or German-Austrian Anschluss have improved the quality of postwar Europe? It is easy to forget how impoverished the vision of Europe's victors was in 1919. Like desperately tired runners, each thought only of itself and then only of taking the next step. The postwar treaties were not the moment of original sin. They were a start, an effort to inaugurate a new era on the assumption that major changes were imperative now and that fur-ther changes would come later. Surrounded by a din of self-serv-ing demands, fearful of revolutionary chaos, and optimistic about the inherent superiority of liberal constitutionalism, Wilson made a stab at the future. The people who followed him did the rest.

States brought on the war, and states triumphed through it. As they funneled resources into the military and blared patriotic messages to justify the human price, democracy and socialism did little more than stoke the war machines. Nationalism, the camp follower, stayed to pick the carrion. With the hollowing out of the Austrian-Hungarian and Ottoman Empires, a variety of nationalist movements—some of them the bitter victims of recent homogenization programs—rushed to fill the spaces. Despite nationalism's reputation in liberal circles as an emancipating force, the peacemakers—champions of central authority to a man—chose state viability over ethnic self-rule. Three of the most important new states were exemplary.

Not only was the Yugoslav idea the product of a few intellectuals who did not even command much support in their own circles; the idea itself had served as little more than a fig leaf for Serbian or Croatian ambitions to swallow the rest of the South Slavs. Croats worked out their identity in a larger context of German speakers and fellow Roman Catholics;, Serbs worked out theirs in a context of Balkan aspirations and Eastern Orthodoxy. On the eve of the Great War, they were less competitive than irrelevant to one another. The last-minute bargaining at the end of 1918 that produced the Kingdom of the Serbs, Croats, and Slovenes (aka Yugoslavia) marked a clear victory of opportunism over nationalism—in fact, the outright frustration of nationalism at its seeming moment of triumph.

Czech nationalism, first as a way of distancing Bohemians from the hated Germans and eventually as a popular movement for independence, had a substantial prewar record, but Slovak nationalism had none at all. In the mean humor of the time, Slovaks were a people with no history, only a past. Certainly no popular movement identified the Slovaks' future in the Czech-dominated state that the United States and then its allies recognized in 1918.

As a final example, the reactionary elite around Roman Dmowski who negotiated Poland's boundaries at the peace conference showed not a scintilla of concern about absorbing Germans to the west or Ukrainians, Belorussians, Jews, Russians, and Lithuanians to the east. Even after the war when Bolshevik Russia pushed back Poland's eastern boundary, a third of the new state's population had no identity as Polish.

In postwar Europe, these and other states ruled their domains with virtually no outside interference, one consequence of which was the oppression of minorities. The Minorities Protection Treaties of 1919, one informed observer noted, were merely "a necessary evil."[5] Moreover, the undoing of the old empires was accompanied by many coerced movements of population (what would later be called ethnic cleansing)—some unprecedently large in scale, all cruel in formulation and vicious in execution. Turks set the new standard by killing perhaps 2.5 million Armenians as the rest fled for their lives. These were years, Hannah Arendt reminded us, that buried the Enlightenment dreams about the Rights of Man. Only states gave rights, and those who gaveth could taketh away. Incidences of statelessness—people devoid of rights—increased dramatically.

These apocalypic hopes and postapocalyptic realities fundamentally transformed nationalism. Like a sudden, eerie silence on the streets, the overwhelming majority of the prewar movements dissolved, some only for a time, others forever. Where nationalist movements had succeeded, the Icarus Effect usually downed them. Now everybody in a new state claimed to be serving the nation, by which they meant serving the state. But even where nationalism fared badly, failure at the critical moment drained energy from almost all of them. In the broadest terms, it mattered crucially that the same improving networks of communication behind nationalism's rise had also been carrying new norms about family planning that sent birthrates into a sharp and seemingly irreversible decline more or less in the wake of nationalism's initial surges. Moving west to east across Europe between 1870 and 1920, one society after another revealed the same sweeping downturn. These long-term alterations in fertility, Susan Watkins reports, represented not a shift from group standards to individual choices but "a shift from social control by a smaller group [the local community] to a larger group"—including, of course, the nation itself.[6] Self-correction? Whatever else, the most likely source for brand new nationalist movements had dried up.

In sum, combined forces that only a few years before seemed about to burst the bounds of Europe slipped instead inside its postwar state system, giving it a temporary look of permanence. The course of Irish nationalism was a case in point.

Under the leadership of Charles Stewart Parnell, its central figure from the mid-1870s to the end of the 1880s, Irish nationalism, like the great trio of movements throughout Europe, systematized. Parnell, a compelling personality, was also a masterful manager. At home he tamed the rough, violent Land League into obedient supporters of his political campaign: Win Home Rule for Ireland by allying with Britain's Liberal party. Abroad he turned North America's magnificent spread of newspapers and societies into a network responsive to his leadership and ready for fund-raising. At the peak of his power, Parnell gave orders to a thriving transatlantic organization. Yet his campaign failed twice over. First, Gladstone's Liberals could not deliver Home Rule. Second, the prospect of a large Catholic majority controlling Home Rule— Rome Rule, its enemies called it—mobilized Protestant opposition in the northern counties. Though Parnell was himself a Protestant, he could do nothing to lessen the religious gap. Even before scandal disgraced Parnell, his time had passed.

What did not change was the movement's increasing bureaucratization. Within a few years after Douglas Hyde founded the Gaelic League to revive Ireland's distinctive language and spark its cultural creativity, political nationalists who knew no more Gaelic than Greek co-opted Hyde's movement to hoist as a banner in their parade. Early in the twentieth century, the political campaign for Irish nationalism, with its empty pretensions to cultural leadership and its burdensome alliance with a papal-centered Catholicism, was as much an orthodoxy as a movement. Socialism might have sharpened it through competition, but following the disastrous defeat of its strongest union in 1913, it too fell in line. Hence when the British promised Home Rule in 1914, Ireland's buttoned-down nationalist politicians thought above all of consolidating their power.

Whatever might have happened, wartime emergency shelved all plans. With no fighting edge in its political wing, the initiative shifted to a handful of conspirators who, in the long but almost lost tradition of calculated martyrdom, stood up to the British on Easter 1916 with little more than sticks and stones. Although few Irish showed an initial sympathy for these archaic heroics, Britain's brutal repression—beating and jailing and hanging dissidents almost at random—changed their minds and, simultaneously, the tone of Irish nationalism. As threats of a military draft in Ireland wiped out the remnants of support for Home Rule, yesterday's radical fringe to Irish nationalism, represented by Sinn Fein, swept to power behind the banner of independence.

Like nationalists everywhere, the Irish anticipated the postwar settlement, with its ideally suited theme of self-determination, as their golden moment. They lost. In the wake of a demoralizing failure at the peace conference, Irish nationalist energies on both sides of the Atlantic turned in on themselves. Should they fight or negotiate? For autonomy or independence? For all the island or most of it? The dominance of secret organizations—Clan na Gael in the United States and Sinn Fein in Ireland—guaranteed little popular input to these decisions. Arguments veiled hatreds, words gave way to weapons. Even further British brutality, still in the name of peace, could not unite the factions. The deteriorating nationalist movement's final gasp was a brief, savage civil war.

What materialized in 1923 was a divided island. The British, faced with the prospects of a Protestant minority in a Catholic state or a Catholic minority in a Protestant state, not surprisingly chose the latter: The government in London reserved the six northern counties of Ulster as a separate dependency and under-wrote there "a one-party [Protestant] state, structured upon religious apartheid."[7] For the rest of the island the Catholic Irish Free State brought to power a military elite who repressed dissenters much as the British had done. Icarus crashed. Ulster Protestants, with the authoritarian Sir Edward Carson as their hero, declared themselves not a distinct nation but pure, loyal Brits. In the Irish Free State, nationalism survived only "in fossilized form, as official symbols" that all parties routinely claimed as their own.[8] It was as if the end defined itself: What happened became ipso facto the fulfillment of what had come before.

In the postwar glory days of state sovereignty, the trend ran strongly toward state embodiment of one of the great trio: that is, a state's claim simply to *be* what those movements had aspired to achieve—socialism, democracy, nationalism. The more tightly each in the trio became bound into the fate of its sponsors, the more it atrophied as a movement. The more thoroughly a state identified itself with one in the trio, the less tolerance it showed for the other two. How states expressed that intolerance varied widely, of course, from little more than a rhetoric of orthodoxy at one end to a relentless crushing of dissent at the other. Moreover, a number of states, including such major ones as France and Britain, remained arenas of tough competition among the trio of movements throughout the interwar years. Nevertheless, by the 1930s the impulse toward monopoly looked as if it would envelop the Western world, and state leaders came under intensifying pressure to declare exclusive loyalties: socialist, nationalist, or democratic, and nothing else. Britain and France seemed the weaker for hedging their answers.

Embodying one of the trio set states along a particular path. First, it entailed eliminating or at least neutralizing the other two. Second, it meant state-izing the one that it claimed to be, that is, encasing nationalism or socialism or democracy in a government's definition, implementation, and protection of it. Two very different embodiments on Europe's flanks—the United States as democracy and the Soviet Union as socialism—illustrated how that process might work itself out. In both countries each movement in the trio had shown new vigor early in the twentieth century. In cities at the European end of Russia, varieties of socialism competed with one another in a struggle to develop popular followings. Hopes for constitutional rights, if not full-blown democracy, flared briefly after the Revolution of 1905, then burst forth in March 1917 with the overthrow of the Romanovs. State patriotism, an essentially traditionalist exaltation of the czar and his ambitions, did borrow from the religious and racial embellishments of prewar nationalism elsewhere, and genuine nationalist stirrings among the empire's minorities exploded with the March Revolution into a chorus of demands for independence from, among others, Polish, Ukrainian, Belorussian, Armenian, Georgian, and Lithuanian spokesmen.

In Russia, all three movements pitted themselves against czarist despotism. In the United States, socialism and nationalism wrestled a place alongside America's dominant democracy. At the start of the century, the ill effects from concentrations of capital, leagues of employers, and large industrial cities finally provided enough impetus to found the Socialist Party of America, which during the next fifteen years joined in the debate over the future of democracy. Dependent on the socialist commitment that migrating Europeans brought with them, the movement was less than the sum of its scattered, disparate parts but definitely growing. At its American end, transatlantic nationalism—overlapping, reinforcing, competing with these socialist segments—rode its own wave of hopes into the war.

A new dispensation began in 1917, with America's declaration of war in April and the Bolshevik Revolution in October. As Wilson and Lenin were quick to realize, Bolshevik socialism for the United States and capitalist democracy for Russia represented precisely the competition that could not be tolerated. Although Lenin's government promised an ongoing dialogue between its ruling cadre and the country's myriad local organizations, as a one-party state the Soviet Union turned elections into mere affirmations of Communist authority. Whatever illusions about Lenin's "democratic centralism" still hung on at the end of the 1920s were completely dispelled with the massive state coercion behind Stalin's first Five Year Plan and its rural collectivization. By the 1930s a vast network of state police lay in wait for dissenters.

The parallel story in the United States was far less bloody and systematic but no less effective. Before 1920, an alliance of courts, police, and vigilantes had already crushed the syndicalist socialism of the Industrial Workers of the World. Political socialism, doubly exposed by the prominence of German Americans in its ranks and by its opposition to American belligerence, also suffered from government persecution, but its own internal weaknesses were at least as crippling. Ridden with factions and cut off from European recruits, socialism shrank to inconsequence, even during the Great Depression. To monitor the remnants, the federal government relied on its own state police, the FBI, spindly next to Russia's but equally secret.

To the challenge from nationalism, both states gave more imaginative responses. Drawing on extensive prerevolutionary debates, in which Lenin took the lead, the Soviet Union from the outset gave an astonishing degree of leeway to its many cultural subgroups. Those with a significant presence and geographical concentration became regional units of the Soviet Union; those too small or scattered to constitute administrative entities still received unprecedented support from the central government: Well into the 1930s, 192 languages had official standing in state policies. Only through their own languages, the communist leadership believed, would it be possible to bring socially backward peoples into the mainstream of socialist consciousness. Even when the centralizing trends of the 1930s eliminated many of these languages from the Soviet menu, ethnicity continued to flourish under party auspices. The peoples who retained official standing were actually instructed to embellish the very ceremonies, celebrations, and histories that identified them as unique. Always the price was obedience to the policies of the central state, with the Communist party, Russian-dominated, the vehicle for overseeing and integrating the regions. As anything resembling independence, nationalism was out of the question. Nevertheless, given the monumental task of ruling a huge landmass with maximum compliance from its disparate population, the Soviet Union could lay claim to Europe's only enlightened nationality policy. In the context of minority persecutions almost everywhere on the continent, the major ethnic components of the Soviet Union, as Ronald Suny, an expert on these matters, summarizes it, were "guaranteed . . . territorial identity, education and cultural institutions in their own language, and the promotion of native cadres into positions of [regional] power."[9]

Ethnicity yes, nationalism no. Under America's very different circumstances, the United States followed similar guidelines. On two counts, the war raised serious questions about the wisdom of the government's long-standing, implicit bargain with the country's many ethnic groups: civic loyalty to the United States, cultural identifications as people chose. For the first time in its history, the United States was positioned to affect the outcome of Europe's contests for power. And for the first time in their history, transatlantic nationalists of all sorts had good reason to anticipate an imminent resolution for their movements. As these curves converged, demands that the American government support various European objectives gave nationalism in America—*hyphenism*—a new, charged meaning. The wartime drives for a uniform cultural code and a heightened state patriotism—*Americanization*—were not just mindless repressions. Leaders in every mobilizing European state expected at least as much from its citizens. What did it mean if millions of people in America routinely identified themselves as Irish or Italian or Serbian or Hungarian and routinely argued over European, not American issues in as many languages as there were groups? Could American democracy even function without a commitment to this country's interests above all others? If the goals of Americanization were misty, so were the grand pluralist visions of John Dewey, Horace Kallen, and Randolph Bourne. Everybody was groping.

The winning answer began by separating out nationalism and repudiating it. To a striking degree, the Wilsonian peace process dismissed the entire output from all the mass meetings, lobbies, resolutions, petitions, and delegations that pressed around it. Individuals did stand a chance of influencing the president. His adviser Louis Brandeis probably affected Wilson's response to Zionist ambitions; the famous pianist Ignacy Paderewski, a friend of Wilson's confidant Edward House, probably elevated an independent Poland in the president's priorities; the philosopher Tomáš Masaryk probably hastened Wilson's recognition of Czechoslovakia. To the noisy public pleas for popular nationalism, however, he turned a deaf ear. As it happened, that was the critical moment to stand fast. By the time Wilson left office, nationalism was collapsing everywhere, and its American reputation was fading fast. As disillusionment with the entire war spread, English American nationalism also lost favor. In the 1920s, a self-consciously American literature, American language, and American law came in vogue.

Ethnicity, on the other hand, thrived in America. If for a short wartime interval isolated German Americans were fair game, those in German American communities never were, nor were Irish Americans inside their urban political fortresses. In the midst of war, Czech and Polish language instruction found its way into Chicago public schools; Norwegian Americans celebrated their brand of patriotism on May 17, Norway's Freedom Day; and a parade down Fifth Avenue on the Fourth of July 1918 brought out New

York City's cultural groups in full ethnic regalia: "The Poles won first prize for the best floats, but the judges also commended the Assyrians, the Bolivians, and the Americans of German Origin."[10] So much for the homogenizers, even at their wartime peak.

Entering the war a fervent multinationalist country, the United States emerged from it a comfortable multiethnic society. The trajectory of Polish American consciousness marked the change. From loose cultural gatherings of fictive kin, Polish American nationalism skyrocketed with the prospects of a Polish state, then subsided as quickly once it sat in place. After the war some migrants returned to Poland; more stayed in the United States where Polonia culture turned away from Europe to concentrate on tight little church-oriented communities. Similar patterns were repeated elsewhere early in the 1920s. No sooner did the Supreme Court establish the right to teach in languages other than English than reliance on those other languages, including German, Norwegian, and Czech, dropped sharply.

The restriction of European immigration through the National Origins Act of 1924, often cited as American bigotry's finest moment, could just as well serve as another illustration of postwar America's multiethnic moderation. At a time when states throughout Europe and Asia Minor were blocking voluntary migrations and forcing involuntary ones in the name of national unity, it would have been extraordinary to the point of craziness for the United States to ignore all of that and swing wide its gates. The challenge was how best to limit the numbers. No one knew how to measure degrees of human need on an intercontinental scale. First come, first serve would have triggered a heartbreaking stampede. In the 1920s, national origins had just the right ring. A mature America would be taking its place in what looked like a congealing Western society filled with states. At the outer boundary, the act excluded people of color, a race line more or less standard everywhere in the white world. Using postwar European states as stand-ins for the white nationalities that made up America's population, it established entry quotas more generous than Europe's, with additional provisions for reuniting families. There were remarkably few complaints inside the United States, even from the nationalities that apparently got shortchanged. In any case the new European states, it was widely believed, would now draw migrants home, not send them out, an assumption that the return of Slavic and Italian peoples seemed to validate. The National Origins Act, in other words, was racist but not a subterfuge for racism. Its purpose was aboveboard: to perpetuate a static white America, a completed United States, in a spirit almost every European state could understand.

As the United States took on the task of regulating population flows in the name of its democracy, the Soviet Union was controlling movements with far greater force in the name of its socialism. Police sealed its borders to entry or exit, and the army shifted entire populations to serve state policy. Millions were trapped in the Ukraine to die of starvation; millions of Cossacks were driven from their homes into Asia. As its own ideologues proclaimed, the Soviet Union was a dictatorship. Whatever ultimate goal it might be serving, into the indefinite future it was ruthless state rule on a scale no czar could have dreamed of achieving. Although a few other states—Sweden and Australia, for example—had a call of their own on socialism, the Soviet Union for all the world embodied it: a state-run socialism that the state ran for itself.

If considerably more states had a right to the title of democracy, the United States remained the world's preeminent example. What the global resonance of the Soviet slogan the Five Year Plan said about the Soviet Union's centrality in socialist hopes, the worldwide appeal of the American slogan the New Deal said about United States as the expression of democracy. Around the Great War, the United States also broke from its past to embody a new-style democracy. The norm in nineteenth-century American had been a strong citizen–weak government democracy. After the Civil War the winning side had experimented briefly with a strong citizen–strong government model, and the losing side had slid into a weak citizen–weak government pattern. Challenges from capitalist developers and populist reformers unsettled both of them, however, and early in the twentieth century, American democracy shifted direction toward a new goal: weak citizen, strong government. Consolidated city administrations, regulatory commissions, and short ballots distanced governments from the voters. Both major political parties, as well as the corporations, unions, and farm lobbies trying to influence them, developed comprehensive organizations that could only deal effectively with one another and with a systematized government. In Europe at the turn of the century, superimposing new democratic politics on old hierarchies held out the promise of more democracy. In the United States, superimposing new hierarchies on old democratic politics only promised more hierarchy. Voting turnouts plummeted. The Republican Walter Lippmann, whose writings in the 1920s set the agenda for informed discussions about democracy, disparaged ordinary citizens for failing "to transcend their casual experience and their prejudice" and advocated instead a rule through experts, with elections as a means for voters to approve or disapprove of their policies—a consumers' democracy.[11] New Deal Democrats implemented those basic principles in the 1930s.

If dictatorial socialism and oligarchic democracy prevailed at Europe's flanks, authoritarian nationalism dominated its heartland. The more monopolistic these versions of socialism, democracy, and nationalism, the more fearful—the more antagonistic—each became of the other two, and more leaders in each case took responsibility for preserving the one correct system from its enemies. Antipopulism prevailed everywhere. Ordinary people, dangerously susceptible, had to be protected against the omnipresent possibility that they would listen to a siren song, make the wrong decision, and simply sell out the truth. To defend against that possibility, leaders for each of the trio claimed to have a corner on the future. Only their system could provide the service, the protection, the welfare, the education, the opportunity that citizens craved.

Even American democrats, unaccustomed to a game of spiraling promises, joined the chorus. "The ideal democracy would, of course, arrange a job for every able-bodied citizen," the New Dealer Henry A. Wallace announced.[12] It was an inherently hostile, mutually exclusive competition that put more and more pressure on all states, whatever their persuasions, to deliver the goods.

Contrary to first impressions, nationalism did not culminate with the postwar settlement. As the old nationalism exhausted itself, a disfigured cousin—this one the captive of the state—roamed the continent in its place, gathering its forces for Armageddon. Where the state set the terms, nationalism provided little more than a rhetoric of justification for the uses of force both inside and outside the state's boundaries. As its interests were twisted into the service of the state, this bastardized nationalism lost any necessary relation to the visions of ethnic self-determination that had given it life in the first place.

In this latest dispensation, nationalism, which had always fed on people's restless desires, manifested itself in two ways. On the weak side, a few dissenting voices accused the state of dulling the national spirit and yearned for its renewal. Usually more reactionary than their ruling opponents, these revivalists squandered most of their energy lamenting the loss of the old, pure truths. If they did take power, they rarely did more than make the state a bit more repressive. Far more postwar nationalists called on the state to complete its mission. In a Europe of ragged boundaries and mobile people, there was still work to do. Once in the hands of the state, however, these ambitions became whatever the state's leaders said they were, as Italy's experience illustrated.

The deep-seated complications of Italy's nationalist politics set the stage. In the middle of the nineteenth century, with the maneuvers to form an Italian state already under way, "the Italian language was perhaps spoken by less than five per cent of the population in the Italian peninsula," the historian Denis Mack Smith has estimated.[13] Small wonder no government could meet the challenge of creating a population of Italians. Divided north,

central, and south, secular capitalist, landed gentry, and reactionary Catholic, white collar, wage earner, and peasant, Italy was
riven with hostilities and inequalities that the sudden introduction
of universal manhood suffrage in 1912 simply laid bare for every-
one to see. The Italian army, once expected to be a culturally
unifying force, slid into the military's familiar role of muscling citizens: "Instead of being the nation's schoolmaster it became the
[state's] policeman."[14] On the eve of the Great War, a radical socialism and a homogenizing nationalism, already at each other's
throats, competed with democrats for the power to eliminate one
another.

Some leaders, realizing how fractured Italy was at home, hoped
to compensate with victories abroad. The upshot was a miserable
war record and a frustrating peace settlement. Serious economic
problems and vicious infighting after the war opened the way for
Benito Mussolini's brutal Fascist forces, which seized power in
1923 with promises of achieving what no other regime had come
close to accomplishing: unity at home and glory abroad. Eliminating democracy and outlawing socialism, the fascists appeared to
be mobilizing the country's resources exclusively behind Italian
nationalism. Indicatively, the nationalist enthusiasm of Italian
Americans, unlike that of other ethnic groups in the United States,
rose to an even higher level than it had reached before the war.
Mussolini looked for all the world like its agent of fulfillment.

On the contrary, Mussolini glorified the state and nothing but
the state. "The nation does not exist"—fascist doctrine read—
". . . [until] the nation is created by the state."[15] From the Bolsheviks Mussolini borrowed the ideal of the new fascist man, root-
less except for his absolute dedication to the state, a measure of
citizenship that made a mockery of nationalism's ancestrally con-
nected kin. Italian nationalism, merely a fig leaf for fascist ambitions, meant what Mussolini said it meant, no more, and Italians
abroad, willy-nilly, were cast in the role of expatriot patriots, not
transatlantic nationalists.

States fundamentally altered by the war were particularly prone to the new brand of authoritarian nationalism. By the 1930s the entire sweep of Central and Eastern Europe—Czechoslovakia excepted—came under the control of dictators employing nationalist rhetoric in behalf of state power. The war's winners—Poland, Yugoslavia, Romania—were as eligible as its losers: Austria, Hungary, Bulgaria. In retrospect, historians find these regimes quite limited in the control they actually exercised in their countries—significantly better at generating terror than running the state. At the time, however, they seemed to be models of total, centralized power. Germany came to embody this kind of nationalism in the same sense that the Soviet Union embodied socialism and the United States democracy. Appropriately, it was Nazi Germany that precipitated the climax of European nationalism, taking the entire system down, once and for all, in the deadly embrace of the state.

Coming into the twentieth century, German nationalism did not appear exceptionally dangerous. By equating membership in the nation with citizenship in Bismarck's Germany and by treating emigrants as deserters, its state-dominated nationalism had cut itself off from potentially important sources of strength abroad. The waves of internal migration from country to city that gave German nationalism its popular strength also invigorated its hot competitors, socialism and democracy, whose movements proved to be better adapted than nationalism to the still-powerful regional loyalties crisscrossing Germany's federated state. In the face of these challenges from socialism and democracy, some prewar conservatives sharpened their weapons, exalting military might and excoriating outsiders in what Hans-Ulrich Wehler has called a "passionate, xenophobic, vulgarized nationalism."[16] Nonetheless, these glorifications of German power did nothing to diminish the strength of socialism and democracy or to compensate for the relatively weak support that nationalism derived from related sources: religion, language, race.

Although Protestant-Catholic hostilities had subsided by the turn of the century, the results said more about Protestants giving up on Catholics than Catholics converting to a Protestant brand of Germanness. The chasm still yawned between them. Language continued to diffuse rather than focus nationalist energies. Too many German speakers divided their loyalties among too many jurisdictions for Wilhelmine Germany to claim language as grounds for its distinctive nation. Race had as many meanings—some hard, more soft—in prewar Germany as it did elsewhere in Europe. An unusually heavy dependence on the state was German nationalism's one ominous quality before the Great War. Even here, the state did not fly a distinctively German flag or recruit a comprehensively German army until the 1890s.

A losing war and a punishing peace scrambled these calculations. In a contest that might have tipped the other way, Germany was treated like a crushed and powerless state: its government overturned, its territory parceled among its neighbors, its economy drained to pay tribute to the victors. First a devastating inflation, then a devastating depression, undermined hopes that either socialism or democracy could show Germans the way out of these harsh, humiliating times. Authoritarian nationalism, by then both a familiar European solution and a thriving brand of German politics, was the alternative. If chance played an important role in bringing the National Socialist party to power in 1933, chance could not account for its appeal. It was the Nazi genius to gather in those once-scattered dividers—race, religion, and language— and stack them one atop the other as reinforcements for its version of the German state.

Nazis, major contributors to the popularizing of a hard, biological racism, were even greater beneficiaries of it. If it served Adolf Hitler's regime as a weapon against both whites and people of color, its immediate targets were Jews. In the long history and recent revival of anti-Semitism throughout Europe, nothing made Germans peculiarly susceptible to it, but then nothing made them particularly resistant, either. What the Nazi regime demonstrated was that persistent racist messages banged home with mounting force gave them wider currency and greater urgency. By the end of the 1930s, public policy used Jews and to a lesser degree Slavs to mark the boundaries of the German people. Doubly important, this racism through a common animus toward aliens and outsiders could serve as a bridge across Germany's critical Catholic-Protestant divide. On the eve of the Nazi takeover, as Margaret Anderson has shown, Catholic areas of Germany were the least likely to support the party. After 1933, however, where race trumped religion it meant that religion, too, fell in line behind the state. The Vatican's benign neutrality helped.

In its initial Bismarckian version, state citizenship defined the German nation. The Nazis reformulated that principle to justify a breathtakingly expansive policy southward and eastward. Now the state would not simply make the nation; it would ratify the nation. The Third Reich would extend its boundaries to incorporate all those people whom the Nazis by assorted cultural criteria designated Germans. The state would cover the nation; the nation would express itself through the state. What had originated as a rule to keep nationalist attention focusing inward, in other words, now sent it coursing outward. Even obvious exceptions, such as German Americans, were courted: At least they were potential Germans, or perhaps Germans in absentia. If Hitler netted almost nothing from that transatlantic appeal, it still stood as one index to his nationalist daring. As a corollary to these radical changes in strategy, the German language, once the common property of people in and out of the German state, became another layer atop German nationalism—both a new line of division and a standing justification for conquest. Self-determination, the Nazis called it, and until 1938 they neutralized a good many foreign critics with that widely respected standard.

The Nazis, in other words, combined every major theme in half a century of European nationalism: the most potent combination of language and race, overlaid with a Christian endorsement; the claim of national incompleteness, compounded by the theft of German land in the postwar settlement; and the need for an aggressive defense against a ring of enemies, italicized by stories of Wilson tricking Germans into the Armistice of 1918. These militantly arrayed reinforcements, in turn, always took their orders from the Third Reich. Whatever the rhetorical merger of the two, in practice the state used the nation, never the converse. As Hannah Arendt emphasized, the Nazis had an undisguised "contempt for the narrowness of nationalism."[17] Its leaders turned their nationalist messages on and off strictly as it served them. Territories they demanded by reason of self-determination served strictly as stepping stones: from the Sudetenland across all of Czechoslovakia, from Danzig through the rest of Poland. Smelling victory in the wind, the Third Reich dropped the issue of self-determination entirely in 1942. As Hitler had written years before in *Mein Kampf*, boundaries simply expressed the fruits of conquest. By the same token, the anti-Semitism that was once anchored to German nationalism cut those moorings when it became a boundless policy of genocide. It made more sense to see Hitler himself as the culmination of a Napoleonic rather than a nationalist tradition.

As the Third Reich collapsed, it carried the authoritarian state's lackey—an utterly dependent, exclusionary nationalism—with it, but not without a final, furious show of force. Wherever German power spread, knots of fascists materialized to invoke nationalist values in behalf of their own bloody vendettas. What they might have mobilized in the long run, nobody knows. In the short run, however, they concentrated on crushing old enemies. Appropriately, these brief, vengeful regimes left a far deeper imprint on their victims than on their supposed beneficiaries. Croat Ustaše, for example, slaughtered hundreds of thousands of Serbs without strengthening a connectedness among the Croats themselves. The Vichy government, bent on a Christian purge of social impurities, made no effort to unite, only to purify the French.

The primary survivor of this fascist cataclysm, Francisco

Franco's regime in Spain, had the weakest nationalist claims of them all. Franco, who precipitated a civil war in 1936 on his way to almost four decades as head of state, took for granted "the weak attraction of Spanish, as opposed to regional or local, identity."[18] Where he made war on regional groups, he was attacking people who were resisting his rule, not opposing a Spanish nation. Like the dictator Primo de Rivera who preceded him in the 1920s, Franco relied on a Roman Catholic Church long hostile to Spanish nationalism and an army indifferent to it. Around that core he cobbled reactionary bits and pieces that he was able to manipulate for his own purposes. Opportunistic above all else, he concentrated nothing on more exalted than personal power. Pius XII, a pope for the age, gave his blessings, even as Franco was crushing Catholic Basques.

A racism that had expanded on the same schedule as the final wave of European nationalism crashed precipitously with it. Despite the repudiation of race theory in intellectual circles after the First World War, its general popularity only increased during the 1920s and 1930s. Radicals were certainly not immune. "Jews had played a leading part in the early phases of all [European] Socialist and Communist parties, but since then they had everywhere been squeezed out. . . . The year before Hitler came to power there was not a single one among the hundred Communist deputies in the Reichstag."[19] Nevertheless, authoritarian nationalist regimes were the primary promoters. Some of these uses, such as Italian Fascism's invocations of a Latin-Mediterranean-Roman race, were largely bombastic. Others, such as the claims to a single Serbian-Croatian-Slovenian race at the heart of Yugoslavia, were just hopeful. Still others, however, such as the Metaxas regime's proclamation of a Greek race, were pointedly vicious from the outset. What distinguished Nazi racism was more the power to act on it than the values behind it. As German power destabilized the continent, it let loose a host of racist demons ready to devour their prey. Sometimes singling out Gypsies, above all cooperating in the wholesale murder of European Jewry, they blanketed the Balkans, settled into Vichy France, and found as much sympathy in conquered Poland as in collaborating Slovakia. Outside of continental Europe, cool responses to the millions of desperate Jews indicated how widespread anti-Semitism was and how well it correlated with the heating of the Holocaust. According to wartime opinion polls, American anti-Semitism peaked in 1943.

Beginning late in the nineteenth century, a new round of color-coded racism gathered strength in the United States on the same schedule as European racism. Blacks who moved north to escape the increasingly elaborate rules of Southern caste faced an increasingly elaborate segregation there, too. Federal policy segregated government work. Migrants from Asia could not become citizens; prospective immigrants were banned entirely. Miscegenation laws, once peculiar to the South, came to cover most of the United States between the 1890s and the 1930s, stigmatizing Asian Americans and Native Americans as well as African Americans and punishing violators as felons. The scientific cousin of those laws, eugenics, which spread from Britain into Germany and the Scandanavian countries, had its widest application America, where by the 1930s forty-one of its forty-eight states criminalized marriage to "inferior people" and in most cases authorized sterilizing them—the fate of over seventy thousand souls. Wartime concentration camps for Japanese Americans capped the era.

Significant differences separated the two sides of the Atlantic, however. Although Nazi Aryanism disparaged people of color, it posed a much greater danger to neighboring Slavs than to distant Africans. In the United States, color coding had all the advantages: Whiteness, after all, had been a defining element of American democracy from the outset. On the other hand, race theories that sorted whites into moral-biological hierarchies—Nordic at the top, Alpine in the middle, Mediterranean below, for example—had only a blaze of prominence in the United States between 1915 and 1925, then faded from public discussion. Anti-Semitism, systematic and deadly in Europe, was never more than desultory and nasty in the United States. Hence many Americans who raised no objections to dismantling the rights of people of color in the United States considered the dismantling of the rights of Jews in Europe the work of lunatics.

Nevertheless, for reasons that remain mysterious, this odd couple that had risen together fell together. Throughout Western society, kinds of racism that had been normal before 1945 rapidly became abnormal after that. Declarations of universal equality were embedded in the founding documents of the new United Nations organization. Racist language lost its acceptability. By the 1960s, ignoring the Holocaust was no longer an option in any Western state. By then also, the United States removed the last legal supports for segregation, and European powers retreated to their last outposts of colonialism. If for the balance of the century a subterreanean layer of Western racism proved remarkably durable, it never regained public legitimacy.

Out of the vortex of war spun one last victory for the movements that had accelerated during the 1890s and crashed a half century later—a coda, as it were, to Europe's state nationalism. Zionism, which in 1939 seemed hopelessly lost, revived to see its cause succeed in less than a decade. Until that sudden recovery, Zionism looked for all the world like a movement that had irremediably missed its turn a generation earlier when in the waning days of the First World War it had glimpsed a glory it simply could not reach. In 1917 the prospect of reviewing boundaries, governments, and systems of authority throughout the old Ottoman Empire gave Zionism an audience that its slight, disputatious movement could never have mustered on its own. Although Arabs, not Jews, had the better claim to self-determination in its usual sense, the assumption that the Jews were one race— an assumption with terrible future consequences—made them competitive for rights in Palestine. Even more significant, the two most important Zionist leaders, Chaim Weizmann in London and Louis Brandeis in Washington, had the ear of the two most important world leaders, Prime Minister Arthur Balfour and President Wilson. It was those relationships, along with Weizmann's persistent bargaining and drafting, that secured the Balfour Declaration, an acceptance of the idea of a Jewish homeland in Palestine just as the British prepared to replace Turkish power in that territory.

A second dazzling prospect appeared alongside the first. To escape contamination from the European war, the headquarters of the World Zionist Organization provisionally relocated in the United States, and as it did, Brandeis—renowned in Jewish and Gentile circles alike as a brilliant lawyer, policy maker, and presidential adviser—gave Zionism an immense boost by committing to the cause. His presence immediately changed Zionism's prospects and tone. The millions of Jews in the United States were Zionism's greatest untapped resource; Brandeis gave the movement instant American credibility. In addition, by focusing on the preparation of Palestine as a home for Jews, he made two more critical contributions. First, he normalized Jewish nationalism. Now like any other nationalism active in the United States, Zionism sought political control over a distant ancestral land, nothing less and nothing more. No sooner had he joined the movement than Brandeis was drumming on the familiar American theme of bilevel loyalties: a people's primal tie to the homeland, a citizen's unswerving attachment to the United States. A number of wealthy American Jews, delighted with the prospect of Jews from the Pale migrating to Palestine rather than to the United States, shelved an earlier anti-Zionism to support what they saw as a safe, philanthropic nationalism, one that Brandeis, famous as a cost-cutting problem-solver, might just accomplish. During the war, membership in the Zionist Organization of America shot up sevenfold, and Brandeis, like a prince in waiting, envisaged the teams of experts that would soon make the desert bloom in Palestine. All Jews, he thought, could enlist in this Zionism.

Great expectations to no avail. After the war, as the vitality drained out of nationalism throughout Europe, Zionism too went flat. The vague phrasing of the Balfour Declaration, strictly a wartime measure that the British matched in private with an equally general endorsement of Arab interests, provided neither a road nor a timetable nor even a precise destination for the Jewish cause in Palestine. Everything depended on a British goodwill that rapidly dwindled. Perhaps Brandeis's drive and optimism could have surmounted that disappointment, but Weizmann and his allies, pushing Brandeis into the shadows as they reclaimed control of the movement, did not have that ability.

The issues between the Brandeis and Weizmann camps were real enough. Brandeis would have Americanized the movement—with efficiency, democracy, and growth the measures of its success in Palestine. He no more pictured himself living in Palestine than he anticipated any appreciable number of American Jews migrating there. Palestine was a homeland for other people. In the guise of a foreign mission, the Americanized movement could accommodate anyone supporting a good cause. Jews who feared that modernity was destroying the distinctiveness of their culture had reason to fear this kind of nationalism as their problem, not its solution. Eastern Europeans, fighting for the soul of their movement, took it back from alien spirits.

Without Brandeis, Zionism lost most of its American members, who concentrated on the United States as the Jews' promised land. Indicatively, almost the only ethnic leaders who opposed the postwar American laws restricting immigration were Jewish. Contributions also dried up, and settlement in Palestine barely inched forward. Even when the Nazis intensified their anti-Semitism, Weizmann was too preoccupied struggling for power with the authoritarian Vladimir Jabotinsky to rethink his strategy. As streams of refugees, washing against stone-cold state boundaries, gave a terrible concreteness to the meaning of a safe place—a homeland—for Jews, Weizmann still clung, hope against hope, to his British benefactors. Then in 1939, the Chamberlain government repudiated the Balfour Declaration, essentially sealed off Palestine to Jewish immigration, and promised primacy there to the Arabs. Weizmann's Zionism collapsed.

Wartime revelations of the Holocaust did not so much revive Zionism as swallow it in a far larger and more complicated process of state-building. After 1942, anything short of complete independence in Palestine became unthinkable to Jews of many different persuasions with many previous attitudes about Zionism. Except perhaps for little Denmark, Jews had no reliable friend in Europe. The very countries that had once led the way in emancipating Jews now appeared as a lineup of enemies: not just Germany but its collaborators in France and a British government that adamantly refused access to Palestine. For the most pessimistic, anti-Semitism in the United States was final proof that, as Herzl had warned, only Jews could secure a safe place for Jews. New leaders—some like David Ben-Gurion in Palestine, some like Rabbi Abba Hillel Silver in America—fashioned a new movement as hard as the world around it, where the first rule was: Don't ask, take. They would turn the pitiless state system that had bottled Jews inside the Nazi domain to their own advantage. High-level discussions of carving a Jewish state out of postwar Germany, as millions of putative Germans were being driven out of other European lands, demonstrated how casually ethnic cleansing entered into great power calculations. Why not in Palestine? Jews of all kinds using tactics of all sorts mobilized their well-situated allies and produced the state of Israel, a final monument to the European values of unregulated state sovereignty that in other hands had come close to killing all European Jews.

CHAPTER 6

# Nationalism Worldwide

As the pulse of nationalism quickened across Europe between 1880 and 1920, interest in it spread globally. By the beginning of the twentieth century, nationalist aspirations had currency among people everywhere who found Europe's might by turns intimidating, horrifying, and fascinating. While Europeans watched and copied one another, handfuls of Chinese, Filipinos, Indians, Iraqis, Palestinians, and many others watched and copied, too. Rather than alienated intellectuals fleeing their failed cultures, as some Western scholars would have it, they were by and large questing individuals who imagined using the techniques of European power against Europeans and in the process preserving the best of their own culture. Some, like the original theoreticians of Vietnamese nationalism, were strictly reactionaries trying to reclaim the past. Some, like the pioneer Chinese nationalist Sun Yat-sen, were progressive reformers who set out to tailor Western principles to their country's need for cohesion and justice. Some, like the early exponent of Egyptian nationalism Mustafa Kemal, were eclectics—in Kemal's case, an admirer simultaneously of

French ideas and Ottoman rule. Whatever their orientation, all predicted future glory for their cultures.

Their visions, however, rarely spread beyond elite circles and often died with them. Despite an occasional moment of glory— Sun Yat-sen's in 1911 on the collapse of the Manchu Dynasty— these exploratory intellectuals essentially kept their own company. None of the subject people they were exhorting mounted a popular nationalist movement along lines they advocated. Popular nationalism came by other routes in other guises. If there had been no Sun Yat-sen, hundreds of millions of Chinese still would have mobilized as Chinese in opposition to the Japanese invasion of the 1930s and 1940s. Appropriately, the only successful transfer of European nationalism to Africa before 1914 consolidated white power in a colonial outpost of Western society. On the same schedule and by the same logic as contemporary Europeans, Boers around the turn of the twentieth century became Afrikaner, replete with a newly constructed language, a heightened sense of racial distinctiveness, and a people's history of sacrifice and triumph that laid claim to South African lands as their ancestral heritage. Among the victims of colonialism, however, popular nationalism made little use of European models. It appeared now here, now there, according to the special circumstances of culturally different people—in a very few cases before the First World War, in several more between world wars, then in a great variety of settings over the balance of the century. Because nationalism worldwide originated as resistance to oppression, imperialist Western societies profoundly influenced it, but rarely by showing it the way to succeed.

The marvel is that nationalism figured prominently in such a large number of these efforts. By contrast, the other two in the grand trio of Europe's movements fared much worse. Democracy had the least success of all. Dependent cultures that managed to elude formal colonization were almost always hierarchical in structure. Nothing in colonialism itself argued in democracy's favor: Neither the rulers' arbitrary authority nor their victims' traditions modeled its possibilities. Imperial governments, by denying their subjects essential civil rights until perhaps the eleventh hour, destroyed the preconditions for building a democracy. A democracy driven underground was a contradiction in terms. Moreover, the process of fighting for independence tended to eliminate democracy's indispensable middle ground where today's winners and losers could accept the prospect of changing places tomorrow. As Rupert Emerson put it, anticolonialism everywhere "is the champion of self-government . . . as opposed to alien rule, but it is only accidentally self-government in the sense of rule by the many as opposed to rule by the few."[1] It was the marvel of independent India that it survived all these hazards to give democracy a try.

Socialism fared somewhat better, largely because of its ideological focus on oppression and resistance. When the armies of Europe set about slaughtering one another in the First World War, anticolonial elites who had once searched for the secret of the imperialists' invulnerability paid increasing attention to their vulnerability, and the explosive possibilities of revolutionary socialism often ranked at the top of the list. Taking Marxism back home, however, was a slippery enterprise, not only because it favored industrial over agrarian societies but also because colonial governance, spreading hardships and indignities indiscriminately, diffused the effects of class. Anticolonialism drew people from all walks of life into capacious resistance movements. Although some anticolonial leaders and some trade unions retained a distinguishably Marxist loyalty, it rarely tapped popular energies. At midcentury South Africa may have been an exception; revolutionary China certainly was.

Ethnic loyalties, on the other hand, did mobilize the millions. Perhaps, as a generation of radical scholars have argued, colonial subjects throughout Asia and Africa failed to comprehend their own interests. Perhaps, as the Africanist John Lonsdale claims for the insurgent Kikuyu under British rule, they mismeasured real "class injustice against imagined ethnic reciprocity."[2] Nevertheless, the social scientist Donald Horowitz's rule of thumb—"the generally greater power . . . of ethnic affiliations in Asia and Africa than in the West"—serves as a useful point of departure, for nothing cemented loyalties or channeled grievances more effectively.[3] Where slave trading had devastated the social order in West Africa, family-kin systems often held a virtual monopoly in organizing public life and providing basic governance even before European colonialism arrived.

In direct competition, ethnic attachments almost always overwhelmed class attachments. Although they might reinforce one another, as they did in the bloody conflicts between Tutsi and Hutu, their combined forces marched under an ethnic banner. When the British in Rhodesia grabbed land and coerced labor from the indigenous Shona, black ZANLA guerrillas rallied local and regional groups into a common anticolonial movement by promising not to redress class injustice but to return Shona land to the Shona people. In mobilizing resistance to the French, the Marxist Ho Chi Minh played upon the "near-religious status" of the Vietnamese family and the "quasi-priestly functions" of its patriarch to assume the national mantle of "Uncle," while his Communist colleagues spoke to their compatriots as "brothers and sisters" and to one another as "elder brother comrade." "Since no one can divide the members of one family," Ho lectured the nation in 1946, "no one can divide our Vietnam." Appropriately, at his death he rose to the pinnacle of honor: "great-grandfather."[4]

Sometimes Europe's powerful generator of nationalism, migration, inspired nationalism elsewhere as it stretched out an ethnic group's kin system. A decade of soaring landlessness and war-driven dislocations in Vietnam produced massive population movements just preceding Ho's sweep to power in 1945. Before nationalism gathered significant support on the China mainland, Sun Yat-sen's strongest partisans came from the relocated Nan-

Yang Chinese in Southeast Asia. Extensive Middle Eastern migration set the stage for Pan-Arabism. The Igbo in Nigeria, the Kikuyu in Kenya, and the Bamileke in the Cameroon, precocious nationalists in their areas, were also outstanding examples of an "overpopulation in the ethnic homeland and the consequent diaspora."[5] At the time of Kenyan independence, two of five Kikuyu lived away. Farther south, ethnic consciousness sharpened where young workers flowed into the fields of Southern Rhodesia (Zimbabwe) and the mines of South Africa—among Tumbuka and Ngoni, for example, who were the leading nationalists in northern Malawi. On the contrary, "in areas from which men did not emigrate in large numbers, such as southern Zambia and central Malawi, the ethnic message has clearly had less popular appeal."[6] By the same token, the closest approximation to a popular nationalist movement among Egyptians, famous for their disinclination to migrate, was loyalty to Gamal Nasser's state, never to the symbols of fictive kinship.

Migration's role, however, changed dramatically in the twentieth century, as states increasingly herded populations to their new destinations or simply dumped unwanted people into the world at large. The South African policy of imposing taxes, seizing lands, and forcing labor from the dispossessed, culminating in the creation of impoverished Bantustan enclaves, no doubt inspired countless tribal dreams of reclaiming a homeland, as a similar plight did among a million Palestinians. Indeed, the world in the second half of the twentieth century teemed with people—perhaps 30 million refugees by 2000—most of whom would never inhabit the places they called home. Nonetheless, these forced-march horrors bore almost no relationship to the nineteenth-century chain migrations behind Europe's popular nationalism. People driven into exile were migrants only in a cruelly restricted sense.

Hence the essential guideline: Nationalism worldwide did not pick up Europe's story and give it global applications. Europeans did not pass the baton to everybody else. People around the world changed what they took from Europe to suit themselves. Borrowing, of course, was always natural, whether it was Frank Lloyd Wright's incorporation of Japanese design, Pablo Picasso's appropriation of African masks, or Béla Bartók's assimilation of Harlem jazz. All cultures borrow, and given the opportunity, all cultures borrow all the time. Then they give what they get a new meaning. Rather than a European concept sitting awkwardly where it did not belong, nationalism opened itself to protean cultural translations, a diversity all the richer because of the near universal centrality of kinship to social structures everywhere.

At the same time, nationalism's very plasticity makes its global history devilishly hard to follow. Before we examine its chameleon qualities through three of its most common guises worldwide—nationalism as a state creation, as a pan movement, and as an anti-imperialist response—let's look briefly at the case of India, which not only contains elements of all three of these categories but also highlights the difficulty of determining where we have lost the thread of nationalism and picked up the story of something else. Our best preparation for a global search after nationalism is a humbling awareness that we can never be quite sure what we have located.

The customary starting point for a history of Indian nationalism is the founding of the Indian National Congress more than a century after Britain's East India Company had first disrupted power relations on the subcontinent. Initially in 1885 and then more or less annually, a small gathering of widely scattered elites met to address the needs of all Indians in the context of imperial rule. Perhaps, as the historian Christopher Bayly has argued, much older traditions of regional patriotism fed into the Congress. Nevertheless, these strands were so territorially vague, so politically indeterminate, and so tactically nebulous they seem more like floating sentiments than nationalist precursors. Congress began something new. Soberly and cautiously, it sought to redress egregious injustices and expand Indian rights in ways that pointed toward self-rule, even though it did not actually articulate that goal until well into the twentieth century.

Unquestionably the Congress's greatest accomplishment was its continuity. Despite times of eclipse and despair, it survived to inherit India's independent government in 1947. Until the Second World War, however, it was never a comfortable or consistent voice for popular nationalism. That role fell to Mohandas K.—more familiarly Mahatma—Gandhi, who initially tapped those feelings just after the First World War in his dangerous, dramatic movements to purge India of impurities: imperial and indigenous, body and soul. Modeling his message of simplicity and sacrifice as he spread it, he drew tens of thousands of ardent followers throughout India and established a moral beacon for millions more. No one more effectively—more creatively—adapted nationalism to the culture around him. The Congress did not prepare the way for Gandhi's popular nationalism; Gandhi taught a skittish Congress how to participate in such a movement. Around 1930 he turned that fading forum for accommodation into the center for a massive civil disobedience campaign that filled the jails and turned all eyes to the Congress for anticolonial leadership. In the process, by bridging the gap between socialist hotbloods like Jawaharlal Nehru and traditional dignitaries like Nehru's father, he helped to sustain enough cohesion in the movement to survive the war, weather partition, and set the Congress on its way to decades of independent rule.

With the colony's partition in 1947 into India and Pakistan, which no leader seemed to want or know how to avoid, Gandhi's Icarus hurtled to earth. In the deadly turmoil that followed, more than 12 million people went in search of new homes and well over a million died. As if it had been scripted, his assassination a year later embodied the fate of his movement. Gandhi the spiritual secularist never wavered in his goal of a united Indian community encompassing all religions, sects, and peoples: hence his tireless appeal for a Moslem-Hindu alliance and his persistent drive for the public rights of women and caste-defined untouchables. But Gandhi the secular spiritualist showed genius only in mobilizing resources out of Hindu culture: in investing pollution and purity with political meaning, in playing both domestic and transcendent aspects of a complex Hindu tradition against male dominance and caste rigidity. When he identified with cow protection, he drew strength from Hindu belief at the expense of Moslem practice. Except for the one occasion in 1920 when he joined Indian Moslems in their own cause—one that pitted Islamic religious authority against British imperial power—he simply had no good ideas about interfaith collaboration, only good intentions. The more talk of independence included plans for an effective central government, with the sop of reserved legislative spaces for religious minorities, the further away the Moslems pulled until, at a critical moment, the unquestioned leader of the Moslem League, M. A. Jinnah, pulled them out entirely.

Was there ever a popular Indian nationalism that was not a Hindu quest in mufti? From the days when officials of the original East India Company listened to Brahman dreams of a whole India, unity invariably devolved into Hindu unity. Indeed the word *Hindu* was meant to comprehend the entire subcontinent. Nothing mitigated nationalism's Hindu character, not even a common hostility to the British. In a classic case of minorities ducking for cover, Sikhs, Christians, and other smaller groups, as well as millions of Moslems, looked beyond Hindu India for their security, often to the British themselves. Nor was there a substitute in India for Hindu unity. Not only did the people of the subcontinent speak scores of languages and hundreds of dialects; these belonged to four entirely different language groups. Myriad regional and local attachments confounded Gandhi as much as they did lesser leaders.

The glory of modern India's history is its unique transition from imperial rule to democratic independence, despite its size and heterogeneity. Several explanations come to mind. The remarkable continuity of the Congress, the impressive preparation of its leaders, and their broad, enthusiastic constituency at the moment of independence provided the new state with a governing party that was equipped for its task. Because British rule had left much of regional and village India intact and because in most cases the Congress party accepted the importance of those traditional networks, there was also a crucial continuity in everyday life connecting colony and independent state. In this regard, Indians reclaimed what they had never lost. Moreover, British standards and Indian personnel gave the new state the inestimable advantages of an army subordinate to civilian government and a civil service capable of administering it. Still and all, the horror behind the wonder of that transition were the herded and brutalized and murdered millions caught in the communal upheavals of partition. It may be that those heartrending human costs were the price of India's democracy. In the half century before independence, neither Moslem nor Hindu leaders had shown any talent in accommodation, and precious little interest in trying. With few exceptions, their communities either separated sullenly or met violently. India had not accumulated the civic resources necessary to reckon with large territorial blocs of mutually distrustful Moslems and Hindus. As it was, the new government relied on Hindu fears of their Moslem neighbors for a cohesion nothing else promised to supply.

With independence, the state laid claim to Indian nationalism. So did Hindu leaders. And so, of course, did the self-styled heirs of the anticolonial movement, especially those who appropriated the memories of Gandhi's campaigns for freedom. But did any of these qualify as nationalism? That pestiferous question trails us as we examine three themes that overlap inside the Indian example: state nationalism, pan-nationalism, anti-imperial nationalism.

## APPROPRIATIONS

Around the turn of the twentieth century, states that were vulnerable to Western power but not actually ruled by it initiated preemptive nationalist movements to preserve their independence. Japan, Turkey, and Mexico were cases in point. All of them followed roughly the same sequence: the overthrow of an aging regime ill equipped to ward off imperialism; a centralization of state power; then the restructured state's mobilization of loyalties, including an attempt to merge people and state. A demonstration of military prowess—or at least a good bluff—added a stamp of authority to the new regime's claims to independence. Among the earliest and most successful nationalist movements outside Western society, these were also by all odds the most attentive to Western models.

Nowhere did the state control nationalism more effectively than in Japan between the 1890s and the 1940s. To the extent such feelings are measurable, Japanese nationalism enjoyed a popularity, at times an enthusiasm, that no roughly comparable venture could command. In broad outline, Japan led the way for those countries exposed to Western imperialism but not colonized by it: Topple an inept regime, wreak havoc with the old order's symbols of authority, modernize state resources, and muster sufficient military strength to stop routine great-power bullying. Japan's state-building adapted the German model.

In addition to its pioneering role, what distinguished the Japanese process was its speed and efficiency. The Meiji Restoration of 1867–68 ousted a floundering Tokugawa government—well aware of neighboring China's humiliation by the West but unable to defend itself—in favor of a purposeful, coordinated elite from the exposed provinces of Satsuma in the south and Choshu in the west, now operating from a new capital in Tokyo, who in a decade swept away Japan's centuries-old regional structure, rationalized taxes, and crushed the one serious rebellion against its authority. By 1895 Japan's military was itself playing the bully in China; ten years later it stunned the world by sinking the best of the Russian navy and staking its country's claim to the rank of great power. Appropriate to the age of imperialism, Japan annexed Taiwan in 1895, then Korea in 1910.

It was this small collaborative elite, with only a few additional recruits, who until the First World War presided as ruling elders—*genro*—over the creation of both state and nation. Unquestionably they inherited special advantages. After centuries of isolation, ethnic homogenity in Japan's core islands was exceptional by any measure. With its cities already well developed, Japan did not suffer a sudden rural-urban rebalancing when its population boomed. Even before 1868, the level of popular education exceeded that of many European countries. As part of that general education, Japanese were taught in the East Asian tradition to view the state as both source and expression of civilization.

*Genro* turned these assets to even greater advantage. Destroying traditional rural privilege in one breathtaking stroke, they won the loyalty of peasants who suddenly became landowners and opened the way for skill rather than family and property to determine government service. Above all, they held the Western powers at bay during the crucial decades when they were consolidating the new state. It helped, of course, that Japan mobilized during a lull in European conquests, which did not pick up again until around 1880. But it mattered even more that Japan's leaders gave highest priority to minimizing friction. With an insight rarely matched in dependent countries, they avoided foreign loans as spiked traps for Japan's sovereignty. Well-established transportation networks abiding by centralized rules kept commerce moving to the satisfaction of almost all foreign merchants. Efficiency here hastened the elimination of the treaty-sanctified privileges that the major powers had imposed on Japan, as Western imperialists did wherever their influence spread. A show of military might and Japan's leaders were able to slip the noose of the unequal treaties.

By the turn of the century, Japan sat at the table with the great powers to negotiate its pacts.

First state, then nation: Everything in its time. Japan was well on its way to nullifying the most obvious threats from abroad by the time its leaders set about cultivating nationalist sentiment. In fact, those careful students of Western society opened their campaign in the mid-1890s precisely as nationalism was expanding and hardening throughout Europe. Japan was joining the club.

Two more advantages facilitated these efforts. One was the availability of spiritual reinforcements. By severing the state's ties to a suspect Buddhism, Japan's new leaders freed the space to create their own religious cult out of the country's diverse, local Shinto practices. Shinto priests, on their part, eagerly petitioned to fill the vacuum. Although the fuzziness of its culture slowed the process a bit, early in the twentieth century a state-sponsored and state-focused Shinto, with systematized rites and consolidated local shrines, entered the mainstream of Japanese nationalism. Now the priests lost out, as schools incorporated Shinto rituals and secular officials presided at worship. Public response was very positive. Citizens from the far corners of Japan, for example, volunteered the money and labor that between 1915 and 1920 constructed the grand Meiji Shrine in Tokyo.

Shinto's greatest asset was its association with the emperor, apex of the nation. In the Tokugawa era local Shinto cults had sometimes invoked the emperor; under the new regime, state leaders put muscle on that spindly tradition by merging Shinto with emperor worship. Now the emperor embodied state authority and spiritual purity alike. As the emperor presided over the prescribed rites at the Ise Shrine, his practices there sanctified rites at all of Japan's Shinto shrines. Worship at those shrines, in turn, glorified the emperor.

The entire scheme congealed as nationalism because the emperor also served as capstone to Japan's encompassing family. "The basic characteristic of the Japanese State structure," the public philosopher Masao Maruyama wrote of the years before the Second World War, "is that it is always considered as an extension of the family; more concretely, as a nation of families composed of the Imperial House as the main family and of the people as the branch family."[7] As state-sponsored Shinto transformed a generalized reverence for the emperor into the claim that he was the ultimate ancestor of all Japanese, it articulated a vision of the nation, united vertically from hearth to throne. Because Shinto's roots lay in a multiplicity of family shrines and those shrines extended the bonds of kinship beyond the grave, an ur-connection between the emperor's timeless family and one's own did not require a vast imaginative leap. "The dead visit the living [in Japanese folklore] and the living communicate with them without fear."[8] It was a pattern of belief familiar through countless variations around the world: Spiritual threads bound the living and the dead into a national family.

In Japan these connections ran up a hierarchy, not laterally to cover those who had left the home islands. Although migration and urbanization were old stories in Japan, the rise in population during the half century after the Meiji Restoration—an increase of around 50 percent—and the country's simultaneous surge of industrialization created strains at a new level. Local ties loosened as migration both within the islands and abroad accelerated. The traditional network of mutual aid among extended families within a community—dozoku—unraveled, and in its stead more and more people migrated in search of wage labor. The state-sponsored "family illusion became an issue," the cultural historian Daikichi Irokawa has written, "only [around 1900] when the actual family structure had begun to disintegrate."[9] Indicatively, between the 1890s and the 1920s—years of heavy population growth and migration—democratic and socialist movements also gained enough strength to compete for Japanese loyalties.

Nevertheless, the nationalist campaign more than matched the competition. By 1910 centrally issued textbooks taught all school

children a single message of the divinely descended emperor presiding over his national family. Cultural cohesion within the islands tightened. To no surprise, then, the social fabric held remarkably well even through crisis times. In their relations with
one another, Japan's mobile urban population gave little evidence
of being any of those things attributed to their Western counterparts: "isolated, atomized, impersonal, frustrated, alienated, an-
omic, deprived, fatalistic, nonparticipant, violent, [or] radical."[10]
The belief in *nihonjinron*—a uniqueness that no outsider could
hope to learn—remained a hallmark of twentieth-century Japanese culture, and a highly sensitized race consciousness deepened
Japanese feelings of distinctiveness. "Nowhere," a widely respected expert, Edwin Reischauer, has concluded, "[was race con-
sciousness] greater than in Japan."[11] Although the numbers of indigeneous Ainu declined rapidly with the development of the north
island, Hokkaido, and the low-caste burakumin never constituted
more than 2 percent of the whole population, mainstream Japanese treated them, along with the immigrant Koreans, as pariahs:
Those not fully in (*uchi*) were fully out (*soto*). Claims that the
Japanese were a pure Yamato race, superior to other mongrel
peoples of Asia, justified their bloody imperialism of the 1930s
and 1940s. Parenthetically, Japan's yellow-skinned racism taught
the Vietnamese not to construe colonialism as simply a form of
white racism.

Loyalties extending from home to palace actually sharpened the
division between those who had left the home islands and those
who stayed. Japanese nationalism did not stretch at all well
abroad. As early as 1636 Japan's rulers had tried to block the return of emigrants for fear they would contaminate their homeland.
In the twentieth century, Japanese who lived for a time abroad
quite literally left the nation behind. *Nihonjinron* could be neither
exported nor copied. Nevertheless, in the process of migration,
these consequences unfolded gradually. Practically all first-genera-
tion Issei in the United States—97 percent in one study—maintained ties of affection and obligation to families in the home is-

lands. Fulfilling duties to an older generation, however, proved almost impossible abroad. Worldwide, a substantial majority of these family-bound emigrants who left between 1880 and 1930 simply returned home. Nationalism reconstrued and reinforced weakening intergenerational connections there, but abroad nothing rewove these family strands, either literally or figuratively. Perforce, those who stayed rerooted themselves. By the 1930s, family ties among more and more Issei and virtually all second-generation Nisei bound them into American-based networks. Proudly Japanese but permanently separated from Japan itself, they, much like their German counterparts, threw their energies into an American life. Assimilate the best in Japanese culture, community leaders told the young, and turn it to success in the United States.

Unlike the Germans, however, the Japanese ran smack into America's racial barriers. Eager to learn Western ways and compete in the American world, they were ridiculed and segregated. By forcing Japanese Americans to live among themselves at the fringes of the economy, white Americans early in the twentieth century validated their own prejudices against the Japanese as clannish, cheap-labor aliens. Because Chinese migrants formed their own distinctive communities, as much by choice as from persecution, white Americans expected all Asians to do the same. But where remarkably similar, insular Chinatowns appeared everywhere along the Pacific Rim, comparable Japantowns, even under duress, did not. Japanese migrants, with their elaborated webs of American-based kinship, were family, not community oriented. Chinese migrants often did maintain ties with kin back home. Their culture, defining them as Chinese by a set of rituals rather than through a mysterious essence, enabled them to reintegrate even after a long absence. Hence while Japanese men sought "picture brides" to establish families in America, many Chinese men hired prostitutes in the United States and returned to father children in their villages of origin. It all looked equally immoral to mainstream white Americans.

Bitter ironies abounded, especially those that tangled the fate of

Japanese Americans with the prejudice against Chinese Americans. The Japanese, migrating in numbers around the turn of the century as racism was hardening everywhere, shared its basic premises: a hierarchy of peoples that gave those above greater rights and respect than those below. Between the 1890s and the 1930s many of them cheered Japan's military exploits, including its savage assaults in China, as a proof of racial superiority. But where the Japanese placed themselves atop an Asian pyramid, white Americans rarely differentiated them from the rest of a yellow horde, all of whom were pictured as unassimilable aliens with loyalties only to their own kind and—most ominous for Japanese Americans—their own country.

White Americans got what they asked for. In the 1930s, as relations between Japan and the United States soured, Japanese Americans were caught in limbo, equally unwelcome in both countries. Marginalized in the United States as aliens in fact (Issei) and fancy (Nisei), they were doubly vulnerable because they congregated in the limited spaces, almost all in the Far West, where they had been able to find homes. More than a quarter of them lived in Los Angeles County alone. Although nothing dictated their wartime imprisonment in concentration camps, not much inhibited that decision early in 1942 either. In a stroke the United States was made safe from a people who posed no threat. Perhaps nothing better demonstrated the depth of their commitment to America than the will with which almost all of them picked up life in the United States after their release. It was not that Japanese Americans were peculiarly docile or enduring. After the war as before, they had no obvious, attractive alternative. They were certainly not Japanese; willy-nilly, they were American. By then public racism was in retreat, and they dispersed across the country. Appropriately, within a quarter century after the camps closed, almost half the offspring of Japanese Americans married outside that group.

Japan's expanding empire threw into relief the question inherent in all versions of a state-dominated nationalism. In that mating of unequals, where nationalism served as agent of the state and never the converse, what did nationalism contribute that state action alone could not explain? Following the Meiji Revolution, state leaders, coolly calculating state interests, took the steps leading to war and imperialism. Geopolitics, not ethnic egoism, drove those decisions. Indeed, it was a familiar pattern. Japan's search between the 1890s and the 1940s for an elusive security in ever-widening circles through Asia and the Pacific had its counterpart in nineteenth-century British, early twentieth-century German, and late twentieth-century United States quests for their own phantom security. Hence an interpretation of the battle on the Asian mainland in 1941 as a contest between "Chinese and Japanese nationalism" missed the crucial difference: The very existence of Chinese nationalism depended on the Japanese invasion, but Japanese nationalism, on its part, was no more than a hired hand.[12]

Almost perversely, a distinctive nationalism materialized only when it sought to purify Japan's state-dominated society. Even before the Meiji Revolution the popular slogan "Expel the foreigners, worship the emperor" expressed that impulse, as did the more ethereal aspects of the nineteenth-century National Learning movement to cleanse the Japanese spirit. Sometimes assassins acted in the name of national purification. Whatever its source, the tenacious resistance to modernizing written Japanese derived from the same general sense of traditional purity. When Japanese nationalism showed a distinctive face, in other words, it turned inward, contemplating its own uniqueness and fearing violation. Its extremes ran toward xenophobia, not imperialism. The state looked for global respect, nationalism for self-celebration.

The devastating results of the Second World War did far more damage to this nationalism than to the state that had inspired it. If the crushing defeat in 1945 eliminated a particular conception of Japan's destiny, it did not repudiate the state itself, which remained central to Japanese cohesion and to the setting of new postwar goals. With an important assist from the American occupying force, the state tamed strong postwar impulses toward socialism and democracy and situated itself to preside over a sustained economic growth. Not all traces of the old nationalism disappeared. Shinto, surprisingly resilient after the war, continued to link households with their god-shelves to a national family, and its festivals still drew large crowds. At the Yasukuni Shrine it was even possible to honor dead soldiers, who were after all ancestors like any other in the timeless chain into the past. In some circles, *nihonjinron* enjoyed a revival in the prosperous 1980s, when the Japanese economy looked as if it would be ruling the roost. Nevertheless, nationalism in late twentieth-century Japan, as in other highly industrialized countries, suggested an atavistic past. What the state gaveth the state now wanted to taketh away. Late in the 1960s, leaders in Tokyo were even more eager than those in Washington to scotch widespread Japanese protests against the United States occupation of Okinawa. By then a decorous patriotism was in vogue: Wave the Rising Sun flag, sing the state anthem, cheer the sports heroes. The state's appetite for social control had not abated, but the robust nationalism that had once fed it, combining religion, language, and race with an eternity of fictive kin on sacred land, had been thinned to gruel.

Turkish nationalism, emerging out of the wreckage of the Ottoman Empire, followed the same basic pattern: toppling the old regime, demonstrating military prowess, modernizing society, and identifying the Turkish people and their sacred land with the new central state. By the turn of the twentieth century, the manifest failure of Ottomanism, a political expression of Islamic unity, and a loose system of imperial tribute, put pressure on leaders throughout the collapsing empire to find an alternative. At the heart of the old system, some elites envisaged a distinctive Turkey, built around its own unique culture. In the 1890s, precisely when national languages were being constructed through-out Europe, linguistic entrepreneurs expunged "a thousand years" of Persian and Arabic usage in the name of purifying the Turkish language and making it accessible to ordinary citizens.[13] The Young Turk coup in 1908 added beef to this nationalist movement by attempting to Turkify people in Asia Minor and the Balkans, much as Hungarians were trying to Magyarize the people in their empire. Nevertheless, it took the humiliation of these same rulers in the Great War to prepare the way for a full-scale state nationalism.

As the Treaty of Sèvres formalized it in 1920, defeat in the war stripped the empire of all territory except a core of Turkish land, left it open to great power intervention, and even denied it Constantinople, which remained under military occupation. Operating from the Anatolian interior, military forces around Mustafa Kemal rode the postwar crisis to power. His provisional government drove the Greek army into the Aegean, neutralized France, Italy, and the Soviet Union with separate settlements, and looked just formidable enough to the British to force a new treaty in 1923, which enabled Turkey to salvage its pride, reclaim some territory in Asia Minor, and then reoccupy Constantinople. Out went the Ottoman sultan and in came the Turkish republic, with Mustafa Kemal as president.

Under Kemal, Turkish nationalism expanded along three fronts. Abandoning the old empire's Balkan ambitions, Turkey reorganized around its Anatolian base. Other ethnic groups were either, like the Armenians and Greeks, eliminated with a savage fury or, like the Kurds, beaten down. (Where states set out to create nations, at best all citizens are members, but at worst only members are citizens.) The new Turkey's capital was lifted from the cosmopolitan grandeur of Constantinople at the fringe to an interior hill site; cities lost their European-style names—Istanbul for Constantinople, the new capital Ankara for Angora, Edirne for Adrianople, and so on; and through a combination of archaeological discoveries and historical adjustments, the nation's official roots were sunk deep in an Anatolian past of Hittites, Sumerians, and even Trojans. As the state's base shifted east, however, its focus turned west. In a stunning sequence from the declaration of a republic in 1923 to the removal of Islam from its constitution in 1928, Turkey discarded the rickety Ottoman scaffolding, secularized education, law, and philanthropy, and Westernized dress, calender, and alphabet. In 1934 women received the vote and the right to hold elective office, unimaginable in other Moslem countries of the time.

Underlying all these changes was the empowerment of the state and the exaltation of its leader, Mustafa Kemal: military hero in the teens, modernizing dictator in the twenties, finally demigod in the thirties, with the signature gargantuan statues and a grand new name, Kemal Atatürk—appropriately, father of the Turks. Borrowing from Italy, Germany, and the Soviet Union alike, he counted on authority at the top to fix values everywhere below. What he miscalculated from the start was the tenacious popular commitment to Islam, which Bernard Lewis estimates remained "the major element in the collective consciousness of a large proportion of the Turkish nation," especially outside the major cities.[14] Unwilling to brook Islam's competition, Kemal set out to constrict its influence, only to attenuate his own base of support in the process. Even before Kemal's death in 1938, state nationalism in Turkey relied far more on naked force, far less on systematized persuasion, than its Japanese counterpart; and after his death, it came to look more and more like just another military dictatorship.

Mexican nationalism also followed the sequence made familiar by formally independent but highly vulnerable countries: New leaders seized power, mobilized resources, and inspired a sense of nationhood that simply had not existed before. In general, Latin America, carved into postcolonial states before the appearance of modern nationalism and home to none of its distinguishing characteristics, was barren ground. It required the insertion of a special force to trigger a nationalist movement of any sort, in Mexico's case its revolution: a bloody contest from 1910 to 1920, then two decades of consolidation. Not only did that transformation set Mexico apart from the rest of contemporary Latin America; it constituted the first and arguably the most successful full-scale revolution of the twentieth century. The Mexican Revolution generated wholesale changes without state terror and harnessed the army to civilian authority. Perhaps most impressive of all it resisted in the 1930s what was besetting other postrevolutionary societies, what was gripping governments throughout the Caribbean and Latin America, and what comparable state experiments in Japan and Turkey were experiencing: police-state dictatorship.

Until the revolution Mexico revealed no significant interest in nationalism, let alone a movement worthy of the name. The long battle for independence, dislodging the Spanish rulers by 1821 but leaving a conservative Creole elite intact, bled the country without mobilizing it. The regional and local attachments that had steeled Mexicans against the Spanish held firm. For at least three decades after independence, onetime officers in the Spanish army dominated Mexican politics, competing more or less as warlords under such openly elitist labels as the Scottish Rite and the York Rite Freemasons. Independence marked out state boundaries as artificial as the ones Spanish imperialists had created. When invading gringos took away more than half that territory in 1848, they replaced one arbitrarily drawn Mexico with another.

A persistent hostility to alien rule constituted a partial exception to this picture. Spain's attempt in 1829 to reclaim its colony did stir a popular Mexican reaction. Again after 1862, when conservatives invited French intervention, ill-armed but stubborn peasant guerrillas fought to free their country. Nevertheless, alien rule had many meanings. Very possibly most of these peasants were risking their lives for a country no larger than their village. Many others battled just as fiercely to protect those same villages from equally alien Creole landlords: alone among Latin American countries, Mexico generated a century-long tradition of such uprisings. Not surprisingly, the wealthy liberals who came back to power with Benito Juárez in 1867 had no desire whatsoever to see that kind of local ethnicity expand in any direction, let alone toward nationalism. So it went until the Revolution of 1910: Mexico's leaders imposed their rule of law and dreamed of development but gave no thought to a Mexican nation.

What did happen after 1870 was an increasing concentration of power in the hands of the state and its favored economic interests. Both camps made money; both kept the capitalist peace. During Porfirio Díaz's uninterrupted rule between 1884 and 1910, Mexico experienced its first extended period of systematic, centralized government. Only after 1900, when a generation that had never known civil war came of age, did opposition to that greedy but stable dictatorship gather general strength. The dating, of course, was familiar. On roughly the same schedule, states everywhere in the Western world were consolidating power. So was Japan. But where the presiding *genro* husbanded Japan's resources to maximize its autonomy, the Díaz government sold one concession after another to foreign concerns that paid the right price to the right people. The price paid by the wrong people—the peasantry—was the disappearance of their villages inside expanding plantations that with the government's cooperation took the land they needed. Eventually, the Díaz regime alienated a range of people sufficient to bring Mexico's free-handed capitalism into bankruptcy: drifting peasants, fattening insiders, coercing soldiers, dissolving legitimacy.

Although it required ten terrible years to make sure that revolutionaries, not warlords, would rule Mexico, there were also impressive accomplishments during that decade: among them, a structure for justice in the 1917 Constitution, a reopening of middle-class opportunities and peasant hopes, a commitment to taming armies, and a momentum toward socially responsive government. Experimenting along these lines during the 1920s and fixing the results in place during the 1930s gave the revived quest for modernization a distinctively Mexican, sometimes a distinctively populist stamp. Meanwhile, the central government, waxing stronger each decade, drew its authority from the revolution, which it did everything it could both to monopolize and to glorify as the grand unifier of the Mexican nation. Securing the central government's power and securing the national revolution were two sides of a single coin.

Antiforeign passions had only minor significance in this national mobilization. In a way roughly similar to Japan's nationalism, Mexico's did not materialize until after the most highly charged foreign threats had passed. A broad desire to assert control over economic resources and opportunities—to reclaim a lost sovereignty—did in fact play an important role in some middle-class circles, as the salience of those issues in the 1917 Constitution attested. Nevertheless, the United States, the one and only great power hovering over Mexico, did not loom large as the revolution's villain. The iron-fisted warlord Victoriano Huerta—no revolutionary he—could not make much of the United States military's temporary occupation of Veracruz in 1914. If in 1916 and 1917 the marauding Pancho Villa was a rough-hewn champion of Mexican independence, as some historians have argued, the United States Army's futile chase after him, deep into Mexican territory, still did not generate much popular sentiment in favor of Villa or against the United States. Major American corporations were generally welcome employers in early twentieth-century Mexico. What did matter was the ability of Mexico's new regime to stand free—to reject the Monroe Doctrine without prompting a war of words, to expropriate Mexico's oil reserves without triggering American intervention, to remain neutral in a world war without facing American retaliation. It helped that in each potential crisis the governments in both Washington and Mexico City wanted to settle differences with a minimum of fuss.

In its effort to mobilize a Mexican nation, the revolutionary state

set out to combat cultural fragmentation, not capitalist imperialism. It was a bootstrap operation. Mexican society offered none of
the advantages that the Japanese state had enjoyed. Rather than
one language, the revolutionary leadership encountered many.
Rather than a compliant religion, it was locked in combat with a
hostile Catholic Church. Rather than an integrated country, it faced
a sprawling one. Rather than a tabula rasa of separateness from
the Western world, it showed the scars of conquest, defeat, dependence, even complicity in Mexico's civil wars. Moreover, before 1910 no one cared to prepare the way. Particularly in the two
decades before the revolution, while nationalist movements elsewhere were fitting linguistic, racial, historical, and ceremonial
components to their causes, Mexicans looked elsewhere. If anything other than a rather routine repudiation of foreign rulers
united them in the late nineteenth century, it was probably a Mexicanized Catholicism, one that accepted myriad village lore under
a broad canopy of common ritual and that above all accommodated the enduring popular cult of the Virgin of Guadalupe. But
that spiritual Indian had been no Joan of Arc, and the church hierarchy that benefited from her was still tarnished by its collaboration with the French.

Under the circumstances, revolutionary leaders demonstrated
considerable creativity in tackling this huge problem during their
first quarter century of rule. At the heart of their enterprise lay
racial concepts that transformed Western society's disparagement
of brown skin into the mark of a distinctive Mexican superiority.
By establishing an inclusive racial model for the nation and by
presuming a neo-Lamarckian racial improvement, revolutionary
ideologues envisaged the best in their indigenous and European
heritages blending into an ever more advanced mestizo homogeneity, simultaneously uniting and modernizing Mexico. The cosmic race, José Vasconcelos, a leader among these advocates,
called it in a moment of nationalist euphoria. Among contemporary reformers, the mestizo ideal inspired visions of a society of

sober fathers, respected mothers, and healthy babies freed from the curse of poverty.

For later partisans of ethnic particularity, mestizo nationalism seemed little short of criminal. Ostensibly honoring indigenous cultures, it deplored their backwardness and anticipated their disappearance. Appropriately, Vasconcelos's plan for universal education relied on the Spanish language alone. Though mestizo brown might be cosmic, a dark Indian brown remained thoroughly mundane. In its time, however, mestizo nationalism, appearing at the crest of Western society's wave of racism, looked quite different in a lineup that included Hitler's Germany, Tōjō's Japan, and Jim Crow's America. Elsewhere in Latin America—in Guatemala, Peru, and Argentina, for example—race concepts cleaved societies. If on one hand the mestizo ideal appeared to be killing local identities with its kindness, at least it imagined all Mexicans contributing to a cohesive and egalitarian outcome. In fact, a very different and all too familiar racism did have its day in Mexico. In 1931 the government drove Mexico's tiny Chinese minority out of the country, satisfying as it did powerful "anti-Chinese feelings . . . [that] had genuine popular roots."[15] Whatever its loose association with modern racism, mestizo nationalism sought to tap another cluster of values entirely.

No evidence indicates that mestizo nationalism ever enjoyed widespread popularity. What did unify Mexico was the revolution itself, an upheaval in rights and privileges that gave a high proportion of the middle and lower classes a stake in the new society, a sense of emerging among the winners. Land reform, above all else, secured that popular base. Informally underway as soon as the revolution began, the redistribution of the great estates advanced far enough under the last of the warlord presidents, Venustiano Carranza, so that by 1920 there could be no return. If, as the historian Alan Knight has argued, two primary urges—land ownership and local autonomy—initially powered the revolution, the former now gobbled up the latter. Especially in the 1930s under President Lázaro Cárdenas, an expansive central government gave its blessings to the complicated transfer of plantations to peasant proprietors, including local collectives—*ejidos*—that by 1940 held almost half of Mexico's farmland. As the government's anticlericalism subsided, the revolution settled securely into the very definition of Mexicanness.

By midcentury, time caught up with the revolution. What worked remarkably well when land topped the agenda had little to contribute as urbanization and industrialization dominated public policy. Mexican outmigration, always heavy and now approaching a flood, had no significant bearing on the nationalist spirit. Once again, state nationalism depended on participation from within. The revolution was Mexico's nation-builder. Identifying through it—as an experience, as a source of material benefits, as a matter of civic pride—created the semblance of one people with a common destiny. In a paler version of the Japanese disowning those who settled elsewhere, Mexican nationalists scorned migrants who gave evidence of relocating in another country— almost always the United States. When they cut their roots, so the charge went, their culture died and their characters softened. Appropriately, as late as the 1970s no more than 6 percent of these migrants were American citizens, the lowest rate among any immigrant group in the United States. Mexicans had homes in Mexico. When chain migration did strengthen long-distance ties, they were usually parochial. Especially among native peoples, the lines ran back to the village or at most to the region. Despite invasions and revolutions, the social order among Mayan peoples in the south showed little change. The loyalty that deepened when laboring migrants left "their 'native' sierra of Oaxaca" in search of jobs was a "self-conscious ethnic identity" as Mixtecs, not as Mexicans.[16]

Nationalism among Mexican Americans, therefore, was doubly weakened—by migration's irrelevance to the nation-building revolutionary synthesis in Mexico and by the migrants' splintering pulls back to innumerable village homes. Regular movements back and forth across the border kept the Mexican sources of ethnicity fresh without encouraging nationalism of any kind. Little wonder that the symbols of irredentism, of primeval rights to the territories lost to the United States, found almost no takers. The revolution itself largely turned its back on Mexican history; at least it chose not to dwell on past failures. Late in the 1960s, the Mexican American firebrand Rudolfo "Corky" Gonzales briefly drew a crowd by demanding a separate Aztlan state out of the conquered territories. "We Declare the Independence of our Mestizo Nation," he asserted in the rhetoric of Mexican racial nationalism. "We are a Bronze People with a Bronze Culture."[17] But the mestizo nation, like the revolution itself, was something to achieve, not to reclaim. Only at rare moments did Mexican Americans tie their dream for the future to a loss from the past. An Aztlan movement never materialized.

## TRANSCENDENCE

As these early nationalist experiments got under way at the edges of Western colonialism, another set of movements, equally precocious but very different in nature, also set out to defend subject people from alien power. These were the pan movements—specifically Pan-Asian, Pan-Arab, Pan-African—which either ignored or repudiated the Western-model state and expected to gather in people by other means. Rather than building regional loyalties from more local ones, including those defined by states, the pan movements each sought an entirely different design, with a logic and a history of its own. They enjoyed greatest currency during times of greatest fluidity: when European wars scrambled imperial rights and dissolved empires, for example, or when Western powers challenged their own state system through so-called international bodies. The utterly arbitrary boundaries that imperialism imposed on so many colonies gave additional impetus to causes that promised to substitute a natural wholeness for those fracturing lines. In some nationalist movements, the geographical goal was clearer than the arguments exhorting people to identify with it: Italian nationalism, for example, or Zionism after the Balfour Declaration. The pan movements reversed that order: Identities were clearer than geography.

Pan-Asianism flared briefly at the beginning of the twentieth century when some Japanese leaders and the Chinese revolutionaries around Sun Yat-sen pooled their common fears of Western power and their common hopes that a regenerated China would join Japan as bulwarks of the yellow race against white imperialism. Japan's own power politics destroyed this vision's appeal. Once Japan pressed the notorious Twenty-One Demands of 1915 on China's ineffectual government, its baldly imperialist ambitions stood exposed, revealing another Asian state, not Western colonialism, as the primary threat to China's independence. Now a humiliated Sun looked for all the world like the enemy's pawn. During the 1920s, racism in the West and chaos in China deepened Japan's isolation. A decade later, when its leaders once more employed a Pan-Asian rhetoric, they cast the Japanese as the superior race and the rest of Asia as servants to their destiny. Japan's tyrannical Greater East Asian Co-Prosperity Sphere during the Second World War was a final mockery of the Pan-Asian dream.

The Pan-Arab movement, which also surfaced early in the twentieth century, had a longer life and greater substance. One of the alternatives to the collapsing Ottoman Empire, Arab nationalism was originally a reactionary movement that invoked a purified Islam, free of any Western taint, as the best defense against corrupting outside influences. Defined initially by a language—the one sanctified as God's medium of revelation—Pan-Arabism remained a rhetorical flourish until the 1930s, when publicists made the first serious attempts at a systematic statement. Now purity of race loomed as large as purity in language. Debates in succeeding decades raised but failed to resolve three central issues. Were the true Arabs only those who lived in Asia Minor or did they include the Arabs of North Africa as well? Was Pan-Arabism fundamentally a secular movement seeking its own state, or was it essentially religious, an expression of the Islamic yearning for *umma*—a comprehensive community of all believers? Secular or not, did it cover Christian as well as Muslim Arabs?

Until midcentury Arab nationalism rose and fell with the fortunes of the elites sponsoring it. It influenced the leadership of the Arab Revolt of 1916, some of whom expected their British patrons to replace Ottoman rule with a Pan-Arabic state. When the Bolsheviks exposed a secret agreement to carve Arab lands between the British and the French and the two powers proceeded to do just that, one phase of the movement dissolved in humiliation. After the Great War, royal houses in Iraq, Jordan, and Arabia incorporated a racial version of Pan-Arabism in various quasi-fascist ideologies they endorsed, ideologies that were part and parcel of their preference for the Axis side in the Second World War. To no one's surprise, as the British and French retired from Asia Minor, the retreating imperial powers divided it into states that gave no quarter at all to Pan-Arab aspirations.

The crucial turn came in 1952 when the Free Officers under Gamal Nasser drove the royal house out of Egypt and opened Arab nationalism's populist era. Pan-Arabist from the outset, Nasser clarified the movement's fuzzy issues in ways that served him brilliantly, only to undercut his successors' prospects. For one thing he made Egypt, marginal if not not outright hostile in the movement's earlier manifestations, the nucleus of an Arab "circle" that arced westward toward the Atlantic as well as eastward toward the Gulf of Arabia. For another he gave the movement an unmistakably secular stamp, using states as the modular units to build Arab unity and relegating Islam to an honorific role. Finally, he popularized the movement. Magnetic in a way no predecessor or contemporary in the region could match, Nasser commanded attention high and low with his promise of a strong, prosperous Egypt, his independence from Cold War loyalties, and his vision of an ever-expanding Pan-Arabism. To cheers throughout the Arab world, Nasser initiated the first step in 1958, when Egypt and Syria joined in the United Arab Republic.

It was a movement with fatal weaknesses, however. A Pan-Arabism that relied on individual states was in the end an oxymoron. Its appeal lay in an overarching, inclusive vision. The Arab nation, one of its advocates wrote, "is a wider conception than the state, greater than the people, and more meaningful than the fatherland," with compelling affinities that gathered in all those who share Arab memories, ideals, and aspirations: "Such is the Arab point of view on the nation and nationalism."[18] States only understood other states, and in this case proved utterly fickle to the Pan-Arab cause. Neither the United Arab Republic nor its successor in 1971, the Federation of Arab Republics, which added Libya, lasted long enough to change anything. Another potential source of Pan-Arabism, the Ba'th (Rebirth) party that appeared in Syria, Iraq, Jordan, and Lebanon, never lost its state-by-state identity. Second, secular Pan-Arabism roused an enemy stronger than itself: Islam remained the most popular, powerful, and enduring source of Arab unity. That alone almost certainly doomed Nasser's Pan-Arabism; his crushing military defeat by Israel in 1967 and his death three years later sealed its fate.

Pan-Africanism had its origins in the diaspora, specifically among the descendants of slaves in the English-speaking lands of North America. Far more than other pan movements, it drew its energy from the challenges of migration and hence shared more characteristics than any of the others with contemporary European nationalism. The horrifying imperatives of slavery prepared the way by throwing together people of many African backgrounds, most of whom by the early nineteenth century retained only splintered memories of their homelands. African-rooted customs were assimilated into slave-bound cultures with loose associations to a general past. The very concept of *Africa*, other than a place for imperialist exploitation, was the creation of North American blacks. Inside slavery the tenuous hold that biological parents had on their children threw wide the net of adoptive families, which could be made to cover an indeterminately expanding fictive family. When slave-quarter kin buried the dead in the expectation that their spirits would now return home across the Atlantic, they were generating the wherewithal for some kind of transoceanic nationalism.

From ideas that were floating about everywhere in the late nineteenth century, postemancipation leaders added the concept of a black race, with Africa its historic but no longer its exclusive home. Wherever they had scattered, blacks retained membership in their race of origin: "an ordinance of nature," declared the West Indian Edward Blyden; a divine mandate, according to the American Alexander Crummell.[19] Race made them kin: "Indeed, a race *is* a family," in Crummell's epigram.[20] From time to time during the nineteenth century, an occasional North American black leader tried to solidify the African end of that race vision, even to the point of claiming Liberia, where white racists from the American Colonization Society had once dumped shipments of free blacks, as the site for his own attempt to reunite blacks from two continents. Nevertheless, race consciousness by itself was not nationalism. Nor did the trickle of migration from North America to Africa have an inherently nationalist meaning. It might be a missionary gesture or simply an escape from North America's white racism. In any case, very few people anywhere cared one way or another about these African schemes.

It required a mass migration of American blacks from south to north during the first quarter of the twentieth century to create a popular base for African nationalism. As it filled ghettoes in major cities from the East Coast through the Middlewest, it brought face-to-face more and more people who were sharing the same migratory experiences: Disjointed community values, stretched kin lines, and a stirring of new identities formed a reservoir of nationalist readiness. The spark to ignite a movement came from the West Indies, where, the sociologist Orlando Patterson explains, migration was a way of life, a common culture that turned the islands into a crucible for nationalist ideas. Edward Blyden, Henry Sylvester Williams, Marcus Garvey, George Padmore, Aimé Césaire, Léopold Senghor, Frantz Fanon, and C. L. R. James—islanders all—constituted a Pan-Africanist honor roll.

Understanding the black African experience as a *diaspora* caught on in the West Indies late in the nineteenth century. Around the turn of the twentieth, a particularly large wave of blacks left the islands to hack out the Panama Canal, hire on with United Fruit, and take other jobs in Central America's flourishing export agriculture. Garvey, the genius of popular Pan-Africanism, came out of that milieu. A migrant himself, he left Kingston, Jamaica, when he was in his twenties to travel about Central America, try London, and in 1916 dock at New York City in the midst of the first great northward flow of Southern blacks, who would provide his primary support. From there he launched the United States branch of his core organization, Universal Negro Improvement Association (UNIA). Harlem was just jelling as the premier center for an emerging black urban culture, and other black ghettos mushroomed in major cities from the East Coast through the Middlewest. If the Caribbean culture of mobility gave Garvey the inspiration to talk, the challenges of an American migration gave his audiences the incentive to listen.

And huge audiences did listen. Not only did UNIA enroll perhaps a million American blacks at its peak; through its grand parades, its leader's charisma, and its simple transportable messages, Garveyism reached millions more in Africa and the West Indies as well as the United States. As harsh a critic as the Marxist scholar C.L.R. James, who called Garvey's movement "pitiable rubbish," granted that he was the one who "made the American Negro conscious of his African origin and created for the first time a feeling of international solidarity" in the diaspora.[21] "I know no boundary where the Negro is concerned," Garvey declared. "The whole world is my province until Africa is free."[22]

Garvey's message turned the expectations of his time on their ear. Where white-dictated legislation outlawed black-white marriages in most American states, Garvey affirmed the same values from the other end of the spectrum: Coal blackness—a standard Caribbean point of reference—gave proof of racial strength, he announced. Where American blacks had been taught to measure their own progress by a Western yardstick, with the consoling postscript that as lowly as they might be in the United States, they stood well above the jungle creatures of Africa, Garvey spun his audience around and pointed away from America to Africa. From Booker T. Washington, Garvey said, he derived his sense of instant progress that swept aside the image of blacks slowly, slowly inching forward as apprentices to their white instructors. The Great War destroyed Western society's claim to be leading the evolutionary march; instead, the future lay with the sleeping giant. Africa's day was dawning now. Ethiopia Awake! Africa for the Africans! Renaissance of the Black Race!

Although Garvey felt the closest affinity to Irish nationalism, which rose from the ashes in 1916 to press for immediate independence, others set his movement next to Zionism. Of course there were similarities. Both preached nationalism to a dispersed people. They shared authoritarian characteristics. Like Herzl, Garvey loved pomp and ceremony, gloried in the role of the great leader, and in a disastrous show of incompetence squandered his followers' money in a joint stock company. Like Herzl's Zionism, Garvey's UNIA offered only a misty sense of the homeland. But to make Garvey peculiarly the borrower verges on a racist slur. Around the turn of the century, movement styles and strategies of all sorts suffused Western society: Every nationalist was a borrower. In Garvey's case, it did not matter whether his preference for colorful regalia and hierarchical titles derived primarily from early Zionism, the Scottish Rite Masons, the Ku Klux Klan, or, most probable of all, the widespread images of regal dress and grand titles among tribal leaders throughout Africa. With the incentive, the constituency, and the wherewithal for nationalism at hand, Garveyism, like Zionism, was a movement waiting to happen.

UNIA's bright hopes—and the savings of many hard-pressed black Americans—dissolved in bankruptcy, the victim of factoring far too many dreams into the company's balance sheet. In an early victory for the federal government's racist secret police, the United States hounded Garvey into jail, then out of the country. The organization beneath it gone, his inspirational message moved with the wind. In Africa, where Garveyism reappeared at unpredictable moments for decades to come, it helped immensely that it carried no taint of the West's Christianity. In the United States it was the final dramatic step in a new identity. Blacks were a race, the race was a family, the family had its homeland: A genuine African American nationalism was born.

A second very different strand of Pan-Africanism—a "rival political ideology" to Garveyism—bore a closer resemblance to Pan-Arabism in its emphasis on an educated elite vanguard, its reliance on periodic gatherings to refine the movement's objectives, and its willingness to use states as building blocks to success.[23] Once again it had a Caribbean point of origin: A Trinidadian, Henry Sylvester Williams, called the first Pan-African Conference for 1900 in London. Booker T. Washington and Bishop Henry Turner, eminences of the nineteenth century, helped give it shape; the scholarly activist W. E. B. DuBois, harbinger of the twentieth, took charge at the conference itself. When nothing came of that conference, it was DuBois who almost two decades later revived the idea in the wake of the war and Garvey's stunning popularity. Congresses in 1919, 1921, 1923, and 1927 represented, with some ups and downs, the DuBois era of Pan-Africanism, even though Caribbeans supplied the bulk of enthusiasts sustaining the cause on a day-to-day basis in London and Paris. Committed to the proposition that there was indeed a black race with its own history and culture, DuBois was equally convinced that its success in Africa depended on the stewardship of a primarily American elite, a mobilization of leaders who could guide the continent into freedom. Inevitably it carried the taint of what the historian Wilson Moses has called "civilizationism," the belief among such leaders as Blyden, Crummell, and Turner that elevating blacks as a race would require Westernized Negroes to raise up the barbarians of Africa. "*Our mission*," Crummell instructed a cadre of West Indian blacks, "*is . . . to make these* [Africans] *civilized and Christian people.*"[24] An inherently divisive message, it had no popular following among Africans, as Garveyism did. When DuBois pulled Pan-Africanism to his side of the Atlantic, it lost touch with its few African adherents and disappeared.

Hence when such prominent anticolonialists as Jomo Kenyatta and Kwame Nkrumah, with crucial assistance from the West Indian Padmore and blessings from the great Nigerian nationalist Nnamdi Azikiwe, reclaimed the name after an eighteen-year gap, they were free to set their own stamp on it. Not only did their Pan-African Congress of 1945 have the sharp political edge that DuBois had shunned; it left the diaspora behind to concentrate on Africa alone. In their formative years, these new Pan-African leaders had been migratory young men, detached from place and suspended between cultures, who redefined themselves and their goals as they moved. Who were they? Malcom [sic] I. Nurse, or alternatively Malcom Ivan Meredith Nurse, became George Padmore; Johnstone Kamau became Jomo Kenyatta. Sometimes Azikiwe was Ben, sometimes Nkrumah was Francis, and sometimes not. A man who influenced both Azikiwe and Nkrumah and who at a critical juncture advised South Africa's African National Congress was James Kwegyir Aggrey—or perhaps he was James Emmanuel Kweggir Aggrey; perhaps Kweggir/Kwegyir was part of his family name, perhaps part of his given name. Self-created, they created Africa, with a people held together by invisible threads of race, culture, and experience. If, as these men discovered in the diaspora, whites treated all of them alike, they needed to be alike, to join together in order to be free.

Living in the United States added a critical dimension to their understanding as Africans. Although Azikiwe, a pioneer of sorts in his journeys through America, witnessed Jim Crow at its worst during the 1920s and 1930s, he focused his attention not on white racism but on black values. Only those aspects of the Harlem Renaissance that emphasized pride over protest interested him. From his experience in the Negro colleges, he learned about the dignity of manual labor; from his mentor Aggrey, he assimilated the motto "Christianity, education and agriculture"; from the writings of Booker T. Washington, the giant looming behind his vision, he extracted a picture of blacks laboring together in their own societies for a common good. Like Garvey before him, Azikiwe read a revolutionary message into the Washington legacy. Pride in oneself, one's land, and one's work, he declared in his famous clarion call, *Renascent Africa* (1937), would transform the mentality of colonial subjects and turn them toward the New Africa—a phrase he probably adapted from the black philosopher Alain Locke's New Negro.

Nkrumah, who arrived in the United States as Azikiwe was leaving, also spent about a decade there, fashioning a more radical creed and laying more concrete plans to implement it. He saw the Pan-African congress movement not simply as a gesture of unity but, with independence pending, as a stage for action. Appropriately, it was Nkrumah who shortly before the congress of 1945 had presided over the symbolic transfer of Pan-Africanism from cosmopolitan America to Africa itself. Officiating at the North Carolina funeral of Aggrey—no friend to DuBois—Nkrumah employed the rites of his ancestors to capture the dead man's spirit for return to its West African home. From then on, African Americans might serve as fraternal delegates, in Nkrumah's phrase, but they could no longer claim to be Africa's teachers. At the pivotal Manchester Congress, DuBois was bracketed as honorary chairman.

Initially, messages that "emphasized Pan-African solidarity rather than territorial identity" drew in a young, educated constituency that floated among the continent's cities.[25] With the spread of independent African states, however, Pan-Africanists abruptly tailored their hopes to suit what they saw around them; in the language of the self-fashioning George Padmore, first "the federation of self-governing states on a regional basis, leading ultimately to the creation of a United States of Africa."[26] It fell to Nkrumah, leader in the new government of Ghana, to explore ways of realizing that idea. In 1958, a year after taking office, he sponsored two Pan-African conferences, followed by a loose union of Ghana with Guinea and Mali in 1961 and an official Organization of African Unity two years later. By then, however, leadership had gravitated across Africa into the aggrandizing hands of Gamal Nasser, who used what indicatively was renamed the Organization of African States to sanctify the continent's postcolonial boundaries, not transcend them. Headquarters were located in Addis Ababa, capital of Ethiopia's conversative and repressive empire. In Ghana itself, first Nkrumah's adviser Padmore was isolated as a meddling outsider, then in 1966 Nkrumah himself was ousted, killing a crippled movement.

In Africa, as in East Asia and the Middle East, pan movements gained momentum only at times of fluidity: an Africa-wide challenge to colonialism, a China up for grabs, an Arab world divided by arbitrary lines in the sand. When states congealed, they either turned the pan movements into playthings or simply crushed them. Surely the fatal error of the pan movements' champions was to relinquish their fate to existing states, under the delusion that these sovereignties would be willing to transcend their own interests. The legatees—Japanese imperialists, for example, or authoritarian Arab rulers—were certainly not an enlightened lot. On an equally dismal note, Pan-Africanist rhetoric degenerated into an excuse to expel people of a different color and culture from the postcolonial states. Rather than an expression of connectedness, it became a rationale for exclusion. On Zanzibar, black migrants from the mainland with no special claim on the island marched to the slogan of Africa for the Africans in 1963 as they slaughtered thousands of longtime resident Arabs.


## FREEDOM

By far the most common forms of nationalism outside of Europe were those generated by European colonialism and its postcolonial successors. Because so much anguish came later, it has become ever more fashionable to underplay the harshness of these colonial regimes: their brutal extraction of labor, crude seizure of land, and violent protection of privilege, all from the fists of alien racists. In their own time they roused a hatred that made passionate, popular anticolonialism self-justifying. Liberalizing colonial rule, as slaveholders had discovered earlier, only whetted the appetite for more: Charitable tyranny won very few converts. If, for example, some Senegalese enjoyed some rights as *citoyens* under the French, the anticolonial leader Léopold Sédar Senghor then demanded all rights for all Senegalese through independence. Although not many colonial subjects openly resisted imperial rule, a great many who had been silent celebrated independence just as ecstatically when it came.

In a mistake repeated over and over again, Western observers commonly called all of these resistance movements nationalism. On the contrary, anticolonialism was the all-encompassing mobilizer, nationalism just one of its expressions. In fact, without critical contributions from the imperialists themselves, nationalism might well have sputtered and stalled. British colonial rule in Africa illustrated that reinforcing process. Encountering many groups in various states of mutual tolerance, competition, and warfare, the British proceeded to freeze by law what had previously been fluid. At its worst, this British ordering "turned the simple fact of ethnic heterogeneity into a source of tension" and heightened hostilities.[27] In John Lonsdale's phrase, colonialism had a way of converting "negotiable ethnicity into competitive tribalism."[28] Moreover, British weaponry dramatically escalated the costs of interethnic violence. Nevertheless, British administration increased the ability of otherwise scattered peoples to resist the very rule it was trying to impose. As the British invested their own language with immense privilege, they also juggled the importance of other languages, sacrificing the distinctiveness of small tribes to such British-enforced linguistic amalgamations as the Shona, Chaga, and Tumbuka in eastern Africa and the Ashanti in the west. By British fiat, the Ndebele in the southeast were transformed from a loose bargaining confederation into an African race. Eventually these larger units provided some of the toughest nationalist bases in the battles for independence. Even among the favored, raising expectations risked highlighting how severely curtailed a colonial's opportunities actually were. Benefits given and stolen away generated a special anger. After creating the Ndebele, for example, British imperialists around the turn of the twentieth century assigned them a territory, only to take it back a quarter century later. After midcentury, that British-designated territory was the homeland Ndebele nationalists claimed as they joined in the battle to free Zimbabwe.

Some privileges for some frustrated others. Sons of the wealthy acquired a cosmopolitan education and, as the local agents of economic development, access to even greater wealth. Through what Mahmood Mamdani has called decentralized despotism, the British passed much of its day-to-day rule to tribal intermediaries who in sum constituted a continental network of petty tyrants, each with his own subsystem of personal patronage. Arabs later slaughtered on Zanzibar had been used in that way. The United

States employed a comparable system in the Philippine Islands. By 1921, 90 percent of the colony's administrative jobs were held by Filipinos, loyal to local oligarchs on whom American—and for a few years Japanese—rule depended. These very advantageous and ostentatiously displayed benefits, coming at the hands of colonial rulers, left dark wells of interethnic hatred behind the retreating imperialists.

As it funneled envy and ambition, in other words, colonial rule created its own sense of time and entitlement. Colonialism's radical imbalance in power set off a dialectic of cultural inventions and counterinventions that eventually worked in anticolonialism's favor. The length of a group's history did not measure the depth of its feelings: Ethnic identities might be tempered far harder by a few decades of imperial governance than by the mere passage of centuries. Moreover, outlawing nationalism, as colonialism almost always did, increased its reliance on mythic, essentialist beliefs and helped account for the firmer grip these colonially forged, half-century-old identities had than the softer networks of connection that apparently prevailed earlier. There was nothing inherently artificial about the process—invasions, impositions, wholesale swallowings of one group by another, were part of every region's history. Moreover, all traditions in all cultures have been invented—that is, given a specific form—at some time or another. What colonialism tended to do was compress patterns of change and harden their outcomes.

Independence brought with it bounded governing structures that carried an imperialist taint and expressed European values: "the prison-house of the sovereign state," the Africanist Ali Mazrui has called them.[29] Emancipated colonials experienced less of an Icarus Effect than European nationalists because anticolonialism, which dominated all else, contained its own resolution: driving out foreign rulers. Nevertheless, where ethnic aspirations still ran strong, the arbitrary boundaries of these new states offered little or no satisfaction. At the moment of revolutionary victory, David Lan writes, there were two entirely different Zimbabwes, one "the spirit province . . . owned by the ancestors of the Shona people in which the Shona have the perpetual, inextinguishable right . . . to live and govern forever," the other a state "the borders of which were drawn by politicians in Britain and Portugal . . . [collecting] the Shona but also the Ndebele, the Shangaan, the whites, and the other marginal ethnic groups" in a system alien to all of their traditions.[30] As Partha Chatterjee, an expert on anticolonial nationalism, has summarized it, "forcible marginalization of many who were supposed to have shared in the fruits of liberation" was a standard outcome.[31]

Like a relentlessly turning wheel, independence within these artificial state frameworks very often replicated the same grim story: one group's rule imposed on others, superior force as the heart of governance, ethnic networks as the basis for resistance, and nationalism as one of its expressions. Rulers extracted wealth and kept the lion's share for themselves: Under colonialism, after all, that was the meaning of good government. In fact, the new leaders tended to improve on the lessons of their former masters: use power even more exclusively for one group's benefit, act even more ruthlessly against any opposition. The moment of independence did not offer an obvious way out of this vicious, downward spiral. Although precolonial Africa had contained a great variety of political systems, most of them much less centralized, a "careful deafricanization" of the state had occurred long before independence.[32] The institutions that imperialism had gutted, either by emptying them of functions or by draining them of respect, could not be resurrected now. The stabilizing rivalry of princes in Burundi, for example, or the free-standing authority of chiefs in Zimbabwe and the Transvaal was gone forever. That was postcolonialism's Humpty-Dumpty Principle.

By default power passed to the local agents of imperialism, that mediating network of chiefs who had assimilated the techiques of colonial rule as they implemented it. But destroying this legacy of imperialism had its own devastating consequences. In one of the most important insights of the anticolonial struggles, the activist-theorist Frantz Fanon formulated what had the appearance of an irrefutable guideline. To repossess their land, he declared, a colonized people had to take it back by force. Otherwise, the local lackeys of imperialism would simply remain in charge through a laying on of hands. Yet where freedom fighters did wrench power from their imperial overlords, as in Fanon's adopted Algeria, they almost always stayed to rule as an army: an interim liberation perhaps, then another tyranny. A peaceful transfer maintained the old despotism, a violent one established a new despotism: That was the Fanon Dilemma.

Preserving their irrational state structures and mimicking their rapacious former masters, suffering from economic marginality and relying on ethnic loyalty, postcolonial leaders governed in a culture of winner-take-all, loser-take-cover. If for a short time the presence of the Big Men of their revolutions—Sukarno in Indonesia, U Nu in Burma, Kenyatta in Kenya, and their counterparts elsewhere—obscured the rootlessness of the states they ruled, the secret was out everywhere by the late 1960s. The two most likely outcomes, by no means mutually exclusive ones, were authoritarian ethnocracy and military dictatorship.

Occasionally, as in Ghana, the contest between rival ethnic groups seesawed. After dumping Ghana's Big Man Nkrumah, now the Ashanti beat the Ewe and took all the spoils, then the Ewe bloodied the Ashanti and did the same. Usually, however, power perpetuated power. In Kenya, for example, the Kikuyu consolidated their hold on the government, assassinated Tom Mboya, the leader of the rival Luo, and laid the groundwork for decades of Daniel arap Moi's iron-fisted kleptocracy. In Guinea, the single-party government of Sékou Touré meant rule by the Malinkè; in Malawi, the authoritarian regime of Hastings Kamuzu Banda empowered only the Chewa.

In Sri Lanka, it was the majority Sinhalese drive for ethnocracy that dominated postcolonial history. After a decade's attempt to fashion an inclusive pluralist government in then-Ceylon, S.W.R.D. Bandaranaiki—celebrated in the West as a world statesman—took power in 1956 at the head of a new party determined to impose Sinhalese culture across the island and to seize economic benefits for Sinhalese people. Hindu Tamils, usually divided between relatively recent immigrants and those with centuries-old roots in the island, united at least in defense of their basic rights in those provinces where Tamils predominated. Under Bandaranaiki, his wife, and their successors, the Sri Lankan government came to embody Sinhalese interests, deporting Tamil workers, investing Buddhism with constitutional authority, subsidizing Sinhalese migration into Tamil regions, and driving Tamil from public service: 60 percent of the government's professionals and 40 percent of its military in 1956, 10 percent and 1 percent by 1970. Then in 1983, Sinhalese officials, out to prove they were the fierciest nationalists of all, let loose communal rioters who killed thousands of Tamil in Colombo and left over a quarter of a million homeless. A population explosion that almost doubled the number of Sri Lankans between 1946 and 1971 stoked the fires of conflict; Sinhalese rulers spread the flames.

Governments in postcolonial states ranging from the Philippines to Burma to Sierra Leone, with virtually no chance of affecting affairs outside their boundaries, turned inward to take advantage of what they could reach. Armies, their primary reliance, preyed on their own people in what became a grimly familiar spiral: siphon the country's wealth into a military whose expansion required ever more wealth. If postcolonial armies often functioned initially as adjuncts to ethnic power, in almost all cases they became power sources in their own right: self-perpetuating, loyalty-generating institutions that enabled men with virtually no other base of authority to rule uncontested. In the coup of 1965 that deposed Sukarno and massacred hundreds of thousands throughout the islands, it was the Indonesian army that triumphed. In

Uganda, a relatively small coalition in the north imposed itself on the more numerous and better-educated BaGanda in the south through the muscle of an army under A. Milton Obote, who in turn was deposed in 1971 by Idi Amin, with an even smaller civilian base that Amin proceeded to shrink even further. Naked force, slaughtering right and left, sustained him for eight years until an invasion from Tanzania finally ended that particular reign of terror.

Whatever model of despotism prevailed, it laid open the public realm—the realm of the state—to those powerful enough to seize its rewards. Almost nothing remained there for long; almost everything drained into kin and client networks loyal to their benefactors. As Sara Berry has demonstrated, public capital, rather than accumulating for development in Africa, was recycled through these private fiefdoms. In the overwhelming majority of cases, the fierce, emotional battles over office were driven by one group's envy of another's advantages, not by anybody's higher standards of civil service. Moreover, the exceptions brought massive problems of their own. In 1962, when Julius Nyerere took power in Tanzania, he set out to create East Africa's own version of a socialist state under the name of *ujamaa*. But there, as in China's preeminent model for postcolonial socialism, increasingly coercive policies through an increasingly arbitrary government set an appalling human price on such experiments. Between 1973 and 1976, perhaps 11 million Tanzanians were corralled from their hills and villages into disastrously unsuccessful collectives. Through what John Markakis has called garrison socialism, Ethiopia's fanatic Col. Mengistu Haile Mariam then copied the Tanzanian failure in the 1980s with even greater violence and hardship.

Nationalism hovered close to these postcolonial despotisms, occasionally playing their servant, more often steeling their opposition. In China, the Communist leadership did play brilliantly on the memory of past invasions and the fear of future ones to maintain a high-pitched nationalist support. Far less successful were rulers in the Philippines, who had little luck using the symbols of independence. This included the nineteenth-century hero José Rizal, and his attempt to rally a Mexican-style state nationalism/patriotism. Emperor Haile Selassie, who set out like an old Balkan potentate to impose Coptic Christianity and the Amharic language on resisting groups in southern Ethiopia, triggered a movement for Eritrean independence that survived the military coup deposing him, then contributed to the fall of his successor Mengistu.

The Ethiopian example was normative: Ethnic groups out of power had to look to their own resources. In a few postcolonial states, such as Tanzania, a multiplicity of small ethnic groups kept any one of them from dominating the central government. But multiethnicity was usually no defense against death and devastation, as the East Timorese adjacent to Indonesia and the Pampanganos—or Hukbalahap rebels—in the Philippines so painfully learned. Both oppressors and oppressed tended to repeat in postcolonial settings the dynamic their colonial predecessors had generated. As the imperialist governors had done, new rulers claimed a monopoly on force, made and broke promises to various constituents at will, and drove their protesting leaders underground. As the anticolonial resistance had done, the new opposition did whatever it took to survive and fight on. Postcolonial states attacked ethnic outsiders far more often than the converse. In the large majority of cases, that is, nationalism was "not a cause but a consequence of [those violent conflicts]."[33] There was no East Timorese nationalism until the Indonesian army generated it, no Tamil nationalism until the Sinhalese government in Sri Lanka mobilized it.

Denied a place in public, resistance slid into private life. Clandestine movements almost by their nature took on revolutionary import. Surfacing, disappearing, resurfacing, they survived by cultivating those special qualities—almost always ethnic qualities—that defined them as a group. Oppressed people "owed no allegiance to the state, its courts, its police, its festivals, and so all the energies which might in [another] society have been dispersed over such wide areas were instead invested in the rituals of the family" and its kin culture.[34] Whether—or at what point—these patterns of resistance translated into nationalism could be an extremely difficult question to answer. The very qualities that made family-kin resistance so tough could very well preclude its development into nationalism, which required attachments sufficiently elastic to cover wider and wider ranges of fictive kin. By and large, the denser the local webs of commitment, the more literal—the less adaptive—the definitions of family. In sections of Africa, even the village exceeded the limits of loyalty: different families, parceling it into their own networks, helped one another only in an emergency, if at all. Cellular social organizations, Goran Hyden calls them. In such settings, fictive kinship was a contradiction in terms.

Operating along the margins between public and private, nationalism melted and merged with other formulations of postcolonial resistance: spiritual/religious, class, or simply pure hatred of the oppressor. Initially nationalism enjoyed its greatest advantage where no civic culture functioned. Ethnic connections most often doubled as civic values because they were the most likely to weather the attempt common among postcolonial governments to destroy all independent public organizations. As a result, kin and client networks in sub-Sahara Africa routinely assumed responsibility for welfare, protection, and taxation that in other societies the government would have taken on itself. Inside the shell of the Ghanaian state in the 1970s, Kwame Anthony Appiah writes, useful law was kinship law: "Disputes . . . were likely to end up in arbitration, between heads of families, or in the courts of 'traditional' chiefs and queen mothers."[35] In effect, these webs of reciprocal obligation, organizing everyday affairs, bestowed a surrogate citizenship on their members. The longer they functioned like governments, the more the prospect of becoming governments was likely to beckon—that is, the more likely ethnic networks would transform themselves into full-fledged nationalist movements.

Once again, states drove the story, as they had so often in the worldwide spread of nationalism—in the ostensible successes of Japan and Turkey and in the ostensible failure of the pan movements alike. States hollowed of everything except military might were the curse of the postcolonial world. As they picked their citizens' pockets—and many of their carcasses as well—they inspired ethnic, perhaps nationalist resistance that as it slipped in and out of public life eluded capture and definition alike. Nigerian history tells just such tale.

There would be no Nigeria if there had been no Western imperialism. Shaped by competing European interests, named at the inspiration of a British journalist, and administered as if its parts were separate countries, the modern state of Nigeria was colonial residue. Britain, Germany, and France drew boundaries around Nigeria in fits and starts after 1885, as the pressure to translate African spheres of influence into colonies mounted. Within that territory, Britain consolidated its authority. By occupying the Benin Kingdom in 1897, it united the government's coastal interests; by revoking two years later the charter of the rapacious Royal Niger Company, a trading firm, it extended the government's reach across a large northern realm. In 1914 Nigeria was officially a colony with quite distinct northern and southern provinces administered under one overseeing governor-general. The port of Lagos, eventually stripped to little more than its island home, remained administratively distinct, and the Cameroons, taken from Germany in 1916, were then appended to the eastern sides of the two main provinces. In 1939, when the south was split roughly by the Niger River into eastern and western provinces, the colony's interior boundaries could finally be said to approximate the most obvious divisions among its inhabitants: the Igbo (Ibo) in the east, the Yoruba in the west, and the Fulani-dominated Hausa in the north.

At every step, European specificity clashed with African reality. Before colonial rule, nobody drew lines: Tribal territory simply expanded and contracted as its power waxed and waned. Imperial borders transformed lives, fracturing tribes and forcing the reconstruction of indigenous trading economies. As late as the First World War, a good map was a luxury. The original boundary between southeastern Nigeria and German-controlled territory was based on a river that did not exist; the original boundary between northeastern Nigeria and French-controlled territory depended on a tree that was never found. When Britain and France conquered the Cameroons, officials in London relied on memory to divide it between them. Administration could be just as arbitrary. The authoritarian Fulani emirs worked so well as intermediaries in controlling the remote north that the architect of British government, Sir Frederick Lugard, futilely sought to impose a comparable structure on the Yoruba and Igbo, whose cultures simply would not sustain it.

Indirect British rule saved money and evaded responsibility. Corrupting rather than crushing tribal chiefs gave the appearance of a softer colonialism, seemingly untainted by its day-to-day consequences. It was equally true, however, that British colonialism did not disrupt an Edenic garden. The backdrops to British rule were chronic civil war spreading misery and generating slaves throughout Yorubaland, and ruthless Fulani warlords, who had already slaughtered and squeezed Hausa people into their emirate hierarchies, perched ready to push farther south if they could. If British penetration of Nigerian territory forced changes in tribal societies, so had trade and conflict with outsiders from time immemorial. Certainly Yoruba slave gatherers and Fulani warlords showed no sensitivity to the societies they ravaged. In any case, a mythic West Africa frozen in isolation boggles the imagination, especially as global exchanges were transforming cultures everywhere.

The mixed results of Britain's rule were played out within its tripartite administrative structure. On the one hand, its attempt to turn southern chiefs into autocrats only distorted provincial power relations. On the other, British encouragement for linguistic unity and educational opportunity reshaped cultural relations in those same southern areas, where a majority of Nigeria's tribal groups resided. To the west, a legacy of endemic warfare gave way to an increasingly cohesive Yoruba identity. In the east, a synthetic Igbo language, with a 1909 translation of the Christian New Testament as its benchmark, served as an effective compromise among myriad local dialects. First the Yoruba, then the Igbo, took advantage of the colonial schools to prepare themselves as merchants, clerks, and petty traders. At the same time, a large proportion in both groups converted to locally seasoned, relatively benign versions of world religion—Muslim and Christian among the Yoruba, just Christian among the Igbo. Substantial numbers of both groups migrated in search of better jobs; migration experiences, in turn, helped to cement those broader identities.

Consolidating regions, however, accentuated divisions. By far the most populous colony in Africa, Nigeria may also have been the most heterogeneous. Although Yoruba and Igbo both derived from the Kwa language group, those two variations had little in common. Hausa, in turn, was a Chadic language linking its speakers not to the Nigerian south but to desert peoples to their north and northeast. Many small tribes understood none of these. Next to the Yoruba, for example, the Edo spoke still another variant of Kwa, and in a middle belt of tribes the language of the Tiv, among others, was Bantu. Imperialist English was the closest thing to a common denominator. Differences in language went hand in glove with entirely different ways of life: the fervently Muslim Fulani emirates operating out of their walled cities; the eclectic Yoruba cohering around their towns; the thoroughly decentralized Igbo diffusing among their villages. Regional hegemony, in other words, further drained a whole Nigeria of meaning.

Demands for independence focused originally in the cosmopolitan port of Lagos, where the pioneer anticolonialist with the wonderfully perverse name of Herbert Macaulay had already bearded the British lion in the 1920s. By the Second World War, anticolonialism spread rapidly throughout the south, raising critical questions about Yoruba and Igbo loyalties. Could they reach out to encompass an entire Nigeria or would they merely harden into a mutually suspicious regionalism? The preeminent voice of Nigerian nationalism was Azikiwe, an Igbo born in the northern province and raised in Igbo land who set out for Lagos at seventeen, went to the United States for an education at twenty-one, returned to the neighboring Gold Coast (Ghana) at thirty, and finally arrived back in Nigeria at thirty-three to join the militant Nigerian Youth Movement and edit Lagos's fieriest anticolonial newspaper. Between 1934 and 1949, the Africanist James Coleman concluded, no nationalist below the Sahara was more important. As the outstanding ideologue of both nationalism and Pan-Africanism, Azikiwe inspired the labor radicals who mobilized under his nickname—the Zikist Movement—and dreamed of an entire Africa rising in the spirit of the thirty thousand Nigerian workers, cheered on by Azikiwe's newspapers, who struck for more than a month in 1945. Militants in the National (Anglican) Church also followed him. As the Second World War was ending, alone among the colony's big men, Azikiwe, an Igbo based in Yorubaland, called on all Nigerians, north and south, to join under a single banner, the NCNC—initially the National Council of Nigeria and the Cameroons, eventually the National Council of Nigerian Citizens—"the first mass nationalist party in Africa south of the Sahara," one scholar has called it.[36]

Cheek by jowl, his leading competitor was Obefami Awolowo, whose ethnic organization, Egbe Omo Oduduwa, helped to deepen a Yoruba consciousness in the 1920s and 1930s and whose animus toward the ambitious Igbo—an aspiring "master race," he called them—helped to turn Yoruba into a counteridentity in the 1940s. (In Yoruba myth, Oduduwa on instruction from the supreme god Olorun came to earth at Ile Ife, where his sixteen sons founded the sixteen Yoruba kingdoms.) The fortunes of Azikiwe's and Awolowo's very different aspirations were clarified

during the relatively smooth process of imperial divestment between 1946 and 1954, when the constitutional provisions for a
British-style central government resting on Nigeria's familiar three
regions congealed. Once independence was certain, Chief
Awolowo knew just what he wanted: to maximize Yoruba power
in the new state. But Azikiwe no longer did. In a fine illustration
of the Icarus Effect, the closer Azikiwe's anticolonial nationalism
came to success, the more his vision blurred. He cut his ties with
the Zikist militants without binding new ones. In stutter steps, he
claimed an identity as Igbo in 1948, reaffirmed his commitment to
a whole Nigeria in 1951, then accepted the provisional premier-
ship of the Igbo-dominated eastern region in 1954. Meanwhile, in
a critical early round of elections in the western region,
Awolowo's Yoruba party, the Action Group, trounced Azikiwe's
NCNC, which, weak in the west and downright feeble in the
north, became what Awolowo's hostile imagination made of it
from the start: the Igbo party. Azikiwe, no longer the quintessential Nigerian, was simply the great Igbo champion of independence who now served as decorous head of state.

The Nigerian state never worked. Initially it was Fulani emirs—
nervous about independence, contemptuous of democracy, and
comfortable with violence—who between 1960 and 1965 subverted the constitution by rigging elections and census counts
alike. With Azikiwe's NCNC standing aside, the north's allies created a new mid-west region from a piece of Awolowo's home
base, then jailed Awolowo himself. When Azikiwe finally did resist northern thuggery, chaos ensued and the army stepped in,
eliminating electoral politics altogether.

The contest shifted to the army. When northern interests gained
control of it, the Igbo military, responding to the murder and mass
exodus of Igbo residents in the north and hoping to trigger a general southern resistance to Fulani aggression, declared the eastern
region the independent state of Biafra. In 1967 it was Awolowo,
free once more and a Yoruba hero, who toyed with the Igbo just

as the Igbo Azikiwe had left the Yoruba dangling a few years earlier. In fact, the proud Igbo chiefs seemed constitutionally unable to maintain alliances of any kind. Suffering casualties several times greater than, say, the United States had experienced during the entire Second World War, the Igbo—isolated, outgunned, blockaded—were starved into submission by 1970. Azikiwe, who had cut his moorings to side with Biafra, drifted into irrelevance.

From the beginning, the rulers of Nigeria sought structural solutions to its ethnic problems. Riding on the momentum of British colonial policy, Nigeria's original tripartite division consolidated mutually exclusive Fulani-Hausa, Yoruba, and Igbo bastions. As competition among the big three broke out of bounds, one alternative was to eliminate regions entirely in favor of a single integrated Nigeria. The first of the military rulers, an Igbo, tried to impose that answer in 1966, only to be killed along with his plan in six months. His successor, Yakubu Gowon, set off in the opposite direction, subdividing Nigeria's regions into twelve states, which by the end of the century had multiplied to thirty-six.

Although a fragmented Nigeria did complicate mobilization for the Yoruba and the Igbo, it rarely enhanced self-determination for the 250 or so smaller tribes, around 40 percent of the total population, who were even more likely to be splintered as the number of states increased. Nigeria offered a particularly dramatic illustration of the Onion Effect that hard, Western-style constitutional structures could set in motion. Peeling off a large ethnic group's power in order to liberate the minority group beneath it only installed that group as the majority over another minority beneath it, and so on indefinitely. The prospect of Biafran independence promised no greater leeway for the scores of small tribes in the southeast. Indicatively, the most committed Nigerians may have been leaders like Gowon, a member of a small middle-belt tribe, who feared that with a total breakdown of Nigeria the northern emirates would swallow his people whole.

As awkward as the constitutional structure sometimes made it for ethnic mobilizations, in the end they organized Nigeria's public affairs. Parties, churches, unions, and the like provided almost no competing, cross-cutting affiliations. What looked like expediency in a chief like Awolowo, veering now toward a central government, now toward regional autonomy, now toward local empowerment, were the tactics of an ethnically rooted self-interest: serve himself, solidify his Yoruba constituency. In the same spirit, Yoruba and Fulani-Hausa distrust of the Igbo never slackened. Thirty years after the outbreak of civil war, no Igbo held a post of any significance in the military and only one occupied a managerial position in the civil service.

Competing ethnic loyalties destroyed public values. No doubt British rule had set the stage. By its nature colonialism taught its subjects to evade the state's power and appropriate its resources. In addition, Nigerians carried three special burdens from British imperialism: the practice of leaving important economic decisions to private companies, a barebones infrastructure, and a desiccated interregional trade. Outsiders dominated the export business. When major oil discoveries were made in the transitional 1950s, the British did nothing to protect them as a tax base for the state. As a consequence, independent Nigeria financed itself through concessions. Nothing invited looting quite so grandly as the ongoing sale of the country's opportunities and resources. Civilian politicians routinely bought elections and stole public funds. When military rulers took power from them, they stole even more freely. In the 1970s when Gowon held the reins of government loosely and in the 1990s when Sani Abacha pulled them tight, corruption ran rampant, just through different channels. Restraint was a personal matter. One of the testimonials offered in memory of Moshood K. O. Abiola, the martyred president-elect of 1993, was that however dubiously he had acquired his immense wealth, he at least kept it in Nigeria. Overall, the results were disastrous. Plagued by crime, ruled by violence, and infested by disease, Nigerians in 1990 averaged an annual income below $300—by contrast, for instance, to $3,170 in Venezuela, another equatorial, oil-rich country.

The biggest winner was not an ethnic group but the army, which aside from the interlude of the Second Republic, 1979 to 1983, ruled Nigeria until 1999. At the moment of independence, nothing had encouraged the army to act as a law unto itself. Early in the 1960s, in fact, it was modest in size and professional in style. Nor, despite the Biafran war, did the Nigerian military acquire importance through warfare. It evolved in the spaces that the few other potentially statewide institutions were too fragile or fragmented to occupy. Once there, the military functioned as a facsimile government, with its own lines of authority, mechanisms of enforcement, and avenues of opportunity. As rule number one, it insulated itself against outside interference. In addition to the standing threat of force, the division of Nigeria into more and more states and the removal of its capital from vibrant Lagos to isolated Abuja scattered and distanced its civilian opponents. Succession to leadership usually meant killing one's predecessor. In many ways, Abaca's mad rule from 1993 to his death in 1997 was the logical outcome. Even after the exposure of the military government's monumental corruption, the army's unmatched organization assured victory for Gen. Olusegun Obasanjo and his People's Democratic party in the elections of 1999.

But if the army functioned as Nigeria's shadow state, it had no standing whatsoever as proxy for a Nigerian nation. The high point of a Nigerian identity came in cheers for its soccer team during the 1994 and 1998 World Cup competition. No myth explained Nigeria's primordial origins. In the end, the state's severely limited meaning helped it survive. The complex webbing of private interests and mutual suspicions that blocked the integration of Nigeria simultaneously checked its dismantling. Like wrestlers tangled on the mat, who would dare to let go first? When the Igbo did in 1967, they paid in blood: No other ethnic group risked demanding an independent state. Nigerians stayed together to serve themselves. Appropriately, as civil government returned at the end of the century, the statesman most often lionized in memory was Awolowo—affectionately, Awo—the master of Yoruba loyalty and political expediency.

CHAPTER 7

## Global Nationalism

In a transformation that pivoted on the years 1967 to 1972, nationalism changed from a worldwide spread of many movements into a global phenomenon with many variations. Each nationalist movement still had its own story, of course. Nevertheless, during these years, the simultaneous eruptions that brought nationalism back to Europe, spread it to North America, and kept it alive in scores of postcolonial settings rendered it implausible to think of nationalism as so many events that just happened to crop up everywhere at the same time. To see what any explanation of this extraordinary flourishing has to reckon with, let us take a tour of nationalist outbreaks in the late 1960s and early 1970s, starting in North America and ending in Asia: first French Canada, then the black ghettos of the United States, Northern Ireland, Wales and Scotland in the United Kingdom, Spanish Basque territory, Belgium, Rwanda and Burundi, Israel, Malaysia, and Vietnam, with glances at Cuba, Brittany, Catalonia, Norway, Czechoslovakia, Yugoslavia, Palestine, and Sri Lanka.

French Canadian grievances had been festering for at least a century. Although the founding act of the confederation in 1867 built bilingualism into the Canadian Parliament, the trend ran strongly toward English monolingualism, especially with the addition of four new provinces extending west of Ontario to the Pacific Ocean, all of which conducted their affairs in English early in the twentieth century. In 1903, as nationalism throughout Europe took its linguistic turn, Henri Bourassa, the extraordinarily durable voice of the Quebecois cause, laid out its case. Canada, founded as two equal nations, was fast falling under the control of the English. Only a monolingual Quebec could protect the French community and its superior Christian culture from dissolution. A few years earlier, Flemish leaders had made almost the same case in Belgium.

Between 1870 and 1950, perhaps the highest birthrates in the Western world in combination with limited economic opportunities encouraged large numbers of Quebec's citizens, especially its young men, to migrate. Migration, in turn, stretched and strengthened a sense of Quebecois connectedness and hence the urge to call it a distinctive nation. Then as opportunities expanded dramatically after 1945, births dropped abruptly, halving the number of babies per adult woman during the 1960s alone and leaving the province with one of the Western world's lowest rates of reproduction. Although French speakers still constituted almost 80 percent of Quebec's population in 1970, fears of slipping into a minority even at home gripped the champions of a Quebecois distinctiveness. It was then that Bourassa's agenda finally translated into a nationalist movement, especially popular among Quebec's young adults, with belligerent demands for something between extensive provincial autonomy and outright independence. By 1970 French was the official language of Quebec and a systematic bilingualism was official Canada-wide policy. With other ethnic groups also pressing for recognition and English speakers in retreat, Prime Minister Pierre Trudeau a year later declared: "[T]here is no official culture."[1]

Beginning with the local struggles of many Southern black groups and evolving into the campaign that Martin Luther King, Jr., led to victory, the civil rights movement mobilized a new black consciousness in the United States, only to lose control of its purposes after the legislative victories of 1964 and 1965. In 1966, as calls for Black Power rang through the urban ghettos, black nationalism resurfaced—inchoate but very much in the mood of the moment. To the accompaniment of riots across the cities in the North, it played on widespread black frustrations over the great deal that had not changed rather than the great deal that had. At the forefront of the new black nationalist assertions was cultural pride: a creativity in the arts, the beauty in blackness, a triumph over the curse of slavery, the celebration of an African heritage. Race, always far more salient in the diaspora than in Africa itself, now returned to American discourse by way of the people who had been most victimized by the concept: appropriate the power of the oppressor.

Leading black nationalists foresaw a sequence: first cultural pride, then economic leverage, finally political freedom. Enthusiasts, however, could not wait. Late in 1966 the Black Panthers, a militant ghetto-empowering group, demanded "a United Nations–supervised plebiscite to be held throughout the black colony in which only black colonial subjects will be allowed to participate, for the purpose of determining the will of black people as to their national destiny."[2] That colonial analogy, bridging American and African experiences and expressing new defiance in a postcolonial age, lay at the center of Black Power as its original theoreticians, Stokely Carmichael and Charles Hamilton, formulated it, and its sweeping sense of change caught on especially among the young activists who turned nationalist rhetoric into everyday speech.

Around 1960, British administrators in Northern Ireland finally realized that the authoritarian spirit of Ulster's founding hero, Sir Edward Carson, had had its day, and for the first time since partition, they opened the issue of Protestant domination a crack for reconsideration. Until then, policies had only hardened the status quo. Eliminating proportional representation in 1929 had left Catholics with a few pockets of local control, no say in the general government, and chronic poverty. British officials in the north turned a blind eye to the everyday evidence of economic discrimination; Irish officials to the south offered nothing more constructive than hollow rhetoric. Then in 1963, moderate British governors poked gingerly into this chasm separating Protestant rulers from Catholic subjects, only to fall headlong into the rush of events. Rioting in 1969 brought troops from Britain; escalating violence in 1970 and 1971 culminated on January 30, 1972—Bloody Sunday—when police fired into a Catholic crowd. In the wake of the police riot, the British took over the government, thereby hardening antagonisms further. The Irish Republican Army, marginal for decades, now emerged from limbo to redefine the conflict as guerrilla warfare and reestablish its fading lines to Irish American fund raisers and munition suppliers.

Meanwhile, Welsh and Scottish nationalism rose from nowhere in Britain itself. Stirrings in Wales dated from the 1880s, when nationalists generated a flurry of interest by calling for the preservation of a distinctively Welsh culture through the Welsh language. Language was still central in 1963, when after a half century's lapse and a relentless decline in Welsh speakers, an assertive, youth-driven movement to mandate its use sparked an even wider interest in autonomy. As Welsh nationalism heated up, interest in Scottish self-government, scarcely an issue earlier, came alive in 1968 with the sudden popularity of its champion, the Scottish National Party, which drew heavily on politically skeptical young people. Already animated by a spirit of modernization, Scottish nationalism received a significant boost from the offshore oil production that commenced in 1973.

Basque nationalism, caught in the crossfire of Spanish politics, stayed alive as a form of resistance to the Franco regime, which did what it could to obliterate the community. Although the Eus-karian language remained its symbolic core, Basque nationalism shed its Catholic, royalist shell and its claims to a distinct race in favor of ties to the political left and claims to an indigenous social-ist spirit. For the first time, non-Euskara speakers—a substantial majority of the Basque population, too—could become adopted members of the movement. After Franco's oppression, all Basque politicians favored greater autonomy, but only the militant ETA, rejuvenated by the mid-sixties, demanded independence. An im-portant source of the ETA's support came from upwardly mobile Basque youth who resented the influence of outside economic interests and the competition from newcomers in the scramble to benefit from the region's recent prosperity. In 1968 the ETA, now in Leninist hands, arranged the assassination of a despised police chief and threw the region into turmoil. The more zealous the ferreting out of the killers, the deeper Basque hostility to external governance grew. When open politics returned in 1975, attitudes toward the conspiratorial ETA still cleaved the community, but Basque nationalism united all parties.

The origin of Belgium's postwar divisions actually dated from the laws of 1931 and 1932, which formalized the tripartite division among a monolingual French Wallonia, a monolingual Flemish Flanders, and a shared Brussels. Demographics eroded the ar-rangement from the start. In 1963, with the Flemish, once the poor relations, now a prospering majority and the Walloons sliding per-manently into a minority, officials negotiated one more in a series of byzantine readjustments of territory that complexified the rules governing Brussels and even carved its suburbs linguistically. Mu-tual anger only mounted. By 1968 it was no longer possible to form a government, and a Belgium beset by dueling nationalisms fell into a prolonged constitutional crisis.

The 1960s did not initiate but did intensify the long, bloody conflict between Tutsi, traditionally the rulers in what became Rwanda in 1961 and Burundi in 1962, and Hutu, energized by the prospect of independence to assert a control over Rwanda that their preponderance in the population seemed to justify. On the eve of independence, with crucial assistance from their Belgian colonial masters, Hutu in Rwanda drove much of the Tutsi establishment into exile and assumed control of the government. By 1962 it was open season on the Tutsi minority, and an abortive invasion of Rwanda the next year by Tutsi exiles only spread the disaster: In retaliation, over ten thousand Rwandan Tutsi were massacred. Burundi power turned the tables in 1965, imposing a Tutsi government in Rwanda, slaughtering Hutu leaders, and thereby consolidating Tutsi control over both countries. Never subtle, Tutsi celebrated their authority over Rwanda by a ceremonial display of "the genitals of defeated Hutu chiefs."[3] The spiral of violence only shot higher. Implementing a plan that had been discussed since 1963, the Tutsi military used an uprising in 1972 as an excuse to murder around 300,000 Hutu, specifically those who had any record of education or attainment. (As a model for this "selective genocide," Tutsi could look to a comparable Portuguese slaughter of trained Africans in Angola between 1959 and 1961.) This time French helicopters and Belgian munitions backed the Tutsi. Hutu nationalism was temporarily crushed.

As Israelis experienced their own surge of nationalism after 1967, Jewish nationalism flourished even more grandly in the United States. For Jews who had faced neither the Holocaust nor the perils of wartime Russia—who had thrived, in other words, while millions of others died—support for Israel served as a kind of reparation. With about half the world's Jewish population and a preponderance of its wealth, American Jews were Israel's mainstay from the outset, contributing sufficient private funds to cover over half of its balance-of-payment deficit during the 1950s and 1960s. In myriad other ways—the use of Hebrew, songs and dances, the lionizing of founders, youth camps and adult visits—the Israeli connection provided critical wherewithal for a Jewish American identity. That alone, however, added up to an enthusiastic partisanship, sometimes no more than a self-congratulatory ritual of cheers and donations.

What transformed ethnicity into nationalism was the outcome of two Israeli clashes with Arab armies: a quick euphoric victory in 1967, a sobering stalemate in 1973. The first triggered a messianic turn in Israeli politics, elevating fundamentalist religion, military glory, and irredentist ambitions to commanding heights; the second plumbed deep doubts about the state's defenses against a ring of enemies. Both moments highlighted Israel's incompleteness in ways that defied fulfillment. Biblical boundaries stretched indeterminately outward; security needs multiplied endlessly everywhere. Here was the stuff of nationalism. Not yet master of its land, not yet safe from its enemies—not yet there, as it were—unfinished Israel invoked the movement spirit, as it mobilized people in the diaspora finally, finally, to complete the task that would never end. Publicity for the plight of Jews in the Soviet Union then underlined the essential message to American Jews who, their consciences told them, had once utterly failed their kin: Never again!

With independence in 1957, Malaya (Malaysia) inherited the superimposed categories and concepts of British imperialism: Malay, the Muslim majority of the population; Chinese, approximately a third of it; and Indian, a small minority. Chinese success as petty capitalists was background to a rising Malay self-consciousness, particularly among young men, that expressed itself in anger at the barriers to communal prosperity. Widespread anti-Chinese rioting erupted in 1969. Violence worked. By 1971 the government's new economic policy restricted Chinese opportunities and expanded them for Malays, transforming the state into both an expression and a source of ethnic differentiation.

An ageless tradition of resistance to outside oppressors—historically the Chinese, in the heyday of colonialism the French, finally the Americans—gave a Vietnam constructed by imperialism and crisscrossed with regional, tribal, and religious divisions a semblance of wholeness. The very intensity of American-wrought destructiveness tightened those loose connections. As the American military extended its operations across the entire country, the opposing armies of the Vietminh in the north and the Vietcong in the south forged links; as predatory militia and arbitrary air assaults wreaked havoc in the south, otherwise scattered peasants rallied around the Vietcong's radical, nationalist local governments; and as the rulers in Saigon used their power to punish dissenters of all kinds, they brought even Buddhists and Marxists into a common anticolonial alliance. The success of the American war in giving these diverse pieces a new cohesion was revealed in striking fashion after 1973, when all the advanced weaponry money could buy did not halt the quick collapse of southern resistance to a national Vietnamese government.

A second, speedier world tour, starting once again in the Western Hemisphere, suggests how many other nationalist currents were swirling around these events. Some movements were already under way; some did not ignite until later; but all of them contributed to this globalizing transformation. The first flush of the Cuban Revolution, heightened by the abortive Bay of Pigs invasion and attempted assassinations of Fidel Castro himself, brought an élan of postcolonial nationalism to the island during the 1960s. A linguistically based Breton nationalism stirred with new life during the mid-sixties. Catalonian nationalism revived in 1969. To the surprise of its European neighbors, a referendum in Norway rejected membership in the European Union. Less expansively but no less revealingly, signs appeared in several dictatorial socialist countries: Czech assertions of independence in 1968; nationalist demands and decentralizing adjustments in Yugoslavia during the 1960s and 1970s; a growing anti-Semitism and a deepening urge among Jews to emigrate that fed on one another in the Soviet Union. In 1974 Greeks and Turks, each invoking the sacred obligations of nationhood, faced off in Cyprus. The war for Biafran independence absorbed Nigerian energies between 1967 and

1970. Seemingly from nowhere, the Palestinian Liberation Organization, under a new cosmopolitan leadership, raised the banner of nationalism in the 1960s and kept it aloft during the 1970s. In 1971, when Pakistan let loose its Punjabi army among aggrieved citizens in the state's separate eastern sector, an Indian invasion checked the slaughter and precipitated the Bengali state of Bangladesh. Early in the 1970s, in the face of relentless Sinhalese aggression, Tamil nationalism congealed into a demand for the separate state of Eelam, with the Liberation Tigers of Tamil Eelam, founded in 1973, as its spearhead.

Those who insisted on treating this worldwide explosion as an aberration could claim the worst was over by the end of the 1970s. Referenda in Wales, Scotland, and Quebec soundly defeated the nationalists there. Out of Belgium's crisis came constitutional revisions giving Walloons and Flemings effective sovereignty in their respective territories. Well before that, Breton nationalism had dissolved and the Black Power movement in the United States had disintegrated, armies had cowed Igbo nationalism in Nigeria and Hutu nationalism in Rwanda, and the Soviet Union had slammed the lid on dissent in Eastern Europe. Even where nationalism remained active, it seemed to have settled into a rut. Endemic violence in Northern Ireland, the Basque region of Spain, and the Arab-Israeli borderlands, like the interminable stalemate in Cyprus, blended into a landscape of self-perpetuating bitterness. As national governments consolidated their power in Vietnam and Cuba, they took on more and more of the characteristics—and the problems—of postrevolutionary authoritarianism.

But it was too late to close the gate. Support for Scottish nationalism doubled between the early seventies and nineties; Quebec nationalism exploded with greater force than ever late in the eighties. Decentralizing compromises only whetted the appetite for more in Belgium and Yugoslavia, which was disintegrating by the end of the eighties. During the last quarter of the twentieth century a kin-laden, exclusionary black-nationalist idiom suffused ghetto life in the United States. Year after year of brutality in Northern Ireland not only hardened Catholic Irish nationalism; for the first time it hammered out a distinctively Ulster nationalism, with Ian Paisley its most prominent spokesman and suspicion of Britain now intrinsic to a new ethnic identity. So it went everywhere. Like men wrestling with a balloon, leaders in Moscow suppressed nationalism here only to have it pop up there: Poland, Hungary, Czechoslovakia again, the Baltic states, finally the components of the collapsing Soviet Union itself. In 1983 the Sinhalese outdid themselves in persecuting Tamil and in the process hardened their competing nationalisms into endless rounds of guerrilla violence and government repression. When Palestinian nationalism lost steam in the 1980s, the rock-throwing youth of *intifada* gave it new energy. At the horrific end of the spectrum, Hutu nationalists, by no means crushed in the "selective genocide" of 1972, organized the slaughter of over half a million Tutsi in 1994.


What can we make of all that? How did the genie of global nationalism escape when it did, and why did it continue to work its magic for years afterward? Not only was this astonishing eruption global in the sense of integrally worldwide; it was global in the sense of comprehensive. All the diverse kinds of nationalism were represented: colonial and quasi-colonial nationalism; class-enhanced nationalism; cultural, linguistic, and religious nationalism; cheek-by-jowl feuding nationalism; and intrastate renewal nationalism; as well as both secular and spiritual pan movements and, finally, tribal protectiveness in places as different as Zululand, the Canadian north, and Chiapas. To the surprise of no one who has been following this account, the core of the answer lies in the relations between the modern state in its great variety and modern nationalism in its great variety.

Logically if not always historically, the explanation follows a three-step sequence: creating a world of inviolable states, rendering them in varying degrees dysfunctional, and opening the way for nationalism to challenge them. The first provides us with a broad setting—our outer ring of explanation. The second, by showing how such a great mix of states shared in a common dilemma, brings us a ring closer to our target; and the third, by focusing on the precipitants of explosion in the 1960s, justifies the dating of globalization's arrival: bull's-eye.

First the outermost circle: the rigidification of the state system as the Cold War commenced. Coming out of the Second World War, cosmopolitan leaders throughout Western society read the history of the recent past and the tea leaves of the foreseeable future as validation of the modern state's centrality. Indeed, failure to defend legitimate states against fascist aggression, it was widely believed, had marked the path to war: There must be no more Manchurias, no more Munichs. The agency charged with monitoring a peaceful world, the United Nations, was itself a league of states. Although the United Nations repeatedly affirmed a set of basic human rights, it just as consistently guaranteed the territorial integrity of its member states. As the flood of refugees demonstrated—about the same number in the first postwar decade alone as had emigrated from Europe during the entire nineteenth century—giving an organization of states the responsibility to oversee the world's unrequited ambitions for self-determination put the chickens in the care of the foxes. Those who hoped the United Nations would transcend its own origins and challenge the predominance of states were quickly marginalized as idealists: Realists backed states.

The state system that fell into place reigned supreme because the world's two superpowers depended on it. In a gargantuan extension of the interwar principle that each Western state would embody one of the great trio—democracy, socialism, nationalism—the United States and the Soviet Union seemed bent on dividing the entire world in such terms, in this case between the two they claimed to embody: democracy and socialism. Appropriate to its ambitions, the United States, traditionally the very model of big country/small state, vaulted near the top of the big states, with a vast centralized government, a mobilized military, and a secretive apparatus for setting and implementing worldwide policies. The essence of what Arthur Schlesinger, Jr., has called America's imperial presidency was its "capture . . . of the most vital of national decisions, the decision to go to war."[4] The European quip of the 1950s—that the United States was the only country in history to move directly from childhood to old age—had less to do with the oft-cited sentientiousness of Secretary of State John Foster Dulles than with this bureaucratic giant's counterrevolutionary oversight of its vast sphere. As the two megastates accumulated clients in an effort to expand the range of their influence, both planned policies in terms of a stable state system. Neither showed much interest in adding loose people to their side—an ideologically allied political party, for example, or a cluster of dissident intellectuals. They coveted determinate states covering determinate territories.

At times it seemed that the United States never saw a state it did not like. Even such jerry-rigged ones as South Korea and South Vietnam and a hypothetical one such as Kuwait acquired inviolable status. Control in the Soviet Union's satellites, in turn, rested on elaborate intelligence networks and massive military force, both extensions of state power. By tacit consent, in other words, the Cold War giants competed for space in a filled globe. Unlike the years between world wars, when a great many state boundaries seemed experimental—tentative enough for reconsideration and soft enough for readjustment—the world map now came complete. Who ruled, even what system of government prevailed, might remain an open question, but the states themselves were fixed in place. If, for example, it had made perfectly good sense for the major powers to create a Kurdish state after the First World War, it made none at all after the Second. By the same token, moves toward splitting established states prompted only dire predictions: The parts of a divided Belgium or Canada would be too small, too constricted. Who in the 1970s would have guessed from these Cassandra cries "that Quebec is comparable to Sweden in population, natural resources, urbanization, and other important indicators"?[5]

Reified states populated an imaginary realm that became the only reality. They were the dominoes that fell one upon the next, the buffers against invasion, the land masses that one side took as the other let slip away, the votes in the United Nations. Millions of people paid a terrible price for living within the most coveted of these units. Nigeria's official government, claiming sovereignty over the most populous and potentially the most valuable of Africa's state units, received funds from the United States and planes from the Soviet Union so that some of the people residing there could kill well over a million of the others who favored a state of their own. Something called Vietnam—not the ravaged Vietnamese—was at stake in the long American war there. Something called Afghanistan—not the brutalized Afghani tribes—was at stake in the long Soviet war there. Lining up states on the right side in the Cold War legitimated almost any action. American complicity in the wars that Central American armies waged against their people and Soviet complicity in the mass starvation of uprooted people in the Horn of Africa suggest the appalling range of human costs.

However harsh their rhetoric and unscrupulous their designs, that is to say, the Cold War megastates found common ground in an implicit set of rules: how to compete, to negotiate, to calculate winning and losing. Whose states promised greater security to more of their citizens? Whose side produced more goods, built bigger rockets, tallied higher votes in the General Assembly? Nationalism broke those rules. If socialism and democracy were now the behemoths grappling for the big stakes, nationalism was the shade from the past that distracted from the real contest. It came out of the Second World War the pariah, repudiated along with race as an organizing principle in a civilized, settled universe. According to both orthodox Marxism and liberal modernization theory, nationalism was a way station, a stage through which societies passed as they progressed, and those backward enough to cling to it had every reason to expect rough treatment in the rush to progress.

Orphaned by the war, nationalism had no champion remotely comparable to the Soviet Union and the United States. To the extent it had a home, it lay scattered among the anticolonial movements in Asia and Africa, scarcely a position of strength in any contest. Never in dialogue, only in tension with the major powers, anticolonialism was an inconvenience that the United States in particular wanted to hurry to completion—that is, into states with places in a global system of states. In effect, wherever a nationalist movement appeared, it was surrounded by the Cold War's worldwide encounter between megastates. Although the Cold War by no means homogenized the many nationalist movements, it did force a common agenda—a framework of power and a set of tactics—on them. Even when a superpower posed as the sponsor of a movement—the United States for Israel, the Soviet Union for Cuba—the relationship devolved into patron and client, each trying to use the other to its own ends. In most cases, megapowers sought to quash nationalism. Sometimes they did; sometimes they only made matters worse. Nationalists, already considered disrupters, used tactics that were standard for the weak against the strong: unpredictable violence, sabotage, guerrilla resistance. Judged even more barbaric for what they did, nationalists faced even harsher attacks, inspiring an even more desperate determination. Postwar British coercion in East Africa, followed early in the 1950s by what Britain and the United States made famous as the Mau Mau emergency, set off eight years of spiraling repression-violence-repression.

What made states dysfunctional—now we are moving a ring closer to the heart of the matter—did not follow self-evidently from this pulling and hauling, however. It was not just the result of too much arbitrary violence or kleptocratic rule or general depravation, but of a more complex relation between expectations and behavior. The crucial fact was that almost no postcolonial state could meet the minimum standards accompanying its creation. Some of the difficulty was simply the deflation of success: too many hopes invested in independence alone. In the postcolonial world, disappointment came armed. The exponential growth in the manufacture and distribution of ever more deadly and compact weapons—a legacy of the Western world's obsession with warfare—fed not only the new governments but also their unreconstructed opponents. Quantities of weapons sent to shore up the state slipped through official hands. Dispirited troops abandoned quantities more. The primary loyalty of soldiers to their fellow soldiers rather than to the state meant that entire segments of an army might shift sides. The stakes in these contests were not better or worse policies; they were legitimate or illegitimate governments—the state of the state, as it were.

In fact, the expectation of all governments rose dramatically after midcentury, wreaking damage among the old established states as well as the new fragile ones. The basic rights of citizens in Western society came to include matters of income protection, medical services, housing subsidies, and expensive education that a generation earlier had been largely shadows on the cave wall: socialist promises, elite benefits. If communist governments still set the standard, capitalist governments followed close behind, with the United States underwriting welfare programs in the patched-up states of Western Europe by, among other means, covering their military costs. What started as a grand expansion of social rights came subtly to encompass higher and higher demands for individual rights as well: justice for each person, each person's equality, even each person's fulfillment. No state, bar none, could keep the pace.

Nationalism, although not the only beneficiary of the state's difficulties, was a major one. Time and again, it offered the most readily available and least contested—in one sense of the term, the most natural—alternative to cowed citizenship. In some post-colonial states it was already activated: Not all ethnic factions disarmed with independence. No one was better than the fervent nationalists at using associations with the past to rally those disenchanted with the present. Where states had lost all legitimacy, ethnic networks could even provide a substitute government. Experiences during the Second World War revealed how applicable these general guides were to Europe as well.

As E. H. Carr observed in 1945, it was Hitler's Europe more than Hitler's Germany that had released the demons in nationalism for all the world to see. The German army, destabilizing as it conquered, opened the way for forces once contained within Europe's states to rise out of the rubble and take power for themselves. With the dismemberment of Czechoslovakia, eager Slovak collaborators under Father Tiso anticipated an independent state within a fascist Europe. Flemish fascists reveled in much the same ambition. The defeat of Yugoslavia unleashed Croatia's fascist nationalists, the murderous Ustaše; Serbian antifascist resistance on its part doubled as a nationalist movement. Fascism gave new life to Breton autonomy and antifascism new life to Basque autonomy. Killing Jews in cooperation with Germany and expelling Germans under the aegis of the Soviet Union transformed Poland into a genuine nation-state. Even when postwar governments capped these destructive energies, an essential message remained: Nationalism would be waiting in case those states weakened.

Now to the center of our target. Why in the context of the Cold War as states of all sorts experienced mounting stress did nationalism globalize at the particular time it did, roughly 1967 to 1973? In one sense the answer retells the story of the emperor's clothes. Only a few people needed to demonstrate that the state, even a powerful state, could be had. Among the disaffected in the postcolonial states that materialized one after another in the 1960s, this insight lay inherent in their previous success against a colonial power and hence immediately available for use against the new independent states. Elsewhere, however, it came literally in a series of news flashes, beamed around the world incident by incident, one atop the other. Bearding Uncle Sam—whether in Oakland, Chicago, or Hue—provided especially electrifying moments. Nothing gave a sharper edge to the message than the so-called student rebellions of the late 1960s, in which risk-taking youth in Europe and America rocked state authority back on its heels. Youth talked to youth. Many of the nationalist movements that erupted between 1967 and 1973—in Basque Spain, Malaysia, Quebec, Scotland, Wales, and the Black Power centers of the United States, for example—drew their strength from contingents of young, militant followers, many of whom had no previous experience, and no faith whatsoever, in politics as usual.

In the tumble of events, both tactics and language quickly standardized. The nationalists' use of news media and vice versa developed into a mutually refined science. Television in particular, excellent at communicating a sense of immediacy and involvement for its global audience, moved restlessly from site to site in search of fresh excitement. Activists, alert to what made news, played to the cameras. Other nationalists watched and learned. If the 1968 Tet Offensive in Vietnam was the most elaborately planned and courageously executed of these events, it still belonged to a worldwide pattern of calculated appeals to a global audience. Nationalists also learned terrorist tactics from young radicals and from one another. Although assassination was at least as old a nationalist tactic as the Serbian shooting of Archduke Ferdinand in 1914, hidden explosives and automatic weapons gave murder a new and far less discriminating meaning in the late sixties. Terrorism, some nationalists hoped, would disrupt, intimidate, and recruit. Nationalists who were imprisoned or executed provided their movements with martyrs. With borrowed tactics went rhetoric that sounded much the same around the world. If the oppression of Bretons and Quebecois seemed remote from the oppression of Igbo and Algerians, they were still joined at the level of a global language. In 1990, when a rebel chieftain in Moslem Kosovo invoked the heritage of the French Revolution in behalf of his cause, he fell into a line of leaders more than two decades long who addressed a far-flung audience through a universalized nationalist idiom.

Just as global nationalism seemed to be gathering into an irresistible force, its fortunes took a strange turn. In the broadest terms, the same conjunction of circumstances producing this global surge in nationalism also circumscribed its effectiveness, another in the self-correcting sequences that dotted nationalism's history. In this case, it was the very means of mass communication powering global nationalism that then limited its success. Media that publicized nationalism also spread the word about other movements—some that competed directly with nationalism, some that simply distracted attention from it. In an ever more crowded field of causes, nationalism's potential recruits dispersed. Screaming the same messages louder and louder tended only to dull public interest: After an initial splash of attention, more was less to a worldwide audience. In particular, nationalism suffered from a backlash against calculated acts of violence. Appropriately, human rights politics, turning the same communications system to its own advantage, developed right alongside nationalism's global phase.

Among the tactics that rose out of the new symbiotic relation between modern media and globalized challenges to authority, guerrilla violence was the most readily copied. Movements—indeed mere handfuls of people—with no connection whatsoever to nationalism flooded the media market with one bloody, destabilizing episode after another until public sympathy for these acts, and for any group associated with them, was completely drained. If nationalism did not stand out as a perpetrator, it did take the greatest burden of blame. Powerful enemies, automatically linking nationalism to bloodshed everywhere, never looked back to correct a mistake. The same forces propelling nationalism into its global phase, in other words, were even more effective in damning its reputation.

For all the fuss about it, nationalism had much greater difficulty achieving minimally secure objectives after the mid-1960s than during its heyday between the 1890s and the 1920s. Tenacious it certainly was, but it left a record heavily freighted with endemic, in-and-out movements rather than progressively successful ones. On balance, the Cold War superpowers and their local-party allies did well in stymieing nationalism, at least outside their own domains. Indeed, states of all sorts that set their minds to it—Nigeria in Biafra, Indonesia in East Timor, Russia in Chechnya—turned their backs on compromise and exacted a terrible price for nationalist resistance.

Only the wholesale disintegration of the Soviet system proved to be a nationalist bonanza. Between 1989 and 1991, in an updated version of anticolonial nationalism, states that Soviet imperialism had held in place since the end of the Second World War, reasserted independence in the name of a nation's freedom: Hungarians, Poles, Czechs, Slovaks, Romanians, and finally Germans on their way to reunification, with Bulgarians still perched somewhere in limbo. Meanwhile, the Soviet Union itself dissolved into fifteen parts—fundamentally, administrative units that over the decades had shaped and cultivated even more than they had expressed ethnic consciousness within the Soviet domain. Here, far more than in the so-called satellite states, the crucial event was a quick, sometimes overnight transfer of power, jurisdictional unit by jurisdictional unit. Some of these, such as the Baltic states of Lithuania and Estonia and the Transcaucasian states of Armenia and Azerbaijan combined a reasonable ethnic integrity with nationalist aspirations. Others, such as Ukraine and Georgia, merely set boundaries around feuding ethnic opponents with competing political ambitions. Still others, such as Belorus and Kyrgyzstan, expressed no nationalist sentiments of any kind worth mentioning. Finally, the transfer of government powers in units such as Uzbekistan and Turkmenistan simply gave new titles to the old local dictators. The explosion of the Soviet system created a blazing moment of glory, to be sure, but only in a few cases, notably along the Baltic, did strong nationalist movements contribute to the outcome. Interestingly, one of the strongest nationalist impulses emerging out of the old Soviet Union appeared in Russia itself, now a wounded country where past glories and irredentist ambitions meet with especially combustible possibilities.

During the last quarter of the twentieth century, it was nationalism's two most prominent competitors—by now no longer socialism and democracy—that enjoyed the most striking success. Where states seriously deteriorated or even disappeared, warlordism—that is, rule by self-sustaining armies—usually bested nationalism. Power in those settings derived from the ready availability of weapons, their awesome destructiveness, and their ease of use. The rise and fall of the Khmer Rouge hinged on warlord decisions. By the end of the 1980s, Somalia was governed by warlords. With the withdrawal of the Soviet army, so was Afghanistan. "The war in Yugoslavia isn't a nationalist war at all," the public philosopher André Glucksmann shrewdly observed in 1996. "It is a war of the army against civilians. Not a war among armies but a war of a single army, split into groups, against civilians."[6] Characterizing the Bosnian slaughter as a struggle among "warlords," the Czech statesman Václav Havel agreed. As the Balkan cases illustrated, warlordism might overlap with nationalism, bringing now one, now the other into sharper focus. Who could say when during the 1990s the armed factions of Kurds became something other than so many warlords? Hutu warlords thrived in the bush and in the refugee camps. During the 1990s, prospects of peace heightened the warlord qualities of the Irish Republican Army. Nevertheless, nationalism always retained some version of Ernest

Renan's everyday plebiscite: a cause sustained by the continually renewed commitment of its participants. Where the choice boiled down to a gun at your head or a gun in your hand, that crucial element of volunteerism disappeared, and warlordism triumphed.

Nationalism's second and even more potent late twentieth-century competitor, religious mobilization, thrived where states with dwindling legitimacy emptied the public realm of almost everything except force. Religious resources had already played crucial roles in a variety of Asian and African anticolonial campaigns, not because those cultures were inherently spiritual but because holy rituals and transcendent beliefs provided the webs of connection that an imperially dominated civic life precluded. In these settings, no clear line divided religious from nationalist movements. Whatever they were called, they acquired formidable new strength when the combination linked the gods above, the ancestors around, and the ground beneath the living in a network of faith, kinship, and tradition. Tibetan persistence against all the odds illustrates that kind of dogged endurance.

After China occupied Tibet in 1951, its culturally distinct Buddhism supplied the cement for a Tibetan identity; and when China's Cultural Revolution made a shambles of its Buddhist institutions, rebuilding them was the indispensable step in reconnecting Tibet's people. While the Dalai Llama took the cause of Tibetan independence around the world, the purifying magic of Khenpo Jikphun's Buddhism provided a magnetic center for Tibetans inside the country. China's governors, keenly aware of religion's subversive power and severe in repressing it, renewed their assault on Tibetan Buddhism—and hence Tibetan nationalism—at the turn of the twenty-first century.

Nationalism's global surge after the mid-1960s seemed to reaffirm the significance of that alliance. One movement after another fed on religious energies: rigidified Protestant and Catholic commitments in Northern Ireland, essentialist French Catholicism in Quebec, dogmatic Buddhism in Sri Lanka, apocalyptic Judaism in

Israel, and so on. By the 1970s, however, the differences between fervent religious and nationalist movements—indeed their mutual antagonism—predominated, and at the beginning of the 1990s the superior power of the religious movements was being reaffirmed in site after site: triumph in Afghanistan, Islamic political victories in Algeria and Tajikistan, resistance to the Gulf War as a holy cause and disobedience to British law as a holy commandment, surges in Hindu politics and Sikh violence, and much more. Nothing highlighted the transition better than the inspirational drive for a new freedom in Iran.

In its origins, the Iranian Revolution was a latter-day version of the state-dominated nationalism that Japan, Turkey, and Mexico had pioneered: disruptive modernizing forces accelerating under an inept, arbitrary government; a revolution; and a comprehensive national mobilization under new leadership. Anti-imperialism added its influence. First Britain, then the United States, gave Iranians an extended education in great power deception and subversion—what the historian Nikki Keddie has called "the inscrutable ways of Occidentals"—and the American role in eliminating the protorevolutionary government of Mohammed Mosaddeq in 1953 marked it decades before the successful revolution of 1979 as the primary obstacle to an independent Iran.[7]

In the long run-up from the anti-British protests of 1891 to the revolution, secular opposition was as important as religious. In the last years of Reza Shah Pahlavi's corrupt, oppressive regime, a wide range of dissident groups with a host of grievances gathered courage from nationalism's global spread to organize extensive urban networks of resistance that in effect took the city streets away from government police. In the final crisis of 1978–79, however, religion took charge. Tradesmen in their family-rooted *bazaaris*, laborers in and around prayers, the mosques themselves, became beehives of religiously stimulated subversion. Shiite Islam's strict rules against pollution from nonbelievers were superb mobilizers against the Shah's Western, secular proclivities: "For many, Shi'ism and nationalism were part of a single blend."[8] With the towering figure of the Ayatollah Khomeini at its center, the revolutionary government silenced its secular critics and imposed a Shiite theocracy.

At its moment of victory, the Iranian Revolution ranked with the most impressive popular uprisings of the late twentieth century. Opposed by the United States and ignored by the Soviet Union, it not only won against the odds; it promptly consolidated both power and popularity. Through attention to the needs of ordinary Iranians, Khomeini, "a Prophet of the outcasts, [highlighted] the failure of yesterday's generation to take in the poor, to build anything beyond some vulnerable islands of affluence."[9] As a nationalist revolution, however, its legacy was to the say the least ambiguous.

The most obvious beneficiary was Islamic fundamentalism—a congeries of movements to make some readings of the Koran the source for all life's rules and punishments—which rose in the 1970s especially where shallow-rooted, kleptocratic states presided over impoverished Moslem populations. To the poor these movements promised purification: of corrupt government, of violated custom, of holy obligation. What Western observers considered extremism, its constituents called justice. Impetus from the Iranian Revolution helped propel Islamic fundamentalism into the most significant new movement of the late twentieth century, challenging the elite's right to rule from Algeria to Egypt and Turkey, pushing south into Nigeria and the Horn of Africa, swallowing Pan-Arabism in the Middle East, placing its stamp on governments in Afghanistan and Pakistan, and penetrating through Malaysia into Indonesia, and by way of migration affecting Islamic life in Europe and North America.

By its nature Islamic fundamentalism sought holistic answers to comprehensive questions. States were sites of convenience, the vehicles through which a sacred cause worked its will but otherwise mere pausing places in the eventual merger of godliness with government. As Steven Feierman has said of Africa and Partha Chatterjee of India, spiritual sensibilities of all sorts, even those religious impulses tightly bound in particular ethnic groups, never showed patience with geographic boundaries. Appropriately, where people had no clear tradition of state sovereignty, religious movements, not nationalist movements, had the advantage. "In the void left by [a humiliated] Arab nationalism in 1967," Martin Kramer writes, "two ideas of community competed for primacy [in the Middle East]. On the one side stood those who argued that the inhabitants of any one state constituted a distinct people. . . . On the other side stood those who believed that all Muslims constituted a universal political community."[10] The absurdity of the first alternative gave a tremendous push to the second. Targeting the state itself as its opponent, Islamic fundamentalism called upon true believers to transcend the restraints that nationalism would place on them. In general terms, the damage that Islam did to nationalism in an arc from Algeria to Indonesia paralleled the damage that Roman Catholicism had done to nationalism a century earlier in Mediterranean Europe.

Religion also swallowed nationalism inside a burgeoning Hindu movement that rose rapidly to power in India during the 1990s. Dating loosely from anti-British Hindu revivals of the late nineteenth century, an organized movement first appeared in 1925, to remain a minor theme in Indian anticolonialism until it almost disappeared in the flood of outrage over Gandhi's assassination. Much like Islamic fundamentalism in the 1980s, Hindu politics, now pursued through the Bharatiya Janata Party (BJP), set itself as the champion of the dispossessed—low-caste India—against the rule of the elite and as the agent of purification, both spiritual and material, against the corruption of the Congress party establishment. As Islamic fundamentalist parties proved in their battles against notoriously vicious regimes in Algeria and Egypt, these appeals struck just the right popular chords in the India of the mid-1990s and vaulted the BJP into statewide power. But the

Hindu movement's nationalist credentials were exceedingly thin. To the extent the BJP played party politics, it was just one aspiring group among many, all claiming to serve India's best interests. To the extent it set itself apart, it did so by promising to make the state the servant of religion. The same applied to the Sikh movement for a separate religious state, Khalistan, a movement demanding territory from both India and Pakistan that also found new energy early in the 1990s. Pakistan itself, originally a secular Muslim state, acquired more and more of the characteristics of a fundamentalist society in the 1990s, even though its rulers continued to hope that they, not the ulama, would keep control over a heterogeneous, multilingual population. All religions were eligible. In Norway, a Christian Democratic party surfaced at the end of the twentieth century demanding government according to its reading of the Bible. Once nationalism had usually carried religion along with it; now fundamentalism increasingly dragged nationalism in tow. Whatever kept multiethnic India from being a nation would not be overcome by a Hindu theocracy, and whatever made Norway a nation did not require a Christian theocracy.

If brute force and religious discipline had the advantage where states were deteriorating, nationalism showed its greatest strength during the last quarter of the twentieth century in well-established ones. These states, too, experience serious problems meeting their citizens' rising expectations. From a peak somewhere around 1960, public confidence in central governments and other institutional sources of statewide cohesion slid steadily throughout the Western world. Tom Nairn, an expert on nationalism within the United Kingdom, attributed the enduring appeal of separatism there to the weakening reputation of the central state. In the United States a string of opinion polls, beginning approximately with the assassination of John F. Kennedy, traced a long decline in citizen trust not just in government but in almost every overarching institution. The eminent scholar Jacques Revel reports a weakening of French identity and, in tandem, a centrifugal spread of loyalties in France over the last quarter of the twentieth century. Neither the African-born nor the European-born maintained their earlier faith that French culture could, or even should, assimilate former colonials as equal citizens.

At the same time, states of this rank did far more than simply push against a rising tide of skepticism. By several criteria, they grew stronger as the century wound down. Even angry citizens who had purportedly given up on politics continued to press demands on their home governments, which grew in size and scope during the 1980s and 1990s despite official claims that they were contracting. What went by the name of global capitalism also shored up the state system, especially in the core capitalist countries. Crucially dependent on the authority and resources of major Western powers to operate, worldwide business interests needed those states even more than the states needed them. Their alternative—corporate governance, with private armies and global rules—never rose above the level of a grade-B fantasy.

In their internal affairs, these same Western states relied on a politics of negotiation and accommodation. However cynical in spirit and imperfect in execution, they prided themselves in their welcome to a great variety of interests, opened government to the demands from those interests, and oversaw the allocation of rights among them. These were optimum circumstances for late twentieth-century nationalists: an unsympathetic, uninspired, unintimidating government that had an ideological commitment and a reserve of civic strength to keep issues under discussion indefinitely. Appropriately, the United States, the model of such a liberal state, housed its version of this late twentieth-century nationalism: the Nation of Islam, a homegrown movement with much greater authority among American blacks than its small size would suggest.

Although also a religious movement, Black Muslims, reminiscent of the nineteenth-century Mormons, incorporated almost all of nationalism's primary characteristics. According to its founder, Elijah Muhammad, the Nation in microcosm was fulfilling the destiny of the black race, a genetically united people superior in all important respects to their implacable enemy, the white race. Black Muslims not only addressed one another but more important treated one another as members of a single family bent on ensuring its collective welfare. As the family patriarch, Elijah expected to pass his autocratic power to a son, and the man who did inherit the power, Louis Farrakhan, struggled mightily to claim that mantle, if only as the founder's adopted son. With generational continuity came economic continuity: The patriarch held sole control over the family's investments. As one observer summarized it, the Nation's leader "combines both spiritual and secular authority": Members "feel that they belong both to a nation and a government of their own."[11] Indicatively, cadres of Black Muslims acted both to enforce discipline within the family and to screen it against dangers from a corrupt society.

Again like the Mormons before them, Black Muslims originated in a chiliastic vision of impending apocalypse, then settled down to consolidating their secular power. By the same token, Elijah's nationalist demand for five Deep South states as the homeland that the labor of slaves had made the blacks' own slipped quietly from the Nation's agenda. Nevertheless, unlike the Mormons, the Nation of Islam showed no interest in entering an American mainstream. If the Mormons eventually posed as just one more Christian denomination, the Black Muslims planted themselves firmly on the outside by allying with other Muslims—notably with a branch of Elijah Muhammad's great black family that had taken another path and followed his biological son Walter. By all indications, the Nation of Islam represented a long-term nationalist challenge inside the United States, vague in its political objectives perhaps but firm in its separatist values.

A second, more complicated example of late twentieth-century nationalism thriving inside Western society's well-established states developed alongside the formation of the European Union. Rather than endangering the states that joined it, the European Union promised them a new life by relieving them of at least some of the expectations they could not possibly meet. At the same time, it opened the prospect for novel forms of administrative autonomy that might satisfy the nationalist ambitions of such veteran agitators as the Flemish and such newcomers as the Lombardy League Italians. On a global scale, states that tried to construct bicultural or multicultural halfway houses on their own— "consociationalism," it was called—compiled a bleak record. Almost invariably, a taste for autonomy developed into an insistence on separation. Attempts at a confederation of this sort, one scholar noted some years ago, "were made in Lebanon, Yugoslavia, Nigeria, Malaysia, Sri Lanka, India, Northern Ireland, and South Africa," to which should be added Cyprus, Canada, and perhaps the final days of the Soviet Union—scarcely a list to inspire confidence.[12] Unlike states one by one, however, a successful European Union might well accommodate a large measure of communal self-government without forcing the issue of independence and ripping apart a state's complex economic network. In fact, the new EU might allow existing de facto divisions to experiment with a more comfortable level of outright autonomy—between Catholics and Protestants in the Netherlands, for example, who already maintain parallel communities covering their own schools, parties, newspapers, unions, clubs, charities, and much more. As the history of the United States illustrated, a successful confederation does not require loving thy neighbors, only making room for them.

That, however, is just a piece of the picture. A quarter century ago, no one would have predicted the global outcome: Nationalism, which still rolls off almost every western tongue as the most formidable enemy of peace and order, continues its decline, with no prospects of reversing the trend. Although an important force worldwide, it increasingly struggles for a place. Better attuned to spiritual than to theological sources of unity, it has watched one variation after another of religious fundamentalism mobilize people who in another dispensation might well have been nationalists. In each late twentieth-century rerun, it seems, the fundamentalist assassin again kills Gandhi. One critical advantage has been fundamentalism's superior ability in using warlord techniques to tame the warlords. If nationalists by and large still try to outmaneuver the warlords, fundamentalists add plans to outshoot them, too, as the victorious Taliban in Afghanistan neatly illustrate. As if coming full circle, nationalism's brightest prospects on the cusp of the new century lie in its original Western European home. Elsewhere, the odds favor its competitors.

CHAPTER 8

## Thinking about the Future

$B$y the end of the twentieth century the great trio—democracy, socialism, and nationalism—no longer structured public life in any major portion of the world. They had risen together; they fell together. What had once been primary solutions for Europeans and a menu of alternatives for people around the world slipped into a crowd of options. Each continued to have its partisans; each powered movements here and there. But an era of dominance, when the three of them shaped popular aspirations on a global scale, had passed.

A decade earlier, as the Cold War ended with the disintegration of the Soviet Union, each had had reasons for optimism. In many Western circles, especially in the United States, it seemed self-evident that democracy had triumphed. From another vantage point, lifting the Soviet incubus promised new life for a liberal brand of socialism. Nationalist movements on their part took hope from diminishing great-power support for the military dictatorships that were blocking their paths. But everybody's crystal ball proved cloudy. Democracy, always the weakest of the trio outside Western society, had only spotty and ambiguous successes elsewhere in the world. Socialists failed to realize how Europeanized they had become, and how dependent on the Soviet bogeyman to stretch public backing for their comprehensive welfare programs. By the turn of the twenty-first century, liberal socialist parties in such states as Germany, France, and the United Kingdom were still liberal but no longer socialist. As for nationalism, it steadily lost ground in competition with the clerics and the warlords.

For people who pictured the end of the Cold War as winner-take-all, winning was losing. Where elected governments replaced authoritarian ones, a sudden dismantling of old systems caused massive hardship, general disillusionment, and chronic instability. Rather than central opponents facing one another in a familiar contest, hostilities fragmented and diffused. Only officials smitten by superpower hubris, such as the American secretary of defense William Cohen, thought it possible to amass military strength so great that one country could dictate the terms of every battle and overwhelm any opponent in any setting. Not even the gods expected that much. As if he had been lifted from a James Bond movie, Western society's quintessential foe at the turn of the twenty-first century was a single, elusive Saudi, Osama bin Laden, made immensely wealthy by the Western demand for oil, who, it was said, plotted the explosion of unpredictable targets on a global scale.

In the face of challenges that no one can anticipate from a bewildering array of culturally different people, Western society, with the United States in the forefront, has four readily available strategies in response. Three of these come immediately to mind: strengthening the state system against a Pandora's box of rogue rulers, terrorists, fanatics, and nationalists; counting on the universal solvent of global capitalism to eliminate parochial barriers and senseless wars; and promoting human rights against violators worldwide. The fourth—welcoming diversity on a global scale—will require more of an explanation.

Reliance on states has all the advantages of inertia. They are there, they are familiar, they hold immense power, and—some believe—they change in response to the changing needs of their citizens. Outside the wall of states, the argument goes, there is only chaos: the world as Bosnia and the Congo. For the new century, interstate cooperation—through such agencies as the European Union, the North Atlantic Free Trade Agreement, G-8 meetings, and of course the United Nations organization—promises to pool state resources as it tames state egos.

There is some truth to the claim that as democracy, socialism, and nationalism have slipped in significance, an expansive worldwide capitalism has emerged the real victor. Global capitalism functions as the great beekeeper: People swarm and work, then from time to time get shaken out of the hives in return for warding off predators, keeping the field full of flowers, and marketing the honey. According to its advocates, liking or disliking the system is not the point. What matters is that on its own terms it works remarkably well and acts simultaneously as a powerful integrator. Ideologues who believe they are witnessing Late Capitalism stand as monuments to the lure of wishful thinking. Nevertheless, global capitalism is only a supplementary force, not an independent one. Without the network of states sustaining it, it would disintegrate, but without capitalism the states would not. Hence the second strategy is really a big state variation on the first.

Much the same is true of the third stategy, universalizing a western standard of individual rights, which without backing from the major powers would have minimal influence elsewhere in the world. Indeed, the demand for individual rights has grown along with those states. The more powerful states grew, the greater their effect for good or ill on individual citizens, who sought protection in a stronger state with even greater effect for good or ill on individual citizens, who sought protection. . . . To break the cycle, activists try to freeze more and more individual rights in place, as if by fiat they could end the struggle to secure them. For an impressive number of educated westerners, some liberal and some conservative, those rights constitute not just the heart and soul of their own society but equally the measure of the good society everywhere.

The United States has weighed in heavily on the side of all three strategies. Charges that Americans, obsessed with stable states, have no appreciation for the suffering of subject peoples elicit indignant reminders that the United States itself originated in a war against colonial oppression and that in the twentieth century no Western power has more consistently championed anticolonialism. What these apologists conflate is the crucial difference between colonialism as distant rule and colonialism as local subjugation. White Americans fought their revolution as subjects in the first sense and masters in the second. Colonialism as distant rule was fundamentally an issue of just government, and its solution was the independent United States; colonialism as local subjugation was fundamentally an issue of extracting wealth, and its solution was the social upheaval that never happened. Borrowing Carl Becker's famous distinction, it was the difference between home rule and who should rule at home. From the beginning, the American state was dedicated to the rule of white men in both capacities. By and large, Americans have stayed true to their heritage. On the one hand, they have favored dismantling European empires (home rule); on the other, their government has bent every effort to hurry the former colonies into conservative, law-and-order states (who should rule at home). Postcolonial resistance to that state structure has been condemned as mere tribalism.

As a corollary to a world ordered by inviolable states, Americans have been promoting global capitalism with ever greater zeal. Indeed, the recent Clinton administration followed the purest version of global capitalist logic in American history. At the receiving end of this juggernaut, global capitalism got hopelessly entwined with Western-style democracy. In those sections of Europe where socialist empires once ruled, for example, democracy plus capitalism has equaled the most severe and least mitigated economic disaster since the Second World War. In a poor country free elections rarely come free: Letting a Western model of democracy in the front door almost always means letting Western corporate favors in the back. The same billions who have reason to doubt Western sympathy for their political aspirations, in other words, have at least as much—perhaps identical—reason to doubt Western sympathy for their economic plight.

At a glance, the United States has had its greatest success with the third strategy, the promotion of individual rights. Around mid-century the rising importance of individualism in American democracy coincided with its powerful appeal as an export. During the Cold War the level of personal risks and restraints were far higher in China and the Soviet empire than in the major states allied with the United States. Even among the legion of authoritarian states in the so-called Free World, democracy as individualism, especially individualized consumerism, could be stretched to hide a multitude of crimes. If on a global scale the United States defined democracy, then democracy equaled individualism.

At the beginning of the twenty-first century, however, yesterday's prospect looks more and more like tomorrow's dead end. As a universe of limitless consumer choices, individualism mocks people in poverty everywhere. In these settings it completes the trinity: democracy, capitalism, individualism, three aspects of a single burden. As a scheme of mandated rights, individualism pits the privileges of people one by one against the group values by which a large majority of the world's population lives—the very majority Westerners have had the greatest difficulty reaching or even understanding. Adding insult to ignorance, educated Westerners have treat the most popular confrontations with individualism as evidences of a collective insanity. Even as informed an observer as Mark Juergensmeyer cannot resist the tired old saw that has trailed nationalism and now fundamentalism through the late twentieth century: "It is no mystery why religious nationalism has become so popular [at the end of the twentieth century]. In times of social turbulence and political confusion . . . new panaceas abound."[1] Who would guess that Islamic and Hindu fundamentalism appeal particularly to educated young people?

As ways of giving coherence to a world of splintered loyalties and fragmented conflicts, strategies relying on fixed states, global capitalism, and individual rights do not look promising. States, lying awkwardly across the multiple attachments of everyday life and accentuating worldwide differences in privilege and power, institutionalize these problems without providing solutions for them. Weaken the state, goes the warning, and you enter a jungle of terrors. But strengthen the state, it is worth emphasizing, and you repeat the familiar horrors. Actions justified in the name of serving the state have taken a toll of innocents to make the angels weep.

Capitalism knows no authority higher than the transactions comprising it. On a global scale, with only a tiny minority situated to benefit from the results, that self-contained morality scarcely augurs a new harmony. Robbing an individual at gunpoint, we all know, is a felony. But as the social philosopher Zygmunt Bauman notes: "Robbing whole nations of their resources is called 'promotion of free trade'; robbing whole families and communities of their livelihood is called 'downsizing.'"[2] Who polices that? At the point where individualism intersects with capitalism, the effects are even less manageable. Although individualism as an idea has a long history, capitalist individualism as an orientation has no past and little future. The transactions people make do not bind them beyond those transactions. What matters is what happens now, and a now culture, as Christopher Lasch famously labeled it, is a culture of narcissism. Where people's relations are no more than the sum of their market decisions, the best simple summary is

Margaret Thatcher's: "There *is* no society." Projected globally, that is the real jungle.

Individualism as a mandated right simply restates the issue of atomization: from each individual alone to all individuals together. What has placed strains on social cooperation in every rich state in the West would shatter community life elsewhere. In the face of charges that they really want to destroy other cultures, some human rights advocates emphasize how limited their objectives are. They have no desire to change everything, they say, only to empower or protect the oppressed, often women and children. A simple incision, in and out. But no culture survives this kind of surgery: Change the family, change everything else. Universally mandated rights may link an individual to another individual, but they set culture against culture in a battle of survival.

The fourth strategy—the encouragement of diversity—has the advantage of taking as its point of departure the world as it is today. Moreover, it can draw an impressive body of supporting evidence from the past century and a half of the world's history. Indeed, the benefits from diversity lie at the heart of this book's findings. However large or small the focus, the availability of alternative ideologies, religions, and economies—aspirations and opportunities of all sorts—has improved the prospects of social health over and over again; and monopoly, either the passion to achieve one or the power to impose it, has spread terrible blight. As socialists, democrats, or nationalists, as capitalists, communists, or god's annointed agents, true believers with sufficient weapons at their disposal have cut vast, bloody swaths across history. Although the analogy may be a bit overblown, the salutary effects of social and cultural diversity on human welfare suggest a comparison to those of species diversity on planetary life in general. The good news: Diversity seems to be on the rise.

As the political analyst Gidon Gottlieb has said of the grand attempts at global management, the past favorites—"domination and equilibrium—are equally beyond us."[3]

Diversity starts with the proposition that people make decisions for themselves and that initially all of those decisions have equal standing. Economic motivations are not inherently rational and village identities are not inherently backward. Ethnic pride is not the mark of a first-class grudge, a second-class citizen, or a third-class mind; it is simply a choice. Voluntary organizations are a diverse world's lifeblood. Whatever people want, including individualism, they must organize to get. Successful relations in a diverse world do not require people to love or even speak civilly to one another. Only in a weapon-saturated environment would someone assume that angry words automatically escalate into violence. The sequence is wrong: Violence, not anger, is the critical issue. Among the concomitants of diversity is bearing witness against deeply offensive behavior, even screaming to the high heavens in protest. Absolutely nothing argues that we should smile benignly in the face of actions we consider cruel, destructive, and unjust.

Diversity does not mean that anything goes. Groups of people forming a common polity require rules in common, and quite naturally, polities give priority to their perpetuation. A polity relying on democratic procedures, for example, has reason to protect those procedures against groups that would like to destroy them. By the same token, polities control entry and membership, and they set rules about a civic language, that is, the language of education, politics, and governance. Not only do polities have the right to defend themselves; their members have every right to protest to the high heavens against actions anywhere that they consider fundamentally unjust and to mobilize as widely as possible in behalf of their outrage. A genuinely diverse world takes clashing values as a matter of course. In the face of this ceaseless pulling and hauling, Samuel Huntington's rule of thumb is both sound and succinct: "Renounce universalism, accept diversity, and seek commonalities."[4]

Forty years ago the historian David Potter warned us about the dangers of privileging loyalty to the state over other loyalties. At the beginning of the twenty-first century much of the world's population agrees with him. Multiple crisscrossing attachments that sometimes stop short of the state and sometimes transcend it, express what people actually feel and how they actually live. The state has only one of the many stalls in this global marketplace, and its wares have not been moving all that well in recent times.

Diversity certainly contains its share of contradictions and conundrums. At one end of the spectrum, the units of diversity can become too small to sustain any polity. An individualized diversity is a self-defeating absurdity. At the other end, systems that contribute to diversity on a global scale may eliminate it entirely within their own domains and in the process diminish the world's diversity. We have no perfect model, no unambiguous principle of diversity available to us. A commitment to diversity is an orientation, an inclination that we only apply as best we can situation by situation. Perhaps it is appropriate to diversity that no single rule encapsulates it. Favoring diversity, moreover, gives no group the right of acting as its guarantor. One brand of diversity imposed by the strong on the weak would be its ultimate contradiction.

By the same token, small-group identities provide no panaceas. There is no promise they will mitigate the abuse of women and the prostitution of children. Communities as well as countries persecute Gypsies. Fascist cells plot violence against their enemies throughout the Western world. It pays to heed the warning of David Morley and Kevin Robbins about an uncritical "celebration of small nationalism and regionalism, a utopianism of the underdog."[5] No one should ignore the authoritarianism deeply embedded in Ireland's paramilitary groups or the Basque ETA or the Liberation Tigers of Tamil Eelam, all of whom have scorned their squeamish constituents and killed according to the Menshevik rule: First murder the people closest to you. Blaming colonialism or capitalism for all the world's small-group cruelty and violence insults the moral capacities of people everywhere.

Despite its problems, small-scale diversity constitutes the world's best hope. Diversity means chaos only if we call it that; it can function just as well as a solution to chaos: a messy order. The primary enemies of a healthy, adaptive society are not competing small groups but the state itself. It is simply not true that a deep skepticism about the state's beneficence inhibits service to its citizens. If nobody should wish to destroy the entire system of states, nobody should trust a one of them. Who still believes in the honesty of a government statement? Worst of all are the military and religious legions that covet the state's authority. It is worth emphasizing that Islam, Hinduism, and Christianity, each with its own rich tradition of diversity, suffer as much as any victims when their fundamentalist branches use state power to choke off difference. Appropriately, the great trio of democracy, socialism, and nationalism, no longer at the center of affairs, live on as resistance movements, channeling aspirations that the current universe of states has frustrated. Shades of the nineteenth century. By the same token, the most admired humanitarian agencies of our time tackle issues of health, poverty, and empowerment not by way of state policies but through small-group initiatives: They help some people take the next step.

Imagine a world freed from the tyranny of guns and gods where diversity wrestles with diversity in a match of wits and dreams, not life and death.

# Notes

CHAPTER 1
**Thinking about Nationalism**

1. Quoted in Deborah J. Coon, "'One Moment in the World's Salvation': Anarchism and the Radicalization of William James," *Journal of American History* 83 (June 1996): 77.

2. Rupert Emerson, *From Empire to Nation* (Cambridge 1960), 378.

3. Alfred Cobban, *The Nation State and National Self-Determination*, rev. ed. (London 1969 [1945]), 280.

4. Karl R. Popper, *The Open Society and Its Enemies*, 2 vols. (Princeton 1963), II:49.

5. Tom Nairn, *The Break-up of Britain*, rev. ed. (London 1981 [1977]), 359.

6. George Mosse, *Nationalism and Sexuality* (New York 1985), 133; Michael Ignatieff, *Blood and Belonging* (New York 1994), 8.

7. *New Yorker*, 71 (May 8, 1995): 45.

8. Arthur M. Schlesinger, Jr., *The Disuniting of America* (New York 1992), 48.

9. Boyd C. Shafer, *Faces of Nationalism* (New York 1972 [1955]), xiii.

10. Mark Beissinger, "Nationalisms That Bark and Nationalisms That Bite: Ernest Gellner and the Substantiation of Nations," in John A. Hall, ed., *The State of the Nation* (Cambridge, Eng., 1998), 176.

11. Anthony Birch, *Nationalism and National Integration* (London 1989), 7.

12. Richard Handler, *Nationalism and the Politics of Culture in Quebec* (Madison 1988), 41.

13. John Breuilly, *Nationalism and the State*, rev. ed. (Manchester 1993 [1982]), 255, 390.

14. Hannah Arendt, *The Origins of Totalitarianism* (New York 1958), 126.

15. Hakan Wibert, "Self-Determination As an International Issue," in I. M. Lewis, ed., *Nationalism and Self-Determination in the Horn of Africa* (London 1983), 43.

16. Michael Oakeshott, *On Human Conduct* (Oxford 1975), 188.

17. Liah Greenfeld, *Nationalism* (Cambridge, Mass., 1992), 5.

18. Anthony D. Smith, "Toward a Global Culture?" in Mike Featherstone, ed., *Global Culture* (London 1990), 180.

19. Handler, *Nationalism*, 126.

CHAPTER 2

European Origins

1. Charles Tilly, "Migration in Modern European History," in William H. McNeill and Ruth S. Adams, eds., *Human Migration* (Bloomington 1978), 57. Italics in original. William McNeill and Charles Tilly are major influences in my thinking on population and migration.

2. Walter Nugent, *Crossings: The Great Transatlantic Migrations 1870–1914* (Bloomington 1992), 3.

3. David Warren Sabean, *Property, Production, and Family in Neckarhausen, 1700–1870* (New York 1990), 37.

4. Quoted in H. Arnold Barton, *A Folk Divided* (Chapel Hill 1979), 124.

5. K. H. Connell, *The Population of Ireland, 1750–1845* (Oxford 1950), 121.

6. Patrick J. Blessing, "Irish Emigration to the United States, 1800–1920: An Overview," in P. J. Drudy, ed., *The Irish in America* (Cambridge, Eng., 1985), 16.

7. Conrad M. Arensberg, *The Irish Countryman* (New York 1937), 82, 84.

8. Connell, *Population of Ireland*, 119.

9. Jay Dolan, *The Immigrant Church* (Baltimore 1979), 7–8.

10. Philip H. Bagenal, *The American Irish and Their Influence on Irish Politics* (London 1882), 107.

11. Sir William Harcourt, quoted by John A. Murphy, in David Noel Doyle and Owen Dudley Edwards, eds., *America and Ireland, 1776–1976* (Westport 1980), 110.

12. Michael Hughes, *Nationalism and Society: Germany 1800–1945* (London 1988), 2.

13. John Breuilly, "The National Idea in Modern German History," in Breuilly, ed., *The State of Germany* (London 1992), 14.

14. Albert S. Lindemann, *Esau's Tears* (New York 1997), 69.


CHAPTER 3
## Changing Contexts

1. Charles Tilly, "The Emergence of Citizenship in France and Elsewhere," in Tilly, ed., *Citizenship, Identity and Social History* (Cambridge, Eng., 1995), 229.

2. Ernest Gellner, *Nations and Nationalism* (London 1983), 24–25.

3. Arthur E. Bestor, Jr., "Patent-Office Models of the Good Society: Some Relationships between Social Reform and Westward Expansion," *American Historical Review* 58 (April 1953): 505–26.

4. Alexis de Tocqueville, *"The European Revolution" and Correspondence with Gobineau*, trans. and ed. John Lukacs (Garden City 1959), 170.

5. Quoted in Denis Mack Smith, *Mazzini* (New Haven 1994), 154.

6. Cynthia H. Enloe, *Bananas, Beaches, and Bases* (Berkeley 1990), 46.

7. Geoff Eley and Ronald Grigor Suny, eds., *Becoming National* (New York 1996), 23.

8. Charles Jelavich, *South Slav Nationalisms* (Columbus 1990), 263.

9. George W. Stocking, Jr., *Victorian Anthropology* (New York 1987), 148.

10. Greece, the initial site for romantic nationalist gestures, did not develop a genuinely popular movement until around 1900, as Michael Herzfeld shows in his *Ours Once More* (Austin 1982). Earlier, authoritarian elites mapped grand imperial plans without rousing any significant popular interest.


CHAPTER 4
## The Case of the United States

1. Speech of July 9, 1958, Chicago, quoted in H. M. Flint, ed., *Life and Speeches of Stephen A. Douglas* (Philadelphia 1865), 106.

2. Yaron Ezrahi, *The Descent of Icarus* (Cambridge 1990), 69.

3. Alexis de Tocqueville, *Democracy in America*, trans. Henry Reeve and Francis Bowen, ed. Phillips Bradley, 2 vols. (New York 1945 [1835, 1840]), II, 4.

4. Sheldon S. Wolin, *The Presence of the Past* (Baltimore 1989), 153–54.

5. James Bryce, *The American Commonwealth*, ed. Louis M. Hacker, 2 vols. (New York 1959 [1888]), II, 398.

6. Alexander Mackay, *The Western World, or, Travels in the United States in 1846–47*, 2$^d$ ed., 3 vols. (London 1850), I, 285–86.

7. Jack D. Forbes, *Africans and Native Americans*, 2$^d$ ed. (Urbana 1993 [1988]), 96–97.

8. James Silk Buckingham, *The Eastern and Western States of America*, 3 vols. (London 1842), III, 38–39.

9. Count Francesco Arese, *A Trip to the Prairies and in the Interior of North America* [1837–38], trans. Andrew Evans (New York 1934), 9–10.

10. "Speech of . . . June 16, 1858," in *The Lincoln-Douglas Debates of 1858*, ed. Robert W. Johannsen (New York 1965), 14. I have taken some liberties with word order.

11. Brian M. Barry, *Democracy, Power, and Justice* (Oxford 1989), 168.

12. Walker Connor, *Ethnonationalism* (Princeton 1994), 46.

13. Cynthia H. Enloe, *Ethnic Conflict and Political Development* (Boston 1973), 269. Italics in original.

14. Michaela di Leonardo, *The Varieties of Ethnic Experience* (Ithaca 1984), 119.

15. Francis D. Cogliano, *No King, No Popery* (Westport 1995), 60.

16. Richard Gottheil, quoted in Melvin I. Urofsky, *American Zionism from Herzl to the Holocaust* (Garden City 1975), 90.

17. Matthew Frye Jacobson, *Special Sorrows* (Cambridge, Mass., 1995), 15; Edward R. Kantowicz, *Polish American Politics in Chicago, 1880–1940* (Chicago 1975), 169.

18. Quoted in Hans Kohn, *American Nationalism* (New York 1957), 156.

19. Quoted in Robert Bruce Flanders, *Nauvoo* (Urbana 1965), 298.

20. Quoted with approval by the dean of modern Mormon historians, Leonard J. Arrington, in *Great Basin Kingdom* (Salt Lake City 1993), viii.

21. Quoted in Emily Greene Balch, *Our Slavic Fellow Citizens* (New York 1969 [1910]), 398.

22. Ellwood P. Cubberley, *Changing Conceptions of Education* (Boston: Riverdale, 1909), 15–16.

CHAPTER 5
Climax in Europe

1. Arthur S. Link, *Wilson the Diplomatist* (Baltimore 1957), 10.

2. December 9, 1917, quoted in Victor Mamatey, *The United States and East Central Europe, 1914–1918* (Princeton 1957), 162.

3. E. J. Hobsbawm, *The Age of Extremes* (New York 1994), 31.

4. Speech of September 5, 1919, St. Louis, in *The Public Papers of Woodrow Wilson,* ed. Ray Stannard Baker and William E. Dodd, 6 vols. (New York 1925–27), V, 62.

5. C. A. Macartney, *National States and National Minorities* (London 1934), 490.

6. Susan Watkins, *From Provinces into Nations* (Princeton 1991), 178.

7. Declan Kiberd, *Inventing Ireland* (Cambridge, Mass., 1996), 195.

8. Tom Garvin, "The Anatomy of a Nationalist Revolution: Ireland, 1858–1928," *Comparative Studies in Society and History* 28 (July 1986): 468.

9. Ronald Grigor Suny, *The Revenge of the Past* (Stanford 1993), 101.

10. John Higham, "The Mobilization of Immigrants in Urban America," *Norwegian-American Studies* 31 (1986): 22.

11. Walter Lippmann, *Public Opinion* (New York 1922), 365.

12. Henry A. Wallace, *New Frontier* (New York 1934), 263, 20.

13. Smith, *Mazzini,* 13.

14. John Gooch, "Nationalism and the Italian Army, 1850–1914," in Claus Bjorn et al., eds., *Nations, Nationalism, and Patriotism in the European Past* (Copenhagen 1994), 210.

15. Quoted in Cobban, *The Nation State,* 134.

16. Hans-Ulrich Wehler, *The German Empire, 1871–1918,* trans. Kim Traynor (Leamington Spa 1985 [1973]), 105.

17. Arendt, *Origins,* 4.

18. Carolyn P. Boyd, *Historia Patria* (Princeton 1997), xviii.

19. Walter Laqueur, *A History of Zionism* (London 1972), 421.

CHAPTER 6
## Nationalism Worldwide

1. Emerson, *From Empire,* 213.

2. John Lonsdale, in Bruce Berman and Lonsdale, *Unhappy Valley* (London 1992), 463.

3. Donald L. Horowitz, *Ethnic Groups in Conflict* (Berkeley 1985), 61.

4. David G. Marr, *Vietnamese Tradition on Trial, 1920–1945* (Berkeley 1981), 191, 173, 132–33.

5. James S. Coleman, *Nationalism and Development in Africa,* ed. Richard L. Sklar (Berkeley 1994), 138. See also Horowitz, *Ethnic,* 153.

6. Leroy Vail, "Introduction," in Vail, ed., *The Creation of Tribalism in Southern Africa* (London 1989), 16.

7. Masao Maruyama, *Thought and Behaviour in Modern Japanese Politics*, rev. ed., ed. Ivan Morris (New York 1969), 36.

8. Kunio Yanagita, *About Our Ancestors*, trans. Fanny Hagin Mayer and Ishiwara Yasuyo (New York 1988 [1970]), 15.

9. Daikichi Irokawa, *The Culture of the Meiji Period*, ed. Marius B. Jansen (Princeton 1985 [1969]), 287.

10. James W. White, *Political Implications of Cityward Migration* (Beverly Hills 1973), 47.

11. Edwin O. Reischauer, *The Japanese Today* (Cambridge, Mass., 1988), 396.

12. Gordon Berger, "Politics and Mobilization in Japan, 1931–1945," in Peter Duus, ed., *The Cambridge History of Japan. Volume 6: The Twentieth Century* (Cambridge, Eng., 1988), 134.

13. Bernard Lewis, *The Emergence of Modern Turkey*, 2$^d$ ed. (London 1968 [1961]),10.

14. Lewis, *Emergence*, 11.

15. Alan Knight, "Racism, Revolution, and *Indigenismo*: Mexico, 1910–1940," in Richard Graham, ed., *The Idea of Race in Latin America, 1870–1940* (Austin 1990), 96.

16. David Nugent, "Introduction," in Nugent, ed., *Rural Revolt in Mexico and U. S. Intervention* (Durham 1998), 11.

17. From "El Plan Espiritual de Aztlán" (1967), quoted in Armando Navarro, *Mexican American Youth Organization* (Austin 1995), 67, 39.

18. Abd al-Latif Sharara, quoted in Sylvia G. Haim, *Arab Nationalism* (Berkeley 1974), 228.

19. Quoted in George M. Fredrickson, *Black Liberation* (New York 1995), 69.

20. Alexander Crummell, *Africa and America* (Miami, Fla., 1969 [1891]), 46.

21. C. L. R. James, *A History of Pan-African Revolt*, 2$^d$ ed. (Washington, D. C., 1969 [1938]), 79, 82.

22. Quoted in Imanuel Geiss, *The Pan-African Movement*, trans. Ann Keep (London 1974 [1968]), 264.

23. George Padmore, *Pan-Africanism or Communism?* (London 1956), 89.

24. Crummell, *Africa*, 422. See also Wilson Jeremiah Moses, *The Golden Age of Black Nationalism, 1820–1925* (New York 1988 [1978]).

25. James Mayall, "Self-Determination and the OAU," in Lewis, *Nationalism and Self-Determination*, 81.

26. Padmore, *Pan-Africanism*, 22.

27. Mahmood Mamdani, *Citizen and Subject* (Princeton 1996), 292.

28. Lonsdale, in Berman and Lonsdale, *Unhappy Valley*, 329.

29. Ali Mazrui, "African Entrapped: Between the Protestant Ethic and the Leg-

acy of Westphalia," in Hedley Bull and Adam Watson, eds., *Expansion of International Society* (Oxford 1984), 289.

30. David Lan, *Guns and Rain* (London 1985), 222.

31. Partha Chatterjee, *The Nation and Its Fragments* (Dehli 1994), 156.

32. Crawford Young, "Ethnicity and the Colonial and Post-Colonial State in Africa," in Paul Brass, ed., *Ethnic Groups and the State* (Totowa, N.J., 1985), 68.

33. John Markakis, *National and Class Conflict in the Horn of Africa* (Cambridge, Eng., 1987), xvi.

34. Kiberd, *Inventing Ireland*, 101.

35. Kwame Anthony Appiah, *In My Father's House* (New York 1992), 168–69.

36. Geiss, *Pan-African Movement*, 227.

CHAPTER 7
## Global Nationalism

1. Handler, *Nationalism and the Politics of Culture*, 125.

2. Quoted in Alphonso Pinkney, *Red, Black and Green* (New York 1976), 105.

3. Leo Kuper, *The Pity of It All* (Minneapolis 1977), 125.

4. Arthur M. Schlesinger, Jr., *The Imperial Presidency* (Boston 1973), ix.

5. Joseph Rothschild, *Ethnopolitics* (New York 1981), 48.

6. Adam Gopnik, "A Paris Journal," *New Yorker* (Feb. 5, 1996): 36.

7. Nikki R. Keddie and Yann Richard, *Roots of Revolution* (New Haven 1981), 41.

8. Keddie, "The Iranian Revolution in Comparative Perspective," *American Historical Review* 88 (June 1983): 585.

9. Fouad Ajami, in Tawfic E. Farah, ed., *Pan-Arabism and Arab Nationalism* (Boulder 1987), 200.

10. Martin Kramer, "Arab Nationalism: Mistaken Identity," *Daedalus* 122 (Summer 1993): 194.

11. Essien Udosen Essien-Udom, *Black Nationalism* (Chicago 1962), 270.

12. James Kellas, *The Politics of Ethnicity and Nationalism* rev. ed. (New York 1998), 77.

CHAPTER 8
## Thinking about the Future

1. Mark Juergensmeyer, *The New Cold War?* (Berkeley 1993), 194.

2. Zygmunt Bauman, *Globalization* (New York 1998), 123.

3. Gidon Gottlieb, *Nation against State* (New York 1993), 7.

4. Samuel P. Huntington, *The Clash of Civilizations and the Remaking of the World Order* (New York 1996), 318.

5. David Morley and Kevin Robbins, "No Place Like *Heimat*: Images of Home(land) in European Culture," in Eley and Suny, *Becoming National*, 459.

*Bibliographical Essay*

My preparation has been one prolonged lesson at the hands of scholars whose evidence underlies this book and whose interpretations of it have stimulated me to formulate my own. If in the end I did not learn enough, it was certainly not the fault of my teachers. By no means do all of their names appear here, where my primary purpose is to invite further reading. To those missing mentors, I can only offer a general heartfelt thanks, with apologies for the need to be selective.

## GENERAL

The contemporary study of nationalism dates from Karl W. Deutsch, *Nationalism and Social Communication* (Cambridge, Mass., 1953) and in summary form *Nationalism and Its Alternatives* (New York 1969), which link its emergence to a society's development of a sufficiently dense and binding network of communication. Among the many scholars who expanded

Deutsch's ideas into a full-scale correlation of nationalism with modernization, Ernest Gellner attracted the most attention with *Nations and Nationalism* (Oxford 1983), which assigns special weight to modern education. See also his final word on the subject in *Nationalism* (New York 1997) and helpful appraisals of his work in John A Hall, ed., *The State of the Nation* (New York 1998).

The two most influential ideas in recent studies of nationalism come from Benedict Anderson's *Imagined Communities*, rev. ed. (London 1991 [1983]) and Eric Hobsbawm's contributions to Hobsbawm and Terence O. Ranger, eds., *The Invention of Tradition* (Cambridge, Eng., 1983), both of which stress the state's ability to deceive and manipulate. Two important counters to these state-based interpretations of nationalism are Walker Connor, *Ethnonationalism* (Princeton 1994), and Anthony D. Smith, *The Ethnic Origins of Nations* (Oxford 1986). For updated summaries of Smith's views and useful bibliographies, including a list of his own extensive writings, see his *Nations and Nationalism in a Global Era* (Cambridge, Eng., 1995) and his *Nationalism and Modernism* (London 1998). John Breuilly's *Nationalism and the State*, rev. ed. (Manchester 1993) and Richard Handler's *Nationalism and the Politics of Culture in Quebec* (Madison 1988) contain valuable insights into the interplay of nationalist movements and state power. Scholars who make other interesting distinctions between nationalism and the loyalties and impulses around it are: James Kellas, *The Politics of Ethnicity and Nationalism*, rev. ed. (New York 1998); David M. Potter, "The Historian's Use of Nationalism and Vice Versa," in Potter, *The South and the Sectional Conflict* (Baton Rouge 1968), 34–83; Dov Ronen, *The Quest for Self-Determination* (New Haven 1979); Maurizio Viroli, *For Love of Country* (New York 1995). At the other extreme, Margaret Canovan, *Nationhood and Political Theory* (Cheltenham 1996), and Liah Greenfeld, *Nationalism* (Cambridge, Mass., 1992), merge the subject with the essential characteristics of the societies they study.

Some scholars, resisting the widespread impulse to condemn nationalism out of hand, defend it as a right to self-determination: Harry Beran, *The Consent Theory of Political Obligation* (London 1987); Will Kymlicka, *Multicultural Citizenship* (Oxford 1995) and his *Politics in the Vernacular* (New York 2000); David Miller, *On Nationality* (New York 1995); and Michael Walzer, "Nation and Universe," in *Tanner Lectures on Human Values*, vol. 11, ed. Grethe B. Peterson (Salt Lake City 1990), 507–56. Julia Kristeva, *Nations without Nationalism* (New York 1993), and Yael Tamir, *Liberal Nationalism* (Princeton 1993), favor sanitized versions of nationalist sentiment.

Overviews of nationalism have multiplied during the last decade. See, for example, Craig Calhoun, *Nationalism* (Minneapolis 1997); Montserrat Guibernau, *Nationalisms* (Cambridge, Eng., 1996); Ernst B. Haas, *Nationalism, Liberalism and Progress,* 2 vols., (Ithaca 1997–2000); and John Hutchinson, *Modern Nationalism* (London 1994). Compare any of these to their early twentieth-century counterpart, *Nationalism: A Report by a Study Group of Members of the Royal Institute of International Affairs* (London 1939). Three fine collections of short pieces supplement these surveys: John Hutchinson and Anthony D. Smith, eds., *Nationalism* (Oxford 1994), which draws largely from mainstream scholarship, and the same editors' *Nationalism* (New York 2000), which surveys the whole field; and Geoff Eley and Ronald Grigor Suny, eds., *Becoming National* (New York 1996), which ranges more widely among disciplines and points of view. It is harder to extract information specifically about nationalism from two other collections: Homi K. Bhabha, ed. *Nation and Narration* (London 1990), and Andrew Parker et al., eds., *Nationalisms and Sexualities* (New York 1992).

Histories of nationalism are in shorter supply. Carlton J. H. Hayes, *Essays on Nationalism* (New York 1926) and *The Historical Evolution of Modern Nationalism* (New York 1931) are pioneer works that trace its European history through stages from the French Revolution to twentieth-century fascism. Boyd C. Shafer, *Faces of Nationalism* (New York 1972), the bulk of which was published in 1955, relies on social psychology—the dismal science at midcentury—for his interpretations. By far the most useful history is E. J. Hobsbawm, *Nations and Nationalism since 1780*, 2d ed. (Cambridge, Eng., 1992 [1990]), just as hostile as Shafer's account but richly grounded and always attentive to chronology. John A. Armstrong's *Nations before Nationalism* (Chapel Hill 1982), with a particularly interesting analysis of the different roots for nationalism in Islamic and Christian cultures, stands out for the depth of its historical probe, but it is not itself a history.

Other useful studies of a general nature are:

Peter Alter, *Nationalism*, trans. Stuart McKinnon-Evans, 2d ed. (London 1994 [1989]).

Hannah Arendt, *The Origins of Totalitarianism* (New York 1951).

Isaiah Berlin, "Nationalism: Past Neglect and Present Power," in *Against the Current* (New York 1979), 333–55.

Michael Billig, *Banal Nationalism* (London 1995).

Edward Hallett Carr, *Nationalism and After* (London 1945).

Alfred Cobban, *The Nation State and National Self-Determination*, rev. ed. (London1969 [1945]).

Terry Eagleton, Fredric Jameson, Edward W. Said, *Nationalism, Colonialism, and Literature* (Minneapolis 1990), especially the introduction by Seamus Deane.

Thomas Hylland Eriksen, *Ethnicity and Nationalism* (Boulder, Colo., 1993).

Joshua A. Fishman, *Language and Nationalism* (Rowley, Mass., 1972).

Clifford Geertz, "The Integrative Revolution: Primordial Sentiments and Civil Politics in the New States," in Geertz, *The Interpretation of Cultures* (New York 1973), 255–310.

R. D. Grillo, Introduction, in Grillo, ed., *"Nation" and "State" in Europe* (London 1980), 1–30.

John A. Hall and I. C. Jarvie, eds., *Transition to Modernity* (Cambridge, Eng., 1992).

John Hutchinson, *Modern Nationalism* (London 1994).

Elie Kedourie, *Nationalism*, 4th ed. (Oxford 1993 [1960]).

Hans Kohn, *The Idea of Nationalism* (New York 1944).

William H. McNeill, *Polyethnicity and National Unity in World History* (Toronto 1986).

K. R. Minogue, *Nationalism* (New York 1967).

John Plamenatz, "Two Types of Nationalism," in Eugene Kamenka, ed., *Nationalism* (Canberra 1973), 3–20.

Peter Scott, *Knowledge and Nation* (Edinburgh 1990).

Immanuel Wallerstein, "The Construction of Peoplehood: Racism, Nationalism, Ethnicity," in Etienne Balibar and Wallerstein, eds., *Race, Nation, Class* (London 1991), 71–85.

For a different way of addressing these general issues, see my "*Imagined Communities*, Nationalist Experiences," *Journal of the Historical Society* 1 (Spring 2000): 33–63. (Please ignore its opening paragraph, which was written by an anonymous editor.)

## EUROPEAN PEOPLE

Two essays in William H. McNeill and Ruth S. Adams, eds., *Human Migration* (Bloomington 1978), are crucial to the origins of nationalism: McNeill, "Human Migration: A Historical Overview," 3–19; and Charles Tilly, "Migration in Modern European History," 48–72. Also helpful are:

Nicholas Canny, ed., *Europeans on the Move* (New York 1994).

Philip D. Curtin, "Migration in the Tropical World," in Virginia Yans-McLaughlin, ed., *Immigration Reconsidered* (New York 1990).

Anthony Pagden, "The Effacement of Difference: Colonialism and the Origins of Nationalism in Diderot and Herder," in Gyan Prakash, ed., *After Colonialism* (Princeton 1995), 129–52.

Frank Thistlethwaite, "Migration from Europe Overseas in the Nineteenth and Twentieth Centuries," in Herbert Moller, ed.,

*Population Movements in Modern European History* (New York 1964), 73–92.

Charles Tilly, ed., *The Formation of National States in Western Europe* (Princeton 1975).

Basic statements about the hardening of nationalism after 1870 appear in: Eric Hobsbawm, "Mass-Producing Traditions: Europe, 1870–1914," in Hobsbawm and Ranger, eds., *Invention of Tradition*, 263–307; and Hugh Seton-Watson, *Nations and States* (Boulder 1977). See also Ralph Gibson, "The Intensification of National Consciousness in Modern Europe," in Claus Bjorn et al., eds., *Nations, Nationalism, and Patriotism in the European Past* (Copenhagen 1994), 177–97; Miroslav Hroch, *Social Preconditions of National Revival in Europe*, trans. Ben Fowkes (Cambridge, Eng., 1985); and Wolfgang J. Mommsen, "The Varieties of the Nation State in Modern History: Liberal, Imperialist, Fascist and Contemporary Notions of Nation and Nationality," in Michael Mann, ed., *The Rise and Decline of the Nation State* (Oxford 1990), 210–26.

Special efforts to understand the Marxist collision with nationalism include Erica Benner, *Really Existing Nationalisms* (Oxford 1995); Walker Connor, *The National Question in Marxist-Leninist Theory and Strategy* (Princeton 1984); Roman Szporluk, *Communism and Nationalism* (New York 1988); and Pierre Vilar, "On Nations and Nationalism," trans. Elizabeth Fox-Genovese, *Marxist Perspectives* 2 (Spring 1979): 8–30. On the rise of racism, see Daniel J. Kevles, *In the Name of Eugenics* (New York 1985); Maria Sophia Quine, *Population Politics in Twentieth-Century Europe* (London 1996); and George W. Stocking, *Victorian Anthropology* (New York 1987). Stuart Mews, ed., *Religion and National Identity* (Oxford 1982)—particularly Bernard Aspinwall on the Scots, Frances Lannon on Spain, Stella Alexander on Yugoslavia, and R. F. G. Holmes on the Ulster Irish—also illuminates post-1870 European nationalism.

On matters that came to a head between world wars, see C. A. Macartney, *National States and National Minorities* (London

1934), and Catheryn Seckler-Hudson, *Statelessness* (Washington, D.C., 1934). Relevant histories are included in these collections: Hans Rogger and Eugen Weber, eds., *The European Right* (Berkeley 1965), especially Weber on France and Romania and Stanley Payne on Spain; Peter F. Sugar, ed. *Native Fascism in the Successor States 1918–1945* (Santa Barbara 1971); and Sugar and Ivo Lederer, eds., *Nationalism in Eastern Europe* (Seattle 1969), especially Stephen G. Xydis on Greece, George Barany on Hungary, and Peter Brock on Poland.

The following are important studies of particular movements, alphabetically arranged by the territories they cover. Stavro Skendi, *The Albanian National Awakening, 1878–1912* (Princeton 1967). On Belgium, Shepard B. Clough, *A History of the Flemish Movement in Belgium* (New York 1930); Maureen Covell, "Ethnic Conflict, Representation and the State in Belgium," in Paul Brass, ed., *Ethnic Groups and the State* (Totowa, N.J., 1985), 228–61; and Aristide R. Zolberg, "Transformation of Linguistic Ideologies: The Belgian Case," in Jean-Guy Savard and Richard Vigneault, eds., *Les États Multilingues* (Québec 1975), 445–72. On Britain and its offshoots, Anthony Birch, *Nationalism and National Integration* (London 1989); Jack Brand, *The National Movement in Scotland* (London 1978); Linda Colley, *Britons* (New Haven 1992); Christopher Harvie, *Scotland and Nationalism*, 3d ed. (London 1998); Michael Hechter, *Internal Colonialism* (Berkeley 1975); Kenneth O. Morgan, *Rebirth of a Nation, 1880–1980* (New York 1981); Tom Nairn, *The Break-up of Britain*, rev. ed. (London 1981); and Gerald Newman, *The Rise of English Nationalism*, rev. ed. (New York 1997). On the Dutch, Rod Kuiper, "Orthodox Protestantism, Nationalism and Foreign Affairs," in Annemieka Galema et al., eds., *Images of the Nation* (Amsterdam 1993), 39–58. On France, Stanley Hoffmann, "The Nation, Nationalism, and After: The Case of France," *Tanner Lectures on Human Values*, Grethe B. Peterson, ed. (Salt Lake City 1994), XV, 215–82; Brian Jenkins, *Nationalism in France* (Savage, Md., 1990); Maryon

McDonald, *"We Are Not French!"* (New York 1989); and Eugen Weber, *Peasants into Frenchmen* (Stanford 1976). On Greece, see Michael Herzfeld's important *Ours Once More* (Austin 1982), as well as the useful volumes of Martin Blinkhorn and Thanos Veremis, eds., *Modern Greece* (Athens 1990), and of Richard Clogg, ed., *The Greek Diaspora in theTwentieth Century* (Houndmills 1999), esp. Clogg's and Renée Hirschon's contributions. On Italy, Alexander DeGrand, *Italian Fascism*, 3d ed. (Lincoln 2000) and *The Italian Nationalist Association and the Rise of Fascism* (Lincoln 1978); John Gooch, *Army, State, and Society in Italy, 1870–1915* (Basingstoke 1989); Denis Mack Smith, *Mazzini* (New Haven 1994). On Scandinavia, particularly Norway, Denmark, and Finland, Rosalind Mitchison, ed., *The Roots of Nationalism* (Edinburgh 1980). On the Soviet Union, Yuri Slezkine, "The USSR As a Communal Apartment, or How a Socialist State Promoted Ethnic Particularism," *Slavic Review* 53 (Summer 1994): 414–52; Ronald Grigor Suny and Michael D. Kennedy, eds., *Intellectuals and the Articulation of the Nation* (Ann Arbor 1999), esp. the essays by Yuri Slezkine and Andrzej Walicki; and Ronald Grigor Suny, *The Revenge of the Past* (Stanford 1993). On the South Slavs, see Loring M. Danforth, *The Macedonian Conflict* (Princeton 1995); Charles Jelavich, *South Slav Nationalisms* (Columbus 1990); and Andrew Wachtel, *Making a Nation, Breaking a Nation* (Stanford 1998). On Spain and its much-studied regional movements, Carolyn P. Boyd, *Historia Patria* (Princeton 1997); Martin Blinkhorn, "Euskadi: Basque Nationalism in the Twentieth Century," in Bjorn et al., eds., *Nations, Nationalism, and Patriotism*, 213–29; Daniele Conversi, *The Basques, the Catalans, and Spain* (Reno 1997); Juan Díez Medrano, *Divided Nations* (Ithaca 1995); William A Douglass, ed., *Basque Politics and Nationalism on the Eve of the Millennium* (Reno 1999), esp. the pieces by Inaki Zabaleta and Douglass; Marianne Heiberg, *The Making of the Basque Nation* (Cambridge, Eng., 1989); Josep Llobera, "Catalan National Identity: The Dialectics of Past and Present," in Elizabeth Tonkin et al., eds., *History and Ethnicity* (London 1989), 247–61; and Ken Medhurst, *The Basques and Catalans*, 3d rev. ed. (London 1987).


## IRISH NATIONALISM

The best introductions to the subject are D. George Boyce, *Nationalism in Ireland*, 3d ed. (London 1995); Robert Kee, *The Green Flag* (New York 1972); and Kirby A. Miller, *Emigrants and Exiles* (New York 1985), which is a genuinely transatlantic study. The same is true of Eric Foner's valuable article, "Class, Ethnicity, and Radicalism in the Gilded Age: The Land League and Irish-America," *Marxist Perspectives* 1 (Summer 1978): 6–55. Sean Cronin's *Irish Nationalism* (New York 1981), another survey, is particularly useful for its treatment of Northern Ireland in the 1960s and 1970s. Declan Kiberd, *Inventing Ireland* (Cambridge, Mass., 1995) discusses the elusiveness of the nationalist vision.

On the origins of Irish nationalism, see especially Conrad M. Arensberg, *The Irish Countryman* (New York 1937); an expansion of that study, Arensberg and Solon T. Kimball, *Family and Community in Ireland*, 2d ed. (Cambridge, Mass., 1968); and K. H. Connell, *The Population of Ireland, 1750–1845* (Oxford 1950). The path to partition is illuminated by John Hutchinson, *The Dynamics of Cultural Nationalism* (London 1987); Tom Garvin, *Nationalist Revolutionaries in Ireland 1858–1928* (Oxford 1987), or its condensation in Garvin, "The Anatomy of a Nationalist Revolution: Ireland, 1858–1928," *Comparative Studies in Society and History* 28 (July 1986): 468–501; and Thomas Hennessey, *Dividing Ireland* (London 1998). Another set of studies traces a parallel story across the Atlantic: Jay P. Dolan, *The Immigrant Church* (Baltimore 1979); Thomas N. Brown, "The Origins and Character of Irish-American Nationalism," *Review of Politics* 18 (July 1956): 327–58, on the 1850s; William D'Arcy, *The Fenian Movement in the United States: 1858–1886* (Washington, D.C., 1947); T. N. Brown, *Irish-American Nationalism, 1870–1890* (Philadelphia 1966); Lawrence J. McCaffrey, *The Irish Diaspora in America* (Bloomington 1976), especially on the Parnell era; Francis M. Carroll, "America and Irish Political Independence, 1910–33," in P. J. Drudy, ed., *The Irish in America* (Cambridge, Eng., 1985), 271–93; and David Montgomery, "The Irish in the American Labor Movement," in David Noel Doyle and Owen Dudley Edwards, eds., *America and Ireland, 1776–1976* (Westport 1980), 205–18.

Further information is available in:

J. C. Beckett, *A Short History of Ireland,* 6th ed. (London 1979).

Dennis J. Clark, *Irish Blood* (Port Washington 1977).

K. H. Connell, *Irish Peasant Society* (Oxford 1968).

Richard P. Davis, *Irish Issues in New Zealand Politics, 1868–1922* (Dunedin 1974).

D. N. Doyle, *Irish Americans, Native Rights and National Empires* (New York 1976).

Steven P. Erie, *Rainbow's End* (Berkeley 1988).

Michael F. Funchion, *Chicago's Irish Nationalists, 1881–1890* (New York 1976 [1973]).

Henry H. Glassie, *Passing the Time in Ballymenone* (Philadelphia 1982).

Maurice Goldring, *Faith of Our Fathers* (Dublin 1987 [1982]).

Michael A. Gordon, *The Orange Riots* (Ithaca 1993).

Arthur Gribben, ed., *The Great Famine and the Irish Diaspora in America* (Amherst 1999).

Thomas E. Hachey and L. J. McCaffrey, eds., *Perspectives on Irish Nationalism* (Lexington 1989), especially the essays by Hachey and R. V. Comerford.

Oscar Handlin, *Boston's Immigrants,* rev. ed. (Cambridge, Mass., 1959).

T. Hennessey, *A History of Northern Ireland 1920–1996* (London 1997).

Noel Ignatiev, *How the Irish Became White* (New York 1995).

Lynn Hollen Lees, *Exiles of Erin* (Ithaca 1979).

Edward M. Levine, *The Irish and Irish Politicians* (Notre Dame 1966).

L. J. McCaffrey, "Irish Nationalism and Irish Catholicism: A Study in Cultural Identity," *Church History* 42 (December 1973): 1–11.

Timothy J. Meagher, "'Why Should We Care for a Little Trouble or a Walk through the Mud': St. Patrick's and Columbus Day Parades in Worcester, Massachusetts, 1845–1915," *New England Quarterly* 58 (March 1985): 5–26.

Brian P. Murphy, *Patrick Pearse and the Lost Republican Ideal* (Dublin 1991).

Thomas H. O'Connor, *The Boston Irish* (Boston 1995).

Alan O'Day, ed., *Reactions to Irish Nationalism 1865–1914* (London 1987).

Patrick O'Farrell, *The Irish in Australia* (Kensington, NSW, 1986).

Joseph P. O'Grady, *How the Irish Became Americans* (New York 1973).

C. H. E. Philpin, ed., *Nationalism and Popular Protest in Ireland* (Cambridge, Eng., 1987).

Charles C. Tansill, *America and the Fight for Irish Freedom 1866–1922* (New York 1957).

Robert J. Thompson and Joseph R. Rudolph, Jr., "Irish-Americans in the American Foreign-Policy-Making Process," in Mohammed E. Ahrari, ed., *Ethnic Groups and U. S. Foreign Policy* (New York 1987), 135–53.

Timothy Walch, ed., *Immigrant America* (New York 1994), especially the essay by David L. Salvaterra.

James B. Walsh, *The Irish* (New York 1976).

Alan J. Ward, *Ireland and Anglo-American Relations, 1899–1921* (Toronto 1969).

## GERMAN NATIONALISM

The intimate role of the state in blocking and creating German nationalism makes it difficult to extract the history of nationalism from the history of state policies generally. The problems that this mating caused in defining the nation are explored in James J. Sheehan, "What Is German History? Reflections on the Role of the *Nation* in German History and Historiography," *Journal of Modern History* 53 (March 1981): 1–23; and J. Breuilly, "The National Idea in Modern German History," in Breuilly, ed., *The State of Germany* (London 1992), 1–28. See also Diana Forsythe, "German Identity and the Problems of History," in Tonkin et al., eds., *History and Ethnicity*, 137–56; and Pieter M. Judson, *Exclusive Revolutionaries* (Ann Arbor 1996).

The starting point for a study of the struggles to give shape to a German nation is Sheehan's *German History 1770–1866* (Oxford 1989). Brueilly's *The Formation of the First German Nation-State, 1800–1871* (New York 1996) is a superior brief survey. Mack Walker, *German Home Towns* (Ithaca 1971) deepens our understanding of particularism. Michael Hughes, *Nationalism and Society* (London 1988), underlines the weakness of popular nationalism during most of the nineteenth century; the essays by Dieter Düding and Adolf M. Birke in Hagen Schulze, ed., *Nation-Building in Central Europe* (Leamington Spa 1987) add insight into its formlessness. Margaret Lavinia Anderson, *Practicing Democracy* (Princeton 2000), and Helmut Walser Smith, *German Nationalism and Religious Conflict* (Princeton 1995), trace continuing sources of division into the early twentieth century.

Several studies highlight the importance of the 1890s in articulating and hardening German nationalism. See especially Geoff Eley's *Reshaping the German Right* (New Haven 1980) and Hans-Ulrich Wehler's *The German Empire, 1871–1918*, trans. Kim Traynor (Leamington Spa 1985 [1973]). Rogers Brubaker, *Citizenship and Nationhood in France and Germany* (Cambridge, Mass., 1992), and Eley, *From Unification to Nazism* (Boston 1986), supplement that story. German history from 1919 to 1945 virtually merges the study of nationalism with the contests over state power and policy. Attempts to give specificity to German nationalism include Alexander J. De Grand, *Fascist Italy and Nazi Ger-*

*many* (London 1995); Guntram Henrik Herb, *Under the Map of Germany* (New York 1997); Woodruff D. Smith, *The Ideological Origins of Nazi Imperialism* (New York 1986); J. P. Stern, *Hitler* (Berkeley 1975); and George L. Mosse, *The Nationalization of the Masses* (New York 1975).

The experience of Germans in the Western Hemisphere begins with changes in their community life at home. David Warren Sabean, *Property, Production, and Family in Neckarhausen, 1700–1870* (New York 1990), is invaluable. See also Gerhard Wilke and Kurt Wagner, "Family and Household: Social Structure in a German Village between the Two World Wars," in Richard J. Evans and W. R. Lee, eds., *The German Family* (London 1981), 120–47. Dirk Hoerder and Jörg Nagler, eds., *People in Transit* (Cambridge, Eng., 1995), addresses the demographics of German migration. On the separateness of these migrants' lives in the United States, see for example: Kathleen Neils Conzen, "Ethnicity As Festive Culture: Nineteenth-Century German America on Parade," in Werner Sollors, ed., *The Invention of Ethnicity* (New York 1989), 44–76; Conzen, "German-Americans and the Invention of Ethnicity," in Frank Trommler and Joseph McVeigh, eds., *America and the Germans*, 2 vols. (Philadelphia 1985), I, 131–47; Frederick Luebke, *The Bonds of Loyalty* (DeKalb 1974); Linda Schelbitzki Pickle, *Contented among Strangers* (Urbana 1996). On socialist and worker rather than nationalist identities in the cities, see Stuart Bruce Kaufman, *Samuel Gompers and the Origins of the American Federation of Labor, 1848–1896* (Westport 1973); Sally M. Miller, *Victor Berger and the Promise of Constructive Socialism, 1910–1920* (Westport 1973); Stanley Nadel, *Little Germany* (Urbana 1990); and Dorothee Schneider, *Trade Unions and Community* (Urbana 1994).


## ZIONISM

David Vital's authoritative three-volume study—*The Origins of Zionism* (Oxford 1980 [1975]), *Zionism: The Formative*

*Years* (Oxford 1982), and *Zionism: The Crucial Years* (Oxford 1987)—is fair, well written, and teleological. Walter Laqueur, *A History of Zionism* (London 1972), is also an intelligent account. Ben Halpern, *The Idea of the Jewish State*, 2d ed. (Cambridge, Mass., 1969), is particularly useful on differences within the movement. George L. Mosse, *Confronting the Nation* (Hanover 1993), singles out Jewish nationalism as the only good one.

Albert S. Lindemann, *Esau's Tears* (New York 1997), and Jacob Talmon, *Myth of the Nation and Vision of Revolution* (Berkeley 1981), examine sources for Zionism, and Shmuel Almog, *Zionism and History*, trans. Ina Friedman (New York 1987), explores the movement's fragmented beginnings. On Ahad Ha'am, see Steven J. Zipperstein's *Elusive Prophet* (Berkeley 1993). Halpern, *A Clash of Heroes* (New York 1987), details the struggle between Weizmann and Brandeis and in the process takes us to the United States.

*American Zionism from Herzl to the Holocaust* (Garden City 1975) by Melvin I. Urofsky, an expert on Brandeis, surveys the field effectively. Yonathan Shapiro, *Leadership of the American Zionist Organization 1897–1930* (Urbana 1971), is much harsher on the Brandeis circle. Essays by Sarah Schmidt and Carol Bosworth Kutscher in Urofsky, ed., *Essays in American Zionism* (New York 1978) illuminate aspects of the pivotal years around the First World War. See also "Democracy versus the Melting Pot," in Horace Kallen, *Culture and Democracy in the United States* (New York 1924), 67–125. Peter Grose, *Israel in the Mind of America* (New York 1983), also sides with Weizmann, this time against his hard-line opponents during the Second World War.

In its contrast to European experiences, the American anti-Semitism that John Higham reviews in *Send These to Me*, rev. ed. (Baltimore 1984), especially pp. 153–74, serves as backdrop to Jewish culture in the United States. The anecdotes in Leonard Dinnerstein, *Antisemitism in America* (New York 1994), do not substantially alter the comparative mildness of that picture. Jenna Weiss-

man Joselit, *The Wonders of America* (New York 1994), empha-
sizes the centrality of family life in a consumer culture, and Steven
M. Cohen, *American Modernity and Jewish Identity* (New York
1983), traces the effect of such adaptations into the 1970s. David
A. Hollinger, "Jewish Intellectuals and the De-Christianization of
American Public Culture in the Twentieth Century," in Hollinger,
*Science, Jews, and Secular Culture* (Princeton 1996), 17–41, an-
alyzes one triumph in that process. See also David Soyer, *Jewish
Immigrant Associations and American Identity in New York,
1880–1939* (Cambridge, Mass., 1997).

Charles D. Smith, *Palestine and the Arab-Israeli Conflict*, 3d ed.
(New York 1996), includes a clear account of the founding of Is-
rael. Erskine B. Childers, "The Wordless Wish: From Citizens to
Refugees," in Ibrahim Abu-Lughod, ed., *The Transformation of
Palestine* (Evanston 1971), 165–202, describes the systematic removal of Palestinians from their homes. See also Benny Morris,
ed., *The Birth of the Palestinian Refugee Problem, 1947–1949*
(Cambridge, Eng., 1987), and his *1948 and After* (Oxford 1990),
both much milder critiques; and Avi Shlaim, *The Iron Wall* (New
York 2000). Inis L. Claude, *National Minorities* (Cambridge, Mass.,
1955), provides a postwar context of Big Power callousness toward ethnic cleansing. For other Jewish concerns about Palestinians, see Nira Yuval-Davis, "National Reproduction and 'the Demographic Race' in Israel," in Yuval-Davis and Floya Anthias, eds.,
*Woman-Nation-State* (New York 1989), 92–109.

The effects of Israel on Jewish American consciousness, especially after 1967, are revealed in Gabriel Sheffer, "Political Aspects
of Jewish Fund-Raising for Israel," in Sheffer, ed., *Modern Dias-
poras in International Politics* (New York 1986), 258–93; Stuart
Svonkin, *Jews against Prejudice* (New York 1997); and Urofsky,
*We Are One!* (Garden City 1978), the second volume in his history
of American Zionism and itself a document on the subject. For the
parallel collapse of institutional anti-Semitism in the United States,
see Dan A. Oren, *Joining the Club* (New Haven 1985).

## THE UNITED STATES

With only a few exceptions I have not duplicated my extensive bibliographical essay on the many subjects relating to American democracy in *Self Rule* (Chicago 1995).

Several scholars have used citizenship and ethnicity as ways of talking about the distinctive characteristics of American society. Richard D. Brown, *The Strength of a People* (Chapel Hill 1996), emphasizes major changes in citizenship early in the nineteenth century. Linda K. Kerber, "The Meaning of Citizenship," *Journal of American History* 84 (December 1997): 833–54, and Rogers M. Smith, *Civic Ideals* (New Haven 1997), analyze limitations and biases. John Higham has devoted a distinguished career to the place of ethnicity in American history. His *Strangers in the Land*, 2d ed. (New Brunswick 1988) remains indispensable; his essay, "From Process to Structure: Formulations of American Immigration History," in Peter Kivisto and Dag Blanck, eds., *American Immigrants and Their Generations* (Urbana 1990), 11–41, is a recent reconsideration giving special attention to the relations between class and ethnicity. Other broad views include John Bodnar, *The Transplanted* (Bloomington 1985); K. N. Conzen et al., "The Invention of Ethnicity: A Perspective from the U.S.A.," *Journal of American Ethnic History* 12 (Fall 1992): 3–41; Oscar Handlin, *The Uprooted* (Boston 1952); Donald L. Horowitz, "Immigration and Group Relations in France and America," in Horowitz and Gérard Noiriel, eds., *Immigrants in Two Democracies* (New York 1992), 3–35; and Walter Nugent, *Crossings* (Bloomington 1992). George M. Fredrickson, "America's Diversity in Comparative Perspective," *Journal of American History* 85 (December 1998): 859–75, places the accent on race. In *Whiteness of a Different Color* (Cambridge, Mass., 1998), Matthew Jacobson combines race, ethnicity, and citizenship in a single synthesis. Efforts to deal with these factors without losing track of what has held American society together include Higham, "Multiculturalism and Universalism: A History and Critique," *American Quarterly* 45 (June 1993): 195–219; David A. Hollinger, *Postethnic America* (New York 1995), and Michael Walzer, *What It Means to Be an American* (New York 1992).

The following studies illuminate the complex interplay between America and Europe in the making and remaking of ethnic identities. For the experience of Norwegian migrants, see Carl Chrislock, *Ethnicity Challenged* (Northfield 1981); Odd S. Lovell, ed., *Cultural Pluralism versus Assimilation* (Northfield 1977); Jane Marie Pederson, *Between Memory and Reality* (Madison 1992); and April R. Schultz, *Ethnicity on Parade* (Amherst 1994). Accounts of other people's experiences include Dag Blanck, *Becoming Swedish-American* (Uppsala 1997); Stanislaus A. Blejwas, "Polonia and Politics," in John J. Bukowczyk, ed., *Polish Americans and Their History* (Pittsburgh 1996), 121–51; Dino Cinel, *From Italy to San Francisco* (Stanford 1982); and Annemieke Galema, *Frisians to America, 1880–1914* (Groningen 1996). Donna R. Gabaccia's *Militants and Migrants* (New Brunswick 1988) traces Sicilians, and Robert P. Swierenga's *Faith and Family* (New York 2000) follows the waves of Dutch migrants.

On the transoceanic conflicts between and among groups, see for example, Ronald H. Bayor, *Neighbors in Conflict* (Baltimore 1978); Francis D. Cogliano, *No King, No Popery* (Westport 1995); Keith P. Dryud, *The Quest for the Rusyn Soul* (Philadelphia 1992); and Victor Greene, *For God and Country* (Madison 1975). The following are particularly sensitive studies of how immigrants and their offspring worked out their destinies inside the United States: Michaela Di Leonardo, *The Varieties of Ethnic Experience* (Ithaca 1984); Suzanne Model, "The Ethnic Niche and the Structure of Opportunity: Immigrants and Minorities in New York City," in Michael B. Katz, ed., *The "Underclass" Debate* (Princeton 1993), 161–93; John T. McGreevy, *Parish Boundaries* (Chicago 1996); and Judith E. Smith, *Family Connections* (Albany 1985). See also M. Jacobson, *Special Sorrow* (Cambridge, Mass., 1995).

Whether ethnicity has value in understanding contemporary America has stirred hot debate. Stephen Steinberg, *The Ethnic Myth*, rev. ed. (Boston 1989), and Brackette Williams, "A Class Act: Anthropology and the Race to Nation across Ethnic Terrain," *Annual Review of Anthropology* 18 (1989): 401–44, condemn its use. Richard D. Alba, *Ethnic Identity* (New Haven 1990), and Herbert Gans, "Symbolic Ethnicity: The Future of Ethnic Groups and Cultures in America," *Ethnic and Racial Studies* 2 (January 1979): 1–20, emphasize its weaknesses. Werner Sollors, *Beyond Ethnicity* (New York 1986), offers the concept qualified support; J. Fishman et al., *Ethnicity in America* (Binghamton 1985); Nathan Glazer and Daniel Patrick Moynihan, *Beyond the Melting Pot*, 2d ed. (Cambridge, Mass., 1970); and Rudolph J. Vecoli, "Ethnicity and Immigration," in Stanley I. Kutler, ed., *Encyclopedia of the United States in the Twentieth Century*, 4 vols. (New York 1996), I: 161–93, are impressed by ethnicity's strength. Vecoli and Russell A. Kazal, "Revisiting Assimilation: The Rise, Fall, and Reappraisal of a Concept in American Ethnic History," *American Historical Review* 100 (April 1995): 437–71, provide overviews.

Like ethnicity, with which it is sometimes paired, race in American history has been exceedingly difficult to grasp whole. Attempts to orient us include Michael Banton, *The Idea of Race* (Boulder 1977); Barbara J. Fields, "Ideology and Race in American History," in J. Morgan Kousser and James M. McPherson, eds., *Region, Race, and Reconstruction* (New York 1982), 143–77; and Thomas F. Gossett, *Race* (New York 1963). James Campbell and James Oakes, "The Invention of Race: Rereading *White over Black*," *Reviews in American History* 21 (March 1993), 172–83, remind us of the importance Winthrop Jordan's pioneering book placed on Thomas Jefferson's ideas. Comparisons across space offer another broad view. G. M. Fredrickson's study of America and South Africa, *White Supremacy* (New York 1981), is exemplary. Anthony W. Marx, *Making Race and Nation* (New York 1998), adds Brazil to his account of racism as rational self-interest.

Another overview moves across color lines. The theme of Carey McWilliams, *Brothers under the Skin* (Boston 1943)—that racism has looked much the same everywhere in American history—continues to dominate scholarly studies. See, for example, John W. Dower, *War without Mercy* (New York 1986); Bill Ong Hing, *Making and Remaking Asian America through Immigration Policy, 1850–1990* (Stanford 1993); Michael H. Hunt, *Ideology and U. S. Foreign Policy* (New Haven 1987), ch. 3; Francis Jennings, *The Invasion of America* (Chapel Hill 1975); and especially Ronald Takaki, *A Different Mirror* (Boston 1993). Studies of the first half of the twentieth century provide strong evidence for this point of view. See, for example, how the evidence accumulates from Roger Daniels, *Asian Americans* (Seattle 1988); David H. Fowler, *Northern Attitudes toward Interracial Marriage* (New York 1987); Mark Haller, *Eugenics* (New Brunswick 1984 [1963]); Desmond King, *Separate and Unequal* (Oxford 1995); Elizabeth Lasch-Quinn, *Black Neighbors* (Chapel Hill 1993); Walter Benn Michaels, *Our America* (Durham 1995); Peggy Pascoe, "Miscegenation Law, Court Cases, and Ideologies of 'Race' in Twentieth-Century America," *Journal of American History* 83 (June 1996): 44–69; and Vernon J. Williams, Jr., *Rethinking Race* (Lexington 1996). Paul R. Spickard, *Mixed Blood* (Madison 1989), however, tells a more complicated story, as do two interesting articles on the ambiguities of color and race: James R. Barrett and David Roediger, "In Between Peoples: Race, Nationality and the 'New Immigrant' Working Class," *Journal of American Ethnic History* 16 (1997): 3–44; and Robert Orsi, "Religious Boundaries of an In-Between People: Street *Feste* and the Problem of the Dark-Skinned 'Other' in Italian Harlem," *American Quarterly* 44 (September 1992): 313–47. Histories of race as a way of understanding differences among European migrants have yet to be written. David Folkmar, *Dictionary of Races or Peoples* (Washington, D.C., 1911), offers a peek.

It is scarcely possible to overemphasize the significance of slavery to the history of race in the United States before the First

World War. David Brion Davis's *Slavery and Human Progress* (New York 1984) helps to orient us, and William Dusinberre's *Them Dark Days* (New York 1996) and James Oakes's *The Ruling Race* (New York 1982) remind us about the institution's operation. Ira Berlin, *Many Thousands Gone* (Cambridge, Mass., 1998), provides an overview of slavery in North America; Leon F. Litwack, *Trouble in Mind* (New York 1998), traces its aftermath into the pit of Jim Crow. See also Peter Kolchin's comparison of slavery with serfdom, *Unfree Labor* (Cambridge, Mass., 1987).

Nationalism has served scholars less well as a point of departure. Hans Kohn's *American Nationalism* (New York 1957) sought an American spirit, much as his contemporaries did: Max Lerner's *America As a Civilization* (New York 1957) and Daniel J. Boorstin's *The Americans*, 3 vols. (New York 1958–73), for example. L. Greenfeld, *Nationalism*, (Cambridge, Mass. 1992) picks up in that tradition. Stuart McConnell, "Nationalism," in Kutler, ed., *Encyclopedia of the United States*, I: 251–71, shows an admirable command of the literature on the subject. Several recent studies explore the rites and rituals of patriotism under the rubric of nationalism. See, for example, Bodnar, *Remaking America* (Princeton 1992); McConnell, *Glorious Contentment* (Chapel Hill 1992); Simon P. Newman, *Parades and the Politics of the Streets* (Philadelphia 1997); Cecilia Elizabeth O'Leary, *To Die for* (Princeton 1999); Len Travers, *Celebrating the Fourth* (Amherst 1997); and David Waldstreicher, *In the Midst of Perpetual Fetes* (Chapel Hill 1997). David R. Shumway's interesting study of American literature as a nationalist artifact—*Creating American Civilization* (Minneapolis 1994)—belongs in this category. John R. Gillis, *A World of Their Own* (New York 1996), explains how this public culture of celebration thinned out in the twentieth century. The scholarship on celebration has paid particular attention to a general American consciousness late in the eighteenth century, a phenomenon that these studies also treat as nationalism: T. H. Breen, "Ideology and Nationalism on the Eve of the American Revolution:

Revisions *Once More* in Need of Revising," *Journal of American History* 84 (June 1997): 13–39; Richard L. Merritt, *Symbols of American Community, 1735–1775* (New Haven 1966); and Max Savelle, "Nationalism and Other Loyalties in the American Revolution," *American Historical Review* 67 (July 1962): 901–23. Another familiar way of construing nationalism is to equate it with comprehensive state policies. See, for example, Gary Gerstle, "Theodore Roosevelt and the Divided Character of American Nationalism," *Journal of American History* 86 (December 1999): 1280–1307, and Michael Lind, *The Next American Nation* (New York 1995). Imperialism as nationalism is also a common approach. Anders Stephanson's *Manifest Destiny* (New York 1995) is a recent example.

Southern nationalism has been just as difficult to bring into focus. A sample of approaches includes Avery O. Craven, *The Growth of Southern Nationalism, 1848–1861* (Baton Rouge 1953); Drew Gilpin Faust, *The Creation of Confederate Nationalism* (Baton Rouge 1988); Eugene Genovese, *The World the Slaveholders Made* (New York 1965); John McCardell, *The Idea of the Southern Nation* (New York 1979); Michael P. Johnson, *Toward a Patriarchal Republic* (Baton Route 1977); and William R. Taylor, *Cavalier and Yankee* (New York 1961). Books that expose the limitations of Southern nationalism include Eric Foner, *Reconstruction* (New York 1988); Gaines M. Foster, *Ghosts of the Confederacy* (New York 1987); Harold M. Hyman, *A More Perfect Union* (New York 1973); Charles R. Lee, Jr., *The Confederate Constitutions* (Chapel Hill 1963); and Mitchell Snay, *Gospel of Disunion* (New York 1993).

The literature on the Mormons is more straightforward. Among contributors to the picture of Mormonism as mainstream American are Leonard Arrington and David Bitton, *The Mormon Experience*, 2d ed. (Urbana 1992); Klaus J. Hansen, *Mormonism and the American Experience* (Chicago 1981); Jan Shipps, *Mormonism* (Urbana 1985); and Grant Underwood, *The Millenarian World of Early Mormonism* (Urbana 1993). Studies that emphasize the clash between Mormonism and prevailing American values include Robert Bruce Flanders, *Nauvoo* (Urbana 1965); Terryl L. Givens, *The Viper on the Hearth* (New York 1997); "How to Become a People: The Mormon Scenario," in R. Laurence Moore, *Religious Outsiders and the Making of Americans* (New York 1986), 25–47; and Kenneth H. Winn, *Exiles in a Land of Liberty* (Chapel Hill 1989).

Arthur S. Link, *Wilson the Diplomatist* (Baltimore 1957), for the defense, and N. Gordon Levin, Jr., *Woodrow Wilson and World Politics* (New York 1968), for the prosecution, set the agenda of debate over the champion of self-determination years ago. In *Modernity and Power* (Chicago 1994), Frank A. Ninkovich, a more appreciative critic, assigns great historical importance to Wilson. For a recent account of the much-studied intervention in revolutionary Russia, see David S. Foglesong, *America's Secret War against Bolshevism* (Chapel Hill 1995). Derek Heater, *National Self-Determination* (New York 1994), and Victory Mamatey, *The United States and East Central Europe, 1914–1918* (Princeton 1957), guide us from old empires to new states. See also Lawrence E. Gelfand, *The Inquiry* (New Haven 1963). Together, Mohammed E. Ahrari, ed., *Ethnic Groups and U. S. Foreign Policy* (New York 1987); Louis L. Gerson, *The Hyphenate in Recent American Politics and Diplomacy* (Lawrence 1964); Joseph P. O'Grady, ed., *The Immigrants' Influence on Wilson's Peace Policies* (Lexington 1967); and Abdul Aziz Said, ed., *Ethnicity and U. S. Foreign Policy*, rev. ed. (New York 1981), are eloquent on the ineffectuality— the sound and fury—of ethnic pressures on the peace process. The effects of war and peace on ethnic groups varied considerable. J. Higham, "The Mobilization of Immigrants in Urban America," *Norwegian-American Studies* 31 (1986): 3–33, and Rivka Shpak Lissak, *Pluralism and Progressives* (Chicago 1990), discuss a strengthened ethnicity in cities; Jon Gjerde, *The Minds of the West* (Chapel Hill 1997), describes a dismantling in the rural Midwest. On different conceptions and assessments of Americanization, see Gary Gerstle, "Liberty, Coercion, and the Making of Americans," *Journal of American History* 84 (September 1997): 524–58; Dietrich Herrmann, *"Be an American!"* (Frankfurt 1996); and John F. McClymer, "The Americanization Movement and the Education of Foreign-Born Adults, 1914–25," in Bernard J. Weiss, ed., *American Education and the European Immigrant: 1849–1940* (Urbana 1982), 96–116.

## NATIONALISM WORLDWIDE

Modernization theory has construed nationalism worldwide as the outcome of European influences—sometimes a direct borrowing, sometimes an indirect consequence of economic penetration. In either case, European-rooted concepts and practices generally apply with little variation. Anderson, Gellner, and Hobsbawm have been the leading influences. Paul Brass's overview, *Ethnicity and Nationalism* (New Dehli 1991), for example, borrows from all three. The exceptions usually turn the story on its head and treat postcolonial nationalism in Africa and Asia as an embittered reaction, evidence of a failure to keep pace in a modernizing world. S. N. Eisenstadt's *Revolution and the Transformation of Societies* (New York 1978) is a leading example.

Edward Said's immensely influential *Orientalism* (New York 1978) is the most common point of departure in challenging this approach. Some have attacked the leading European-grounded modernizers frontally. See, for example, James M. Blaut, *The National Question* (London 1987); Partha Chatterjee, *Nationalist Thought and the Colonial World* (London 1986); and Sally Falk Moore, "The Production of Cultural Pluralism As a Process," *Public Culture* 1 (1989): 26–49. A series of articles in *Comparative Studies in Society and History* nicely illustrates the spirit and substance of these clashing approaches: Gyan Prakash, "Writing Post-Orientalist Histories of the Third World: Perspectives from Indian

Historiography," 32 (April 1990): 383–408; Rosalind O'Hanlon and David Washbrook, "After Orientalism: Culture, Criticism, and Politics in the Third World," 34 (January 1992): 141–67; and Prakash, "Can the 'Subaltern' Ride? A Reply to O'Hanlon and Washbrook," ibid., 168–84. Daniel A. Segal and R. Handler, "How European Is Nationalism? *Social Analysis* 32 (December 1992): 1–15, and Handler, "Is 'Identity' a Useful Cross-Cultural Concept?" in J. R. Gillis, ed., *Commemorations* (Princeton 1994), 27–40, raise fundamental questions less polemically. However, as penetrating as these criticisms of exported European concepts have been, they have not articulated an alternative way of generalizing about nationalism outside of the Western world. Perhaps by design, particularism triumphs.

Two excellent examinations of that particularism are Donald L. Horowitz, *Ethnic Groups in Conflict* (Berkeley 1985), and Joseph Rothschild, *Ethnopolitics* (New York 1981), both directly relevant to a study of nationalism. See also P. C. Emmer and Magnus Mörner, eds., *European Expansion and Migration* (New York 1992), and Jumari Jayawardena, *Feminism and Nationalism in the Third World* (London 1986).


## SOUTH ASIANS

Judith M. Brown, *Modern India*, 2d ed. (Oxford 1994), is an excellent survey up to independence. See also Brown's one-volume biography, *Gandhi* (New Haven 1989), and Richard G. Fox's *Gandhian Utopia* (Boston 1989) for the limitations of this extraordinary man's vision and tactics. Partha Chatterjee's *The Nation and Its Fragments* (Princeton 1993) is an imaginative re-creation of Indian nationalism's private sources. C. A. Bayly, *Origins of Nationality in South Asia* (Dehli 1998), and John R. McLane, *Indian Nationalism and the Early Congress* (Princeton 1977), examine the roots of nationalism, and Joan M. Jensen, *Passage from India* (New Haven 1988), notes its early appearance among migrants in North America. P. R. Brass, *Language, Religion and Politics in North India* (London 1974); Leonard A. Gordon, *Bengal: The Nationalist Movement 1876–1940* (New York 1974); and Francis Robinson, *Separatism among Indian Muslims* (London 1974) set the stage for partition. Also see the interesting exchange between Brass and Robinson in David Taylor and Malcolm Yapp, eds., *Political Identity in South Asia* (London 1979), 35–77, where religion provides the key in both accounts. Stephen P. Cohen, "State Building in Pakistan," in Ali Banuazizi and Myron Weiner, eds., *The State, Religion and Ethnic Politics* (Syracuse 1986), 299–332, deals with the ambiguities of a secular Islamic state. Harry Goulbourne, *Ethnicity and Nationalism in Post-Imperial Britain* (Cambridge, Eng., 1991), and Peter van der Veer, *Religious Nationalism* (Berkeley 1994), extend the story of communal division into the 1990s.

On India's island neighbor Sri Lanka, the essays by Robert I. Rotberg, Chris Smith, and David Little in Rotberg, ed., *Creating Peace in Sri Lanka* (Washington, D. C., 1999), 1–56, provide an excellent introduction, belying the book's hopeful title. Robert N. Kearney and Barbara Diane Miller, *Internal Migration in Sri Lanka and Its Social Consequences* (Boulder 1987), includes important background information, and K. M. De Silva, *Religion, Nationalism, and the State in Modern Sri Lanka* (Tampa 1986) focuses on the political origins of conflict. Bruce Kapferer, *Legends of People, Myths of State* (Washington, D. C., 1988), judges nationalism in Sri Lanka by western standards, and Michael Roberts, "Nationalism, the Past and the Present: The Case of Sri Lanka," *Ethnic and Racial Studies* 16 (January 1993): 133–66, warns against just that.


## JAPANESE

Volume 5 (1989, ed. Marius B. Jansen) and Volume 6 (1988, ed. Peter Duus) of *The Cambridge History of Japan* are basic resources for the nineteenth and twentieth centuries, especially politics. Delmer Brown, *Nationalism in Japan* (Berkeley 1955), applies a modernization model. Michio Umegaki, "Epilogue: National Identity, National Past, National Isms," in James W. White, ed., *The Ambivalence of Nationalism* (Lantham, Md., 1990), 251–64; White, *Migration in Metropolitan Japan* (Berkeley 1982); and Kunio Yanagita, *About Our Ancestors—The Japanese Family System*, trans. Fanny Hagin Mayer and Ishiwara Yasuyo (New York 1988 [1970]), combine to form a context for Japanese nationalism. The crucial importance of elite policies between the 1880s and the 1910s emerges clearly from Carol Gluck, *Japan's Modern Myths* (Princeton 1985); Helen Hardacre, *Shinto and the State, 1868–1988* (Princeton 1985); and Daikichi Irokawa, *The Culture of the Meiji Period*, ed. M. B. Jansen (Princeton 1985 [1969]). Kevin M. Doak, "What Is a Nation and Who Belongs? National Narratives and the Ethnic Imagination in Twentieth-Century Japan," *American Historical Review* 102 (April 1997): 283–309; and Fred C. Notehelfer, "Ktoku Shsui and Nationalism," *Journal of Asian Studies* 31 (November 1971): 31–39, discuss an early twentieth-century nationalism in tension with the state. See also Kosaku Yoshino, *Cultural Nationalism in Contemporary Japan* (London 1992). Akira Iriye, *After Imperialism* (Cambridge, Mass., 1965); Masao Maruyama, *Though and Behaviour in Modern Japanese Politics*, ed. Ivan Morris, rev. ed. (New York 1969); and Richard J. Smethurst, "Japan's First Experiment with Democracy, 1868–1940," in George Reid Andrews and Herrick Chapman, eds., *The Social Construction of Democracy* (New York 1995), 71–89, guide us into the Second World War; and John Dower, *Embracing Defeat* (New York 1999); I. I. Morris, *Nationalism and the Right Wing in Japan* (London 1960); and Edwin O. Reischauer, *The Japanese Today* (Cambridge, Mass., 1988), tell different stories of postwar changes and continuities.

Peter Duus, "Nagai Ryotar and the 'White Peril,' 1905–1944," *Journal of Asian Studies* 31 (November 1971): 41–48; M. B. Jansen, *The Japanese and Sun Yat-sen* (Cambridge, Mass., 1954); and Mark R. Peattie, "Japanese Attitudes toward Colonialism, 1895–1945," in Ramon H. Myers and Peattie, eds., *The Japanese Colonial Empire, 1985–1945* (Princeton 1984), are helpful on Pan-Asianism, its variants and corruptions.

In *Chinatown and Little Tokyo* (Millwood, N.Y., 1986), Stanford Morris Lyman highlights Japanese American adaptability. On the complex story of Issei attachment to Japan and isolation from it, as well as the Nisei leadership in fixing a Japanese American identity, see Brian Masaru Hayashi, *"For the Sake of Our Japanese Brethren"* (Stanford 1995); John Modell, "The Japanese American Family: A Perspective for Future Investigation," *Pacific Historical Review* 37 (February 1968): 67–82, and "Tradition and Opportunity: The Japanese Immigrant in America," ibid. (May 1971): 163–82; and Sylvia Junko Yanagisako, *Transforming the Past* (Stanford 1985). R. Daniels, *Concentration Camps USA* (New York 1971), with its pinpointing title, remains the standard account of Japanese American imprisonment. Despite its title, Charlotte Brooks, "In the Twilight Zone between Black and White: Japanese American Resettlement and Community in Chicago, 1942–1945," *Journal of American History* 86 (March 2000): 1655–87, describes a strikingly smooth reentry into American society, even during wartime. See also Lon Kurashige, "The Problem of Biculturalism: Japanese American Identity and Festival before World War II," ibid., 1632–54.

## MEXICANS

The strength throughout the nineteenth century of both regionalism and localism and the consequent weakness of a separate Mexican identity emerge from Timothy E. Anna, *Forging Mexico 1821–1835* (Lincoln 1998); D. A. Brading, *The Origins of Mexican Nationalism* (Cambridge, Eng., 1985 [1973]), and "Liberal

Patriotism and the Mexican Reforma," *Journal of Latin American Studies* 20 (May 1988): 27–48; Daniel Cosío Villegas, *The United States Versus Porifio Díaz*, trans. Nettie Lee Benson (Lincoln 1963 [1956]); and Jaime E. Rodríguez O., *The Independence of Spanish America* (New York 1998).

The starting point for a study of the revolution is Alan Knight, *The Mexican Revolution*, 2 vols. (Cambridge, Eng., 1986), in combination with his "The Peculiarities of Mexican History: Mexico Compared to Latin America, 1821–1992," *Journal of Latin American Studies* 24 (supplement 1992): 99–144; and "The Rise and Fall of Cardenismo, c.1930–c.1946," in Leslie Bethel, ed., *Mexico since Independence* (Cambridge, Eng., 1991), 241–320. For an alternative reading, see John Womack, Jr., "The Mexican Revolution, 1910–1920," in ibid., 125–200, which should be compared with his much more sanguine *Zapata and the Mexican Revolution* (New York 1969). See also Douglas W. Richmond, *Venustiano Carranza's Nationalist Struggle, 1893–1920* (Lincoln 1983). Diane E. Davis, "Uncommon Democracy in Mexico: Middle Classes and the Military in the Consolidation of One-Party Rule, 1936–1946," in Andrews and Chapman, eds., *Social Construction of Democracy*, 161–92, ends Mexico's revolutionary phase on a positive note. Specifically on the shaping influence of the United States, see D. Cosío Villegas, *American Extremes*, trans. John P. Harrison (Austin 1964); Friedrich Katz, *The Secret War in Mexico*, trans. Loren Goldner (Chicago 1981); A. Knight, "The United States and the Mexican Peasantry, circa 1880–1940," in Daniel Nugent, ed., *Rural Revolt in Mexico and U. S. Intervention* (Durham, N.C., 1998), 25–63; and Robert Freeman Smith, *The United States and Revolutionary Nationalism in Mexico, 1916–1932* (Chicago 1972).

For aspects of Mexico's brief ethnonationalist project, see Shirley Brice Heath, *Telling Tongues* (New York 1972), A. Knight, "Racism, Revolution, and *Indigenismo*: Mexico, 1910–1940," in Richard Graham, ed., *The Idea of Race in Latin America, 1870–*

*1940* (Austin 1990), 71–113; Florencia E. Mallon, *Peasant and Nation* (Berkeley 1995); and Nancy Leys Stepan, *The Hour of Eugenics* (Ithaca 1991). Regional, local, and cultural resistance is discussed in A. Knight, "Peasants into Patriots: Thoughts on the Making of the Mexican Nation," *Mexican Studies* 10 (Winter 1994): 135–61, and "Popular Culture and the Revolutionary State in Mexico, 1910–40," *Hispanic American Historical Review* 74 (August 1994): 393–444; and Claudio Lomnitz-Adler, *Exits from the Labyrinth* (Berkeley 1992). For the persistence of that resistance, see for example, Roger Bartra, *The Cage of Melancholy*, trans. Christopher J. Hall (New Brunswick 1992); Michael Kearney, "Mixtec Political Consciousness: From Passive to Active Resistance," in Nugent, ed., *Rural Revolt*, 134–46, and the section on Mayan peoples in Manning Nash, *The Cauldron of Ethnicity in the Modern World* (Chicago 1989). Ronald P. Dore's brief in Japan's behalf, "Latin America and Japan Compared," in John J. Johnson, ed., *Continuity and Change in Latin America* (Stanford 1967), 227–49, addresses issues relevant to the Mexican case.

The best guide to the experiences of Mexican Americans in towns and the countryside is *Anglos and Mexicans in the Making of Texas, 1836–1986* (Austin 1987); the best guide to their urban experiences is George J. Sánchez, *Becoming Mexican American* (New York 1993). See also Josef J. Barton's forthcoming study of Mexican peoples in motion, *The Edge of Endurance*. Andrés Reséndez, "National Identity on a Shifting Border: Texas and New Mexico in the Age of Transition, 1821–1848," *Journal of American History* (September 1999): 668–88, shows the limitations of the conqueror-conquered model; Robert F. Heizer and Alan J. Almquist, *The Other Californians* (Berkeley 1971), demonstrates that model's applicability. Walker Connor, ed., *Mexican-Americans in Comparative Perspective* (Washington, D.C., 1985); David G. Gutiérrez, *Walls and Mirrors* (Berkeley 1995); and Armando Navarro, *Mexican American Youth Organization* (Austin 1995), make sense out of the historical inconsequence of Mexican American nationalism. In "The New Era of Mexican Migration to the United States," *Journal of American History* 86 (September 1999): 518–36, Jorge Durand, Douglas S. Massey, and Emilio A. Parrado suggest the hardening of a Mexican American identity.

## PAN-ARABISM

C. Ernest Dawn's *From Ottomanism to Arabism* (Urbana 1973) and his reconsideration, "The Origins of Arab Nationalism," in Rashid Khalidi et al., eds., *The Origins of Arab Nationalism* (New York 1991), 3–30, construe Pan-Arabism as a response to western imperialism. Zeine N. Zeine, *The Emergence of Arab Nationalism*, 3d ed. (Delmar, N.Y., 1973), examines its indigenous sources, and Munif al-Razzaz, *The Evolution of the Meaning of Nationalism*, trans. I. Abu-Lughod (Garden City, N.Y., 1963), illustrates that spirit. See also Sylvia G. Haim, ed., *Arab Nationalism* (Berkeley 1974 [1962]). Janet Abu-Lughod, "Recent Migrations in the Arab World," in W. McNeill and R. S. Adams, eds., *Human Migration*, 225–38, has useful contextual information. Martin Kramer's *Islam Assembled* (New York 1986), reveals how little support the early twentieth-century versions enjoyed, and his "Arab Nationalism: Mistaken Identity," *Daedalus* 122 (Summer 1993): 171–206, explores its weaknesses generally. The battle over its legacy continues. See for example, Tawfic E. Farah, ed., *Pan-Arabism and Arab Nationalism* (Boulder 1987), and Bassam Tibi, *Arab Nationalism*, trans. Marion Farouk-Sluglett and Peter Sluglett, 3d ed. (London 1997). Rashid Khalidi, *Palestinian Identity* (New York 1997), traces the Arab-based nationalist movement that did catch fire.

On Turkish nationalism, see David Kushner, *The Rise of Turkish Nationalism 1876–1908* (London 1977), and especially Bernard Lewis, *The Emergence of Modern Turkey*, 2d ed. (London 1968 [1961]). On Iranian nationalism, see Nikki R. Keddie, "The Iranian

Revolution in Comparative Perspective," *American Historical Review* 88 (June 1983): 579–98, and Keddie and Yann Richard, *Roots of Revolution* (New Haven 1981).

## PAN-AFRICANISM AND BLACK NATIONALISM

The best guides to what may or may not have been precursers to black nationalism and Pan-Africanism in the United States are Floyd J. Miller, *The Search for a Black Nationality* (Urbana 1975); Wilson Jeremiah Moses, *The Golden Age of Black Nationalism, 1820–1925* (New York 1988 [1978]); and Sterling Stuckey, *Slave Culture* (New York 1987). Alexander Crummell's *Africa and America* (Miami 1969 [1891]), expresses the spirit of these ventures. For the Caribbean sources of twentieth-century movements, see Winston James, *Holding Aloft the Banner of Ethiopia* (London 1998), and especially Orlando Patterson, "Migration in Caribbean Societies: Socioeconomic and Symbolic Resource," in W. McNeill and R. S. Adams ed., *Human Migration*, 106–45.

The Garveyite branch of Pan-Africanism has yet to find its historian. E. David Cronon, *Black Moses* (Madison 1969 [1955]), is still a useful narrative. Judith Stein's *The World of Marcus Garvey* (Baton Rouge 1986) is more wide-ranging and more hostile. John Henrik Clarke, ed., *Marcus Garvey and the African Vision* (New York 1974), stresses the later, futile years; Robert A. Hill and Barbara Bair, eds., *Marcus Garvey, Life and Lessons* (Berkeley 1987), emphasizes his lessons, not his life. George M. Fredrickson, *Black Liberation* (New York 1995), provides a transcontinental overview. See also Hill and Gregory A. Pirio, "'Africa for the Africans': The Garvey Movement in South Africa, 1920–1940," in Shula Marks and Stanley Trapido, eds., *The Politics of Race, Class and Nationalism in Twentieth-Century South Africa* (London 1987), 209–53. Emory J. Tolbert, *The UNIA and Black Los Angeles* (Los

Angeles 1980), illustrates how contentious everything about Garvey was. For the migration feeding Garveyism, see James R. Grossman, *Land of Hope* (Chicago 1989), and Nicholas Lemann, *The Promised Land* (New York 1991). Carol Stack's *All Our Kin* (New York 1974) and her *Call to Home* (New York 1996) describe how blacks reconstructed kinship in the course of migrating.

Imanuel Geiss, *The Pan-African Movement*, trans. Ann Keep (London 1974 [1968]), is a solid chronicle of the branch that ran from W. E. B. DuBois to Kwame Nkrumah. See also Colin Legun, *Pan-Africanism*, rev. ed. (New York 1965), a document from the movement with valuable information on its arrival in postcolonial Africa. A further sample of Pan-Africanism writings includes Nnamdi Azikiwe, *Renascent Africa* (London 1968 [1937]); DuBois, *Africa* (Millwood, N.Y., 1977 [1930]); the final chapter in C. L. R. James, *A History of Pan-African Revolt*, 2d ed. (Washington, D.C., 1969 [1938]), a revealingly retitled revison of his *A History of Negro Revolt* (1938); and George Padmore, *Pan-Africanism or Communism?* (London 1956). On Padmore, see also James R. Hooker's *Black Revolutionary* (1967). On the collapse of this Pan-Africanism, see James Mayall, "Self-Determination and the OAU," in I. M. Lewis, ed., *Nationalism and Self-Determination in the Horn of Africa* (London 1983), 77–92.

The thinness of an American black audience for African affairs before the 1960s is revealed in Joseph E. Harris, *African-American Reactions to War in Ethiopia, 1936–1941* (Baton Rouge 1994); Brenda Gayle Plummer, *Rising Wind* (Chapel Hill 1996); William R. Scott, *The Sons of Sheba's Race* (Bloomington 1993); and Penny M. Von Eschen, *Race against Empire* (Ithaca 1997). James T. Campbell's *Songs of Zion* (New York 1995) traces a deeper Christian level of involvement. For the explosion of American interest in black nationalism during the 1960s, see Stokely Carmichael and Charles V. Hamilton, *Black Power* (New York 1967), Harold Cruse, *The Crisis of the Negro Intellectual* (New York 1967), and Alphonso Pinkney, *Red, Black and Green* (New

York 1976). More recent expressions that emphasize a diasporic nationalism include Molefi Kete Asante, *Afrocentricity* (Trenton 1988 [1980]), and Josephine Moraa Moikobu, *Blood and Flesh* (Westport 1981). The most useful studies of the Nation of Islam are Claude Andrew Clegg III, *An Original Man* (New York 1997); Essien Udosen Essien-Udom, *Black Nationalism* (Chicago 1962); and Mattias Gardell, *In the Name of Elijah Muhammad* (Durham 1996). See also Joe Wood, ed., *Malcolm X in Our Own Image* (New York 1992).

## NIGERIANS

Despite its incredible optimism, Harold D. Nelson, ed., *Nigeria, A Country Study*, 4th ed. (Washington, D.C., 1982), contains a wealth of basic information. Michael Crowder, *West Africa* (London 1968), remains a sound introduction. So is John E. Flint, "Nigeria: The Colonial Experience from 1880 to 1914," in Lewis H. Gann and Peter Guignan, eds., *Colonialism in Africa 1870–1960*, 5 vols. (Cambridge, Eng., 1969–75), I: 220–60. Robert Heussler's *The British in Northern Nigeria* (London 1968) is that rarity, a brief in behalf of British rule. J. R. V. Prescott's *The Evolution of Nigeria's International and Regional Boundaries* (Vancouver 1971) is a fascinating factual study in imperial geography.

Larry Diamond, *Class, Ethnicity and Democracy in Nigeria* (Syracuse 1988), traces the fall of the original republic. See also Richard L. Sklar, *Nigerian Political Parties* (Princeton 1963). Robert Melson and Howard Wolpe, eds., *Nigeria* (East Lansing 1971), and S. K. Panter-Brick, *Soldiers and Oil* (London 1978), mark the path into civil war. Different aspects of Nigerian segmentation are examined in Michael S. O. Olisa and Odinchezo M. Ikejiani Clark, eds., *Azikiwe and the African Revolution* (Onitsha 1989), and J. D. Y. Peel, *Aladura* (London 1968) and his "The Cultural Work of Yoruba Ethnogenesis," in Tonkin et al., eds., *History and Eth-*

*nicity*, 198–215. Richard A. Joseph, *Democracy and Prebendal Politics in Nigeria* (Cambridge, Eng., 1987), discusses the impoverished civic life of the short-lived Second Republic; A. A. Ujo, *Citizenship in Nigeria* (Kaduna 1994), lays a foundation of hope for the Third. Okwudiba Nnoli, *Ethnic Politics in Nigeria* (Enugu 1978), attacks Nigerian particularism from the left; Joseph A. Umoren, *Democracy and Ethnic Diversity in Nigeria* (Lantham, Md., 1996), attacks it from an Afrocentric perspective. Setting aside its misleading title, Karl Maier, *This House Has Fallen* (New York 2000), provides useful background on contemporary problems in Nigeria.

## AFRICANS

Three standard accounts identify nationalism in Africa with its colonial boundaries and its postcolonial states: James S. Coleman, "Tradition and Nationalism in Tropical Africa," in Coleman, *Nationalism and Development in Africa*, ed. R. L. Sklar (Berkeley 1994), 117–52; Basil Davidson, *The Black Man's Burden* (New York 1992); and Thomas Hodgkin, *Nationalism in Colonial Africa* (New York 1965 [1956]). Two others emphasize the distorting effects of that colonial legacy: Mahmood Mamdani, *Citizen and Subject* (Princeton 1996), and Ali Mazrui, "Africa Entrapped: Between the Protestant Ethic and the Legacy of Westphalia," in Hedley Bull and Adam Watson, eds., *Expansion of International Society* (Oxford 1984), 289–308. How colonialism distorted cultural differences is the subject of Peter Ekeh's valuable essay, "Social Anthropology and Two Contrasting Uses of Tribalism in Africa," *Comparative Studies in Society and History* 32 (October 1990): 660–700, and Crawford Young's informed summary, "Ethnicity and the Colonial and Post-Colonial State in Africa," in P. Brass, ed., *Ethnic Groups*, 57–93. See also Young's *The Politics of Cultural Pluralism* (Madison 1976) and his valuable bibliographical essay, "Nationalism, Ethnicity, and Class in Africa: A Retrospect," *Cahiers d'Études africaines* 26 (1986): 421–95. Leo Kuper, *The Pity of It All* (Minneapolis 1977), and Benyamin Neuberger, *National Self-Determination in Postcolonial Africa* (Boulder 1986), report on the grim consequences in various settings.

Attempts to reconsider the relationship between European concepts and African realities include Frederick Cooper, "Conflict and Connection: Rethinking Colonial African History," *American Historical Review* 99 (December 1994): 1516–45; John Markakis, *National and Class Conflict in the Horn of Africa* (Cambridge, Eng., 1987); and T. Ranger, "The Invention of Tradition Revisited: The Case of Colonial Africa," in Ranger and Olufemi Vaughan, eds., *Legitimacy and the State in Twentieth-Century Africa* (London 1993), 62–111. I. M. Lewis and other contributors to Lewis, ed., *Nationalism and Self-Determination*, are clear about the sharp separation of state and nation in the Horn of Africa. P. F. De Moraes Farias and Karin Barber, as editors of *Self-Assertion and Brokerage* (Birmingham, Eng., 1990), explore the possibility of liminal figures mediating the creation of an indigenous nationalism in Africa, an approach that in very different ways Jean Marie Allman's *The Quills of the Porcupine* (Madison 1993) applies to Asanti nationalism, David Lan's *Guns and Rain* (London 1985) applies to Shona nationalism, and John Lonsdale's chapters 11 and 12 of Bruce Berman and Lonsdale, *Unhappy Valley* (London 1992), apply to Kikuyu nationalism.

More or less in the alphabetical order of their African settings, here are other useful works: Richard A. Joseph, *Radical Nationalism in Cameroun* (Oxford 1977); Kwame Anthony Appiah, *In My Father's House* (New York 1992), especially chapter 8 on Ghanaian life inside a crumbling state; Sharon Stichter, *Migrant Labour in Kenya* (London 1985); and also on people in Kenya, Susan Pederson, "National Bodies, Unspeakable Acts: The Sexual Politics of Colonial Policy Making," *Journal of Modern History* 63 (December 1991): 647–80. On a related subject, see Helen Callaway, "Purity and Exotica in Legitimating the Empire: Cultural Constructions of Gender, Sexuality and Race," in Ranger and Olufemi, eds., *Legitimacy and the State*, 31–61; Gérard Prunier, *The Rwanda Crisis*, 2d ed. (London 1998). In South Africa, two studies help understand Afrikaner nationalism: T. Dunbar Moodie, *The Rise of Afrikanerdom* (Berkeley 1975), and D. J. Kotzé, *Nationalism* (Cape Town 1981). On black African nationalism there, see the introduction to Marks and Trapido, eds., *Politics of Race, Class and Nationalism*, 1–70; Peter Delius, *A Lion amongst the Cattle* (Johannesburg 1996); and the excellent essay by Leroy Vail and Landeg White, "Tribalism in the Political History of Malawi," in Vail, ed., *The Creation of Tribalism in Southern Africa* (London 1989), which deals with it tangentially. On Tanzania, see two superior studies: Steven Feierman, *Peasant Intellectuals* (Madison 1990), and Goran Hyden, *Beyond Ujamaa in Tanzania* (Berkeley 1980). Also see, T. Ranger, *The Invention of Tribalism in Zimbabwe* (Gweru 1985), and *Peasant Consciousness and Guerrilla War in Zimbabwe* (Berkeley 1985). Finally on French colonialism, a subject underrepresented in my study, two books help to fill the gap: William B. Cohen, *The French Encounter with Africans* (Bloomington 1980), and Gwendolyn Wright, *The Politics of Design in French Colonial Urbanism* (Chicago 1991).

## ASIANS

Chalmers A. Johnson, *Peasant Nationalism and Communist Power* (Stanford 1962), is still a basic on Chinese nationalism. See also Prasenjit Duara, *Rescuing History from the Nation* (Chicago 1995), Germaine A. Hoston, *The State, Identity, and the National Question in China and Japan* (Princeton 1994), and especially James L. Watson, "Rites or Beliefs? The Construction of a Unified Culture in Late Imperial China," in Lowell Dittmer and Samuel S. Kim, eds., *China's Quest for National Identity* (Ithaca

1993), 80–103. On Chinese in migration, see Clarence E. Glick, *Sojourners and Settlers* (Honolulu 1980); Ung-Ho Chin and Minority Rights Group, *The Chinese of South-East Asia*, 3d ed. (London 2000); Edgar Wickberg, "The Chinese As Overseas Migrants," in Judith M. Brown and Rosemary Foot, eds., *Migration* (New York 1994), 12–37; and Judy Yung, *Unbound Feet* (Berkeley 1995). Elsewhere in Asia, Rupert Emerson, *From Empire to Nation* (Cambridge, Mass., 1960), is still helpful. See also Michael Adas, *Prophets of Rebellion* (Chapel Hill 1979); Benedict Anderson, "Cacique Democracy in the Philippines: Origins and Dreams," in Vincente L. Rafael, ed., *Discrepant Histories* (Philadelphia 1995), 3–50; David Brown, *The State and Ethnic Politics in Southeast Asia* (London 1994); Melvyn C. Goldstein and Matthew T. Kapstein, eds., *Buddhism in Contemporary Tibet* (Berkeley 1998); David G. Marr, *Vietnamese Anticolonialism 1885–1925* (Berkeley 1971), and *Vietnamese Tradition on Trial, 1920–1945* (Berkeley 1981); and Thongchai Winichakul, *Siam Mapped* (Honolulu 1994). Roland L. Guyotte and Barbara M. Posadas, "Celebrating Rizal Day: The Emergence of a Filipino Tradition in Twentieth-Century Chicago," in Ramón A. Gutiérrez and Geneviève Fabre, eds., *Feasts and Celebrations in North American Ethnic Communities* (Albuquerque 1995), 111–27, describes an event shared across the Pacific; and Linda Basch, Nina Glick Schiller, and Cristina Szanton Blanc, *Nations Unbound* (Langhorne, Pa., 1994), examines loyalties among migratory people of color with dual homes.

## RECENT TRENDS

Echoing the 1690s, the 1790s, and the 1890s, the 1990s were filled with end-of-the-century intimations of impending catastrophe. Three with special relevance to the study of nationalism are Benjamin R. Barber's relentlessly pessimistic *Jihad versus McWorld* (New York 1995), an account of people everywhere complicit in their own disempowerment; Samuel P. Huntington's Spenglerian *The Clash of Civilizations and the Remaking of the World Order* (New York 1996), a thoughtful examination of the globe's deep divisions with a Ridley Scott epilogue; and Robert Kaplan's enthusiastically gloomy trilogy, *Balkan Ghosts* (New York 1993), *The Ends of the Earth* (New York 1996), and *The Coming* Anarchy (New York 2000). In "Peoples against States: Ethnopolitical Conflict and the Changing World System," *International Studies Quarterly* 38 (September 1994): 347–77, Ted Robert Gurr counters the catastrophism of Huntington and Kaplan, only to add evidence of his own in Gurr and Barbara Harff, *Ethnic Conflict in World Politics* (Boulder 1994). Stephen Holmes, "Liberalism for a World of Ethnic Passions and Decaying States," *Social Research* 61 (Fall 1994): 599–610, and Michael Ignatieff, *Blood and Belonging* (New York 1994) and his *The Warrior's* Honor (New York 1998), are equally grim on the state of the world. Sometimes the worst news is in the title: William Pfaff, *The Wrath of Nations* (New York 1993), and Michael Walzer, "The New Tribalism: Notes on a Difficult Problem," *Dissent* 39 (Spring 1992): 164–72, are by no means eye-rolling condemnations. Crawford Young, "The Dialectics of Cultural Pluralism: Concept and Reality," in Young, ed., *The Rising Tide of Cultural Pluralism* (Madison 1993), 3–35, is a useful overview of what others deplore.

Religious fundamentalism under one label or another has elicited particular concerns. See Mark Juergensmeyer, *The New Cold War?* (Berkeley 1993), and Bassam Tibi, *The Challenge of Fundamentalism* (Berkeley 1998). Dale E. Eickelman, "From Here to Modernity: Ernest Gellner on Nationalism and Islamic Fundamentalism," in John A. Hall, ed., *The State of the Nation* (New York 1998), 258–71, is a cooler account.

Making sense out of globalization has preoccupied scholars and pundits of various persuasions. Thomas Friedman's *The Lexus and the Olive Tree* (New York 1999) gives a cheery account of an American-led globalization. By contrast, Zygmunt Bauman's *Glob-*

*alization* (New York 1998) pictures an amoral few dominating the rest. Between the two, Saskia Sassen, *Losing Control?* (New York 1996), inventories some of the basic unanswered questions in a globalized future. In a volume that I did not encounter until after I had drafted my text, Carole Fink, Philipp Gassert, and Detlef Junker, eds., *1968* (New York 1998), interpret all the uprisings of that year as aspects of a global fight for freedom. Philip Schlesinger, *Media, State and Nation* (London 1991), especially chapter 8, explores the meaning of contemporary communication to popular movements, and Kenneth Cmiel, "The Emergence of Human Rights Politics in the United States," *Journal of American History* 86 (December 1999): 1231–50, analyzes the way a cause gets promoted through modern media. Stuart Hall, "Old and New Identities, Old and New Ethnicities," in Anthony D. King, ed., *Culture, Globalization and the World-System* (Minneapolis 1997), 41–68, and Anthony D. Smith, "Toward a Global Culture?" in Mike Featherstone, ed., *Global Culture* (London 1990), 171–92, put their fingers on the other end of the scale, emphasizing rootedness and adaptability in human culture.

A sample of studies on nationalism in the realm of the European Union, beyond those already cited under country names, includes Michael Keating's challenge to the old Marxist cliché, "Do the Workers Really Have No Country?" in John Coakley, ed., *The Social Origins of Nationalist Movements* (London 1991); exemplary essays on a much-discussed alternative to nationalism by Val Lorwin and Arend Lijphart, in Kenneth D. McRae, ed., *Consociational Democracy* (Toronto 1974); E. A. Tiryakian and R. Rogowsky, eds., *New Nationalisms of the Developed West* (Boston 1985); and Patrick Weil's prediction of a xenophobic reaction to the new union, "Nationalities and Citizenships: The Lessons of the French Experience for Germany and Europe," in David Cesarani and Mary Fulbrook, eds., *Citizenship, Nationality, and Migration in Europe* (London 1996), 74–87. Charles Kupchan, ed., *Nationalism and Nationalities in the New Europe* (Ithaca 1995), and Robert

Pynsent, *Questions of Identity* (London 1994), illustrate the confusion the issue generates.

In addition to the studies by Will Kymlicka, David Miller, and Michael Walzer already cited, general cautions about state centralization and encouragements to ethnic diversity include Gidon Gottlieb, *Nation against State* (New York 1993); John Gray, "After the New Liberalism," *Social Research* 61 (Fall 1994): 720–35; Patricia Mayo, *The Roots of Identity* (London 1974); and James C. Scott, *Seeing Like a State* (New Haven 1998). In the American context, Lawrence H. Fuchs, *American Kaleidoscope* (Hanover, N.H., 1990), describes assertions of diversity; M. Elaine Burgess, "The Resurgence of Ethnicity: Myth or Reality?" *Ethnic and Racial Studies* 1 (July 1978): 265–85, vouches for their authenticity; and Philip Gleason, *Speaking of Diversity* (Baltimore 1992), explains how cultural diversity became incorporated in an American self-understanding. Where multiculturalism is used as a code word for race, Richard Bernstein, *The Dictatorship of Virtue* (New York 1994), and Arthur M. Schlesinger, Jr., *The Disuniting of America* (New York 1991), deplore it; while Lawrence W. Levine, *The Opening of the American Mind* (Boston 1996), and George Lipsitz, "The Possessive Investment in Whiteness: Racialized Social Democracy and the 'White' Problem in American Studies," *American Quarterly* 47 (September 1995): 369–87, deplore the sources of resistance to it. Like John Higham's essays already cited, D. A. Hollinger's *Postethnic America* (New York 1995) seeks a middle ground that accepts diversity within unity; and Wendy Katkin et al., eds., *Beyond Pluralism* (Urbana 1998), reflects the influence of Hollinger's approach.

# Index

Abacha, Sani, 179, 180
Abiola, Moshood K. O., 179
abolition movement, 75–77
Act of Union (1801) [Britain], 22
Action Group, 177
Adolph, Gustav, 18
Afghanistan Taliban, 210
Afghanistan War, 194, 201
Africa: Hutu-Tutsi conflict in, 186–87, 191, 201; nationalism generated by colonialism of, 164, 170–71, 172–73; Nigerian nationalism experience in, 173, 174–81; slavery experience of, 95, 156–57; tribal territory of, 173–74. *See also* black Africans; European colonialism
African American nationalism, 160
African Americans: migration from south to north by, 157–58; miscegenation laws and, 122; race consciousness/nationalism of, 157, 184, 190, 191, 198, 207–8
African ethnic loyalties, 129–30
African forced patterns, 131
African nationalism, 131, 156–64, 173–81

African tribes: British colonialism impact on, 174–75; conflict of Hutu-Tutsi, 186–87, 191, 201; impact of European colonialism on territory of, 173–74
Aggrey, James Kwegyir, 161
Algeria, 168
American anti-Semitism: of late 1880s, 94; W.W. II, 122–23
American citizenship: combination of constitutional federalism and, 67–70; limited obligations of nineteenth century, 86; social cohesion through, 69–72. *See also* state citizenship
American Colonization Society, 157
American democracy: changes of nineteenth century, 113–14; development of early, 67–71; as international model, 46–48; public policy issues of nineteenth century, 93–94; race problem and, 72–80; social cohesion through, 69–71; Southern secession (1860–61) as threat to, 78–79; strong citizenship/constitutional federalism and, 67–70, 71. *See also* democracy

Cuba, 189, 195
Cubberley, Ellwood, 96
Cyprus, 189
Czech nationalism, 61, 103, 197

Dalai Llama, 202
Danish nationalism, 17
Daughters of Norway (1897), 18
Davitt, Michael, 26
democracy: citizenship exercised through, 45; Cold War ideological struggle between socialism and, 192–97; collaboration between nationalism, socialism and, 51–53; difficulties of global attempts at, 128–29; French and American models of, 46–48; global capitalism entwined with, 214–15; impact on European history by, 38; impact on transformation of nineteenth century Europe, 38–48; mobilization of late nineteenth century, 49–53; nationalism in context of, 3; post–Cold War fate of, 211–12; promise held by, 40–41; state identification/path toward, 107–8; state vision under, 48–49; strengths and weaknesses of, 42. *See also* American democracy; nationalism; socialism
Devoy, John, 26
Dewey, John, 111
Díaz, Portifiro, 148
diversity: basic assumptions regarding, 218; contradictions/conundrums of, 219; limitations of, 218–19; salutary effects of social and cultural, 217–18, 220; small-group violence and, 219–20. *See also* global diversity stabilization strategies; racial divisions/racism
Dmowski, Roman, 103
Douglas, Stephen A., 67
*dozoku* kinship network (Japan), 139
*Dred Scott* decision (U.S. Supreme Court), 69
Dreyfus affair (France), 58, 59

DuBois, W.E.B., 160, 161, 162, 163
Dulles, John Foster, 193
Dumont, Louis, 14
Durkheim, Emile, 14

East India Company (Britain), 132, 134
East Timorese nationalism, 171
Easter Rebellion (Ireland), 26
Eastern European Jewish migration, 34–36
Egyptian nationalism, 155–56
Emerson, Rupert, 2
Emmet, Robert, 23
Enlightenment, 24, 104
Enloe, Cynthia, 48, 81
*Escape from Freedom* (Fromm), 3
ETA (Basque militant organization), 186, 219
Ethiopia, 171
ethnic consciousness: of American ethnic groups, 86–87; anticolonialism mobilization of, 129–30; comparing Swede and Norwegian, 17–18; as element of nationalism, 15–16
ethnicity: American nationalism derived from, 80–84; American nationalism vs., 110–14; growing importance of fictive kin or, 14–15; nineteenth-century America view of, 81
eugenics, 57–58
Europe: American society compared to, 63–65; cultural dividers of, 37–38; early interactions between Japan and, 137–38; impact of migration on, 13–14; impact of Wilson world view on states of, 98–102; influence of French ideal on, 46–47; post–Great War struggle of great trio in, 114–17; racial divides of nineteenth century, 55–58, 95; rising anti-Semitism of nineteenth century, 32; state reconstruction during early twentieth century, 100–101;

transformation of citizenship notion in, 39–41; transformation of three great movements of, 38–41

European colonialism: anticolonalism resistance against, 164–65, 171–72; British impact on tribalism during, 165; despotism model following end of, 167–71; Humpty-Dumpty Principle following, 167; impact on Nigeria, 173, 174–81; impact on tribal territory by, 173–74; as local subjugation vs. distant rule, 214; nationalism generated by, 164, 170–71, 172–73; patronage system under, 165–66. *See also* Africa; postcolonial states

European nationalism movements: authoritarian nature of post–Great War, 117–23; collaboration between socialism, democracy and, 51–53; factors determining scope of, 5–6; French and U.S. exported, 46; as function of modernization, 6–8, 19–21; global spread of (1880–1920), 127–35; impact of religious involvement on, 59–60; impact of socialism, democracy and, 38–48; impact of war on European, 18–19; kinship/political objectives of, 5; mobilization of late nineteenth century, 49–53; nation-state birth through, 44–45; Nazi Germany, 117–20, 121–23; post-Great War transformation of, 104–7, 114–17; racial elements of, 55–58; similarities of American and, 82; similarities/differences of, 60–62; socialism and democracy contexts of, 3; state language agendas and, 53–55; state militarism and, 4–5, 7, 52–53, 61–62; state vision under, 48–49; strength of kinship ties and, 19; strengths and weaknesses of, 42; varieties of, 44–45. *See also* democracy; nationalism; socialism

European Union (EU), 209

Euskara language, 55

Ezrahi, Yaron, 68

*The Family of Man* (photographic exhibit), 2

Fanon, Frantz, 158, 168

Farrakhan, Louis, 208

Federation of Arab Republics, 156

Fédération Régionaliste de Bretagne (Breton nationalism), 54

Feierman, Steven, 205

Fenianism, 25–26. *See also* Irish nationalism

Flemish nationalism, 54–55

Fourier, Charles, 43

Fourierite communities, 43

France: citizen-patriot indoctrination in, 52; colonial slavery ended by, 76; competition of great trio in, 107; Jacobin language mandate in, 53; lack of transforming migration of, 45–46; nationalism exported by, 45–46; nationalism feelings in late twentieth century, 207; W.W. II Vichy government in, 120

Franco, Francisco, 120–21, 186–87

*Freemen's Journal*, 25

French Canadian separatists, 182–83, 190

French Revolution: Jacobin language mandate following, 53; modern citizenship invented during, 46; nationalism following, 40, 44; nationalism prior to, 12–13

Fromm, Erich, 3

Fulani-Hausa (Nigeria), 177, 178, 179

Gaelic language, 55

Gaelic League (Ireland), 105

Gandhi, Mahatma, 133–34, 135, 205, 210

Garvey, Marcus, 158, 159, 160, 162

Garveyism, 158–61

Gellner, Ernest, 41

*genro* (Japanese ruling elders), 137, 148

human rights: global stabilization strategy of, 213–14; U.S. promotion of, 215–16; values originating, 9
Huntington, Samuel, 218
Hussein, Saddam, 8
Hutu-Tutsi conflict (Africa), 186–87, 191, 201
Hyde, Douglas, 55, 105
Hyden, Goran, 172
hyphenism, 110. *See also* American nationalism

Icarus Effect, 7, 104, 177
Igbo (Ibo) [Nigeria], 173, 174, 175, 176, 177, 178, 180
Ignatieff, Michael, 4
Indian Moslems, 134, 135
Indian National Congress, 132
Indian nationalism, 132–35
indigenous people of color: exploitation of, 73–74; readiness rule applied to, 101–2. *See also* Native Americans
individual responsibility, 3–4
individual rights: global stabilization strategy of, 213–14; U.S. promotion of, 215–16
Indonesia, 169
Ipsilandis, Prince Alexander, 44
IRA (Irish Republican Army), 185, 201
Iranian Revolution, 203–5
Irish American Fenian Canadian invasions (1866, 1870), 87
Irish Americans: Civil War service of, 86; during Great War, 111; Irish freedom promoted by, 24–25; migration of, 22, 24
Irish Home Rule campaign, 26, 105–7
Irish National Land League, 26
Irish nationalism: British rule impact on, 22–23, 184–85; "Catholic rent" (1825) funding, 23; compared to German and Jewish, 36; demographics and, 15, 21–22, 24; Famine (1845–55) impact on, 21, 22, 23–24; Fenianism expression of, 25–26, 87;

Gaelic language and, 55; kinship adaptation to migration and, 22; post–Great War transformation of, 105–7; transatlantic nature of, 26
Irish Republican Brotherhood (or Fenians), 26, 87
Irokawa, Daikichi, 139
Iron Law of Oligarchy, 50
Islamic fundamentalism, 204–5
Israel, 187–88, 195
Italian Americans, 82
Italy: nationalism transformed by Mussolini, 116; nationalist politics of nineteenth century, 115–16

Jabotinsky, Vladimir, 125
Jackson, Andrew, 45
James, C.L.R., 158
Japanese Americans: kinship relations of, 141–42; miscegenation laws and, 122; W.W. II internment of, 142
Japanese Meiji Revolution (1867–68), 136–37, 139, 143
Japanese nationalism: compared to Chinese nationalism, 143; early development of, 136–41; *genro* rulers and, 137, 148; *nihonjinron* belief and, 140–41, 144; post-W.W. II, 143–44; role of Shinto cults/ emperor in, 138–39, 144
Japanese Twenty-One Demands of 1915, 154
Jefferson, Thomas, 70, 77
Jewett, Sarah Orne, 92
Jewish homeland, 33–34, 186–87. *See also* Zionism
Jewish nationalism, 187–88
Jewish people: anti-Semitism against, 32, 58–59, 94, 118–19, 122–23; Jewish consciousness of American, 83; post–W.W. II Palestine homeland for, 124–26
*The Jewish State* (Lueger), 32
Jim Crow laws (U.S.), 95, 162
Jinnah, M. A., 134

Mazzini, Guiseppe, 45
Mboya, Tom, 168
Meade, George, 87
Meiji Restoration of 1867–68 (Japan), 136–37, 139, 143
*Mein Kampf* (Hitler), 120
mestizo nationalism (Mexico), 151–52
Mexican Constitution (1917), 148–49
Mexico: land reform issues, 151–52; nationalism of, 146–53; outmigration from, 152–53; war between United States (nineteenth century) and, 84–85
Michels, Robert, 50
Middle Eastern migration, 131
migration: of African Americans to north, 157–58; between Mexico and United States, 152–53; Eastern European Jewish, 34–36; forced African, 131; from Germany to U.S., 28–30; German nationalism and, 27, 28–29; impact on European society by, 13–14; impact of *nihonjinron* belief on Japanese, 140–41; Irish Famine and Irish, 24; Irish successful adaptation to, 22; of Jews from Russia, 31; kinship relations reconceived in U.S., 82–83; of mixed population to U.S., 66–67, 72; Mormonism, 88; National Origins Act of 1924 and U.S., 112–13; Pan-Arabism from Middle Eastern, 130; relation between nationalism and, 16–22; Soviet Union control over population, 113; triggered by soaring populations, 15–16
Minorities Protection Treaties of 1919, 104
miscegenation laws (U.S.), 122
modernization/nationalism connection, 6–8, 19–21
Monroe Doctrine (U.S.), 149
Morley, David, 219
Mormonism nationalism, 88–92, 208
Mosaddeq, Mohammed, 203
Moses, Wilson, 161

Mosse, George, 4
Muhammad, Elijah, 208
Muhammad, Walter, 208
Mussolini, Benito, 116

*Nabucco* (Verdi), 50
Nairn, Tom, 3, 206
Napoleonic Empire, 40, 42
Nasser, Gamal, 155–56, 163
Nat Turner's Rebellion (South Carolina), 76
Nation of Islam, 207–8
nation-state: ethnic-linguistic, 101, 102; illusive nature of, 8; linguistic movements of, 53–55; nationalism as origins of, 44–45. *See also* states
National (Anglican Church), 176
National Association for the Advancement of Colored People (NAACP), 95
*National Geographic*, 2
National Origins Act of 1924 (U.S.), 112–13
National Socialist party (Nazi Germany), 118
nationalism: declining appeal of modern, 209–10; defining, 5; early history of, 12–18; global spread of (1880–1920), 127–35; global spread of (1967–1972), 182–210; impact of war on, 18–19; new ethnic consciousness element of, 15–16; pan movements of, 153–64; post–Cold War fate of, 211–12; power mobilized by appeals to, 97; relation between migration and, 16–22; shaped by modern state, 6–8, 19–21; state identification/path toward, 107–8; three propositions regarding, 10; value of examining history of, 10–11; weaknesses and strengths of, 42; Western intellectual demonizing of, 1–5. *See also* democracy; socialism
nationalism movements: African, 131, 156–64, 173–81; African American

Pierce, Franklin, 69
Pinsker, Leo, 32
Pirenne, Henri, 57
Pius XII, Pope, 121
Poland, 60
Polish Americans, 86, 87, 112
Polk, James Knox, 84
Popper, Karl, 3
population density: comparing French and U.S., 45–46; European migration triggered by, 15–16; Irish Famine and nationalism links to, 15, 21–22, 23–24
postcolonial states: despotism of, 167–71; expectations-behavior gap and nationalism of, 196–97. *See also* European colonialism
Potter, David, 80, 219
power: American democracy as distribution of, 70–71; nationalism appeals to mobilize, 97
Prussia, 17, 27, 28, 39

Quebec nationalism, 182–83, 190

race consciousness: African American, 157, 184, 190, 191, 198, 207–8; Japanese *nihonjinron* belief and, 140–41, 144
racial divisions/racism: American, 94–96, 122; American democracy and, 73–80; colonial, 73–74; European, 55–58, 95; of Germany (1880s Nazi regime), 117–23; of U.S. National Origins Act of 1924, 112–13; W.W. II/post–W.W. II, 119–23
"readiness rule," 101–2
Reischauer, Edwin, 140
religion: American cultural tolerance of plural, 85–86; impact on nationalism movements by, 59–60; Irish nationalism relation to, 24–25; Roman Catholic, 24–25, 59–60, 85–86, 121, 150
religious nationalism: global nationalism (1967–1972) role by, 202–6;

modern appeal of, 215–16; Mormon, 88–92, 208
Renan, Joseph Ernest, 57, 201–2
*Renascent Africa* (Azikiwe), 162
Renner, Karl, 51
Revel, Jacques, 207
Revolution of 1905 (Russia), 108
Revolution of 1910 (Mexico), 148
Revolution of 1917 (Russia), 108
Rivera, Primo de, 121
Robbins, Kevin, 219
Rochdale Plan, 43
Roman Catholic Church: American tolerance toward, 85–86; anti-Semitism role played by, 59–60; Irish nationalism relations to, 24–25; Mexicanized, 150; Spanish nationalism and, 121
Roosevelt, Theodore, 100
Royal Niger Company, 173
Russia: anti-Semitism of, 32, 58; Jewish migration from, 31; revolutions (1905, 1917) of, 108; triumph of socialism over democracy/nationalism in, 108–9. *See also* Soviet Union
Rwanda, 186–87

Sabean, David, 14
Saint-Simon, Henri de, 43
Scandanavians: migration of, 17; national consciousness among, 17–18
Schlesinger, Arthur, Jr., 4, 193
Schurz, Carl, 86
Scott, Sir Walter, 79
Scottish National Party, 185
Scottish nationalism, 185, 190
Second Republic (1979–1983) [Nigeria], 180
Sedition Act (U.S.), 68
Selassie, Emperor Haile, 171
self-determination: disruptive outcomes of, 10; growing nationalism role of, 60–61; Irish Home Rule campaign for, 26, 105–7; Nazi Germany rhetoric of, 119, 120; Nigerian

self-determination (*continued*)
experience in, 178; Wilson's world
view on, 100, 101–2. *See also* states
Senghor, Léopold Sédar, 158, 164
Serbia: Eastern Orthodox clergy nationalism role in, 60; linguistic
movement of, 55; post–Great War
creation of, 103; state-based nationalism of, 52–53, 197
Shinto state-focused cults (Japan),
138, 144
Silver, Rabbi Abba Hillel, 125
Sinn Fein (Ireland), 106
slavery: abolition movement to end
U.S., 75–77; American institutional-
ism of, 75–76; American society division over, 76–80; sub-Sahara
African, 95, 156–57
Slovak nationalism, 103
Smith, Anthony, 10
Smith, Denis Mack, 115
Smith, Joseph, 88, 89, 90, 91
social class, 39
social contract myth, 42
socialism: Cold War ideological struggle between democracy and, 192–
97; collaboration between nationalism, democracy and, 51–53; failure
to establish American, 65–66; global
attempts at, 129; impact on European history by, 38–48; labor force
and, 39; mobilization of late nineteenth century, 49–53; nationalism
in context of, 3; post–Cold War fate
of, 211–12; state identification/path
toward, 107–8; state vision under,
48–49; strengths and weaknesses
of, 42; triumph in Russia of, 108–9;
twentieth century revolutionary,
100–101; varieties of nineteenth
century, 43. *See also* democracy;
nationalism
Somalia, 201
Sons of Norway (1895), 18
South Africa, 129–30, 131
Southern Confederacy, 78–80

Southern Rhodesia, 131
Soviet Union: global nationalism and
Cold War role by, 192–97; global
nationalism and disintegration of,
200–201; migration movements
controlled in, 113; nationality policy
within, 109–10; socialism of, 108–9.
*See also* Russia
Spain: Franco regime of, 120–21, 185–
86; Mexico's independence from,
147–48
Sri Lanka, 168–69, 171
Stalin's Five Year Plan, 109, 113
state citizenship: exercised through
democracy, 45; Revolutionary
France creation of modern, 46;
transformation of European notion
of, 39–41. *See also* American
citizenship
state-based nationalists, 52–53
states: African postcolonial despotism
model of, 167–71; authoritarian nationalism movements of post–Great
War, 117–23; Big Man system mimicking, 168; comparing democratic,
socialism, nationalism ideals of, 48;
controlling chaos by strengthening,
212–13; difficulties of establishing
Mexican, 150; expectations-behavior
gap of postcolonial, 196–97; German nationalism related to, 26,
27–28; global nationalism and rigidification of Cold War, 192–95; Holocaust as unregulated sovereignty
of, 126; identification with/path toward one of great trio by, 107–8;
Islamic fundamentalism vision of,
204–5; Japanese nationalism and Japanese, 137–40; late nineteenth
century norms for successful, 93;
Mussolini's glorified vision of, 116;
nationalism and militarism of, 4–5,
7, 52–53, 61–62; nationalism opening through dysfunction of, 195–99;
nationalism shaped by modern, 6–
8, 19–21; nationalism in well-